Educational sciences

Cultural anthropology and education

C. Camilleri

Prepared for the
International Bureau
of Education

Kogan Page

in association with

In the series 'Educational sciences':

Landsheere, G. De. *Empirical research in education.* 1982, 113p.

Zverev, I.D. *Teaching methods in the Soviet school.* 1983, 116p.

Kraevskij, V.V.; Lerner, I.Y. *The theory of curriculum content in the USSR.* 1984, 113p.

Léon, A. *The history of education today.* 1985, 117p.

Mialaret, G. et al. *Introduction to the educational sciences.* 1985, 110p.

Camilleri, C. *Cultural anthropology and education.* 1986, 171p.

Published by Kogan Page
in association with the United Nations
Educational, Scientific and Cultural Organization,
7, place de Fontenoy, 75700 Paris, France
ISBN: 92-3-102339-X

© Unesco 1986

British Library Cataloguing in Publication Data
Camilleri, C.
  Cultural anthropology and education.
  1. Educational anthropology.
  I. Title
  370.19   LB45
  ISBN 1-85091-165-7

Printed and bound in Great Britain by Biddles, Guildford

Contents

Preface *p.iii*

Chapter I The convergence of anthropological culture and education *p.7*
Cultural anthropology p.7
Anthropological culture p.8
Academic culture p.14
Anthropological culture and education: obstacles to convergence p.15
The synthesis in the United States p.16
The synthesis in other countries p.19

Chapter II From simple societies to complex societies: general approaches to the problems posed *p.25*
Socialization and acculturation p.26
Personality development and acculturation p.27
Functions, aptitudes and acculturation p.36
The educational process as a comprehensive system p.45
The anthropological method in practice p.47

Chapter III Schools and national culture problems in the West *p.54*
The educational subculture and social class subcultures p.55
The conflictualist interpretation p.62
Criticism against the conflictualist theory p.63
Other avenues of investigation p.65
Classroom subcultures and national subcultures p.66

Chapter IV　　Educational problems raised by ethnic minorities *p.79*
　　　　　　　Problems of adaptation in Western industrialized countries p.79
　　　　　　　Immigrants and the host society's school p.84
　　　　　　　Participation and specific aspects of the scholastic world p.88
　　　　　　　The socio-economic variable and the cultural variable p.98

Chapter V　　Culture and educational problems in the Third World *p.107*
　　　　　　　Typical situations p.107
　　　　　　　Decolonized societies in the Third World p.110
　　　　　　　Education and the family p.112
　　　　　　　Education and the school p.115

Chapter VI　　Special problems: language and testing *p.132*
　　　　　　　The influence of speech and other forms of language on culture p.132
　　　　　　　Communication language and the school: national problems p.135
　　　　　　　Testing and culture p.148

Conclusion　　Towards intercultural teaching *p.162*

Appendix　　Additional reading *p.170*

Preface

It is now more than half a century since cultural anthropology first made its appearance in North America. Yet it is not at all unusual even today to note that there is still some confusion in the use of such terms as ethnology, anthropology, social anthropology, psychological anthropology, cultural anthropology, etc. It was Margaret Mead who, beginning in 1928 and particularly with *Coming of age in Samoa*, tried to explain the particular psychological characteristics of certain peoples by referring to the specific features of their culture and thus came to blaze a trail for the new discipline. At the same time Malinowski, by emphasizing the role of individual behaviour in the explanation of social factors and by approaching cultural factors from a psychological — even psychoanalytical — point of view, rather than concentrating on social structures, founded cultural anthropology as we know it today in the United States. Some have tried to trace the birth of this new discipline as the simple extrapolation of the thoughts and writings of Marcel Mauss, the French ethnologist and sociologist who wrote *L'Essai sur le don* in 1932.

After the Second World War the field of cultural anthropology underwent an explosive development. Sociologists, psychologists, educators and economists all added to the increasing interest of a discipline which began by assuming that culture is the foundation of social structures themselves and that every institution manifests itself in the final analysis as a system of behaviour imposed on individuals, which they must share, learn and transmit. Since learning and transmission form the basis of any educational activity, it is not difficult to understand the International Bureau of Education's interest in this discipline which has had far-reaching consequences for education and the effects of which, particularly on the education systems of those countries where cultural confrontations or social adaptation of colonial origin are still familiar, could have a very unpredictable effect.

When one considers that the various social sciences each study one aspect of culture — in its anthropological meaning — and that cultural anthropology sets out to grasp this culture as a whole, it is easy to understand why such a subject is profoundly multidisciplinary and renders such service to education, which is both a basic element of culture and at the same time the principal vehicle of its transmission. Hence the multiplicity of studies which set out to understand education systems and behaviours in various societies with a view to understanding not only the mechanics but also to situate this mechanism in the overall social dynamic. This is apparently an impossible task if one imagines the complexity of any social dynamic. Nevertheless, this effort must be made if educational thought is to be more than a dream based on an idea propounded by a philosopher or an educational researcher.

It was with a view to increasing the awareness of a large, knowledgeable audience that the International Bureau of Education asked Professor Carmel Camilleri to try to give in this monograph an overall view of this new discipline by attempting as far as possible to draw attention to the educational outcomes. A hazardous venture or an impossible task: nevertheless, the lengthy experience of Professor Camilleri in the study of contacts between cultures and intercultural relations, as well as his keen powers of analysis and summary, singled him out for such a challenge. And we consider that he has succeeded admirably. However, while renewing the expression of our gratitude, we would like to remind the reader that the author is responsible for the views expressed in this book, which are not necessarily those of the Organization and that the designations employed and the presentation of material throughout the book do not imply the expression of any opinion whatsoever on the part of Unesco concerning the legal status of any country, territory, city or area or of its authorities, or concerning the delimitations of its frontiers or boundaries.

CHAPTER I

The convergence of anthropological culture and education

Cultural anthropology

Cultural anthropology emerged in the wake of ethnology, a discipline with which it is still often confused, at least in practice, and perhaps even in theory, given the number of authors who leap from one term to the other without warning. Yet the two disciplines are not identical, even if they overlap to a significant degree.

Indeed, ethnology is a particular form of study which has from its earliest origins concentrated on the analysis of societies whose limited size, relatively simple structures and slow rate of change — so slow in fact that many believe it to be nonexistent — enabled researchers to attain the prized goal of being able to study these groups as self-contained wholes. Moreover, the apparent absence of the unmanageable confusion of variables involved in the socio-historical dynamics of larger, more complex societies made it easier to perceive in these societies a near obvious variable which we shall discuss here: the so-called 'cultural' factor which, in this context, would ultimately appear to be quite autonomous. This is perhaps the main reason for the misconception which has been vehemently criticized in the case of the 'culturalists' or a good number of them: the belief that this dimension can be treated as an independent factor for explaining social reality, the most important such factor, or even the only one. In any case, ethnology, using its own methods, was indisputably the originator of the 'invention' of culture in the sense we are about to define.

Anthropology, meanwhile, if we wish to remain consistent in our choice of terms, is something far broader because it comprises all the sciences of man (*anthropos*) and thinking in other fields of knowledge concerning man. Cultural anthropology though brings together all the contributions from three different sciences to the study of human cultures. As J. Stoetzel said: 'its objective... is to both describe and understand cultural phenomena in relation to individual and collective behaviour. . . . To this extent it is situated among the series of attempts at interdisciplinary synthesis.'[1] Indeed, insofar as it attempts to organize these contributions into a conceptually coherent whole can it claim to be a science and take its place within anthropology. Need we add that this is an objective, ongoing process rather than an accomplished fact?

Anthropological culture

It remains to define culture, a multivocal concept if ever there was one, the description and use of which have not been sufficiently rigorous. As early as 1952 Kroeber and Kluckhohn estimated that no less than 160 definitions had been given between 1871 when *Primitive culture* by E.B. Tylor was published and 1950.

It is not our purpose here to review in detail the evolution of this notion.[2] A thorough historical and critical analysis was made by E. Vermeersh (1977) and, more recently, by M. Mauviel (1983). Here we will simply present the principal connotations it has acquired.

First of all, the term has always been used to denote that which, with man, is distinct from 'nature', that is, produced by him. 'Culture,' said Herskovits, 'is the man-made part of the environment.'[3] The general idea is that man, unlike animals, is not prisoner to his biological make-up. The latter, thanks to its unique plasticity, is highly manipulable: sufficient evidence has been produced to show that our psychological state is less determined by a collection of inalterable instincts than by a set of malleable inclinations and a multitude of relatively flexible needs. Everyday experience reveals the degree to which we are able to mould them: take, for example, psychoanalytic theories on the repression, redirection and sublimation of the 'libido'. But we know that in addition to the ability to act upon ourselves, we can also act upon the environment, thus using it as an outlet for the multifaceted human ego, from the manufacturing of tools to the creation of institutions. It is precisely by means of this twin series of transformations, which separates man from the repetitive biosystem of animals and makes history possible, and at the same time takes place in it, that that which is specifically human emerges and man's potentialities are fulfilled.

Everyone recognizes this fact and, seen in this light, human culture, when thus spoken of in the singular, becomes *artifact*. When, in addition, the word culture is written with a capital letter, as was the case with the vast panoramas brushed by German philosophers and ideologists on *Kultur*, it acquires the connotation of a progression of values, thus becoming practically indistinguishable from the concept of 'civilization'. The latter notion, which was commonly employed until the beginning of the present century, automatically incorporated the idea of a hierarchy. Authors were fond of ranking civilizations according to the values that each of them was believed to promote throughout history: at the top of the scale were the European civilizations or that of a particular European country (usually that of the author).

At a more modest and less ideologically biased level, agreement as to what is specifically man-made has led to a definition of culture which is now commonly used by authors. If culture is that which man himself has created, then explicitly or implicitly the culture of a group of people includes everything they do which is not strictly biological. Culture thus defined becomes so broad that it loses all specificity and becomes impossible to circumscribe; because, if we are to remain consistent, any act, anything created, the appearance of anything new in the life of the group becomes a part of culture, even if only for a few instants. Culture thus becomes completely diluted, namely, into a number of products studied individually by each of the social sciences, and it becomes difficult to see how a science of its own could be defined. In fact, we would only be dealing with a general science on the composition of groups and the object of cultural anthropology would be the same as that of social psychology.

What we must do, therefore, is to set the boundaries of this as yet poorly defined field. However, before doing so, we ought to mention a point directly related to our subject: if it is true that culture involves the accumulation and organization of man-made creation, then it is, for this very reason, potentially transmissible, but by non-genetic means of transmission. It is also modifiable, and these modifications can also be transmitted. Because of these characteristics, the cultural fact is of immediate interest to education, and the manner in which man 'pieces together' his relationship with his own nature, that is, his biological self, has to be integrated into this 'constructed' reality. That is why a more profound cultural analysis provided by any discipline whatever can obviously have a direct or indirect impact which the educator must take into consideration. Specifically, it is important that he learn that a given aspect of the intellect which was heretofore believed to be 'natural', ie part of instinct, for example, is, in fact, a product of society crystallized in culture. On the other hand, it has been observed that, in a particular society or certain smaller groups, some aspects of the intellect, although fundamentally biologically determined, actually admit of a degree of artificial manipulation with respect to their orientation and realization: in all these instances, the psychic process in question falls within the realm of the educable. Cultural anthropology abounds in examples of this type. Thus, one of its main goals was, and still is, to bring psychology out of the naturalist and universalist perspective into which it tends to fall spontaneously, so that it takes into account those parts of its subject of study that have social origins: it is precisely in this way that this incessantly changing field interests the educational sciences.

Having said that, let us return to the question at hand. How can the history of the concept of culture help us to define a way of collecting and organizing human achievements without allowing that concept to be swallowed up by a much broader category embracing all social creation?

A great number of authors dealing with this problem have relied on methods which try to describe the *content* of cultures. The result has been a tedious succession of *extensional definitions* all too familiar to anthropologists. They are without fail disappointing for, as M. Mauviel observed,

extensional definitions have a major drawback: they run the risk of being incomplete and thus inadequate. As it is impossible to list all cultural objects, authors are generally content to give subclasses of a general class of objects considered to be constituent elements of culture.[4]

We might add that these subclasses themselves stand little chance of ever being exhaustive.

The study by Kroeber and Kluckhohn (1952)[5] gives an idea of the indefinite character of these constituent elements via the five categories in which these authors try to classify them: mental states and psychological operations, which includes evolutive and normative attitudes; types of behaviour, including mores, customs and habits which groups have always relied on to differentiate themselves; the various kinds of skills, ranging from communication codes and languages to modes of utilizing tools and aspects of the environment; the immense category of the products of human activity, including tools and works of art, for which the modes of utilization apply; finally, the variety of institutions and the means of collective organization, both formal and informal.

It can be shown how difficult it is to differentiate clearly these overlapping categories which are incompletely formulated and ultimately arbitrary.

But what list can avoid these pitfalls? This brings us to another interesting point relevant to our discussion. As long as cultural content as a complete package is placed within the open-ended category of everything which is capable of receiving the stamp of man, all things are potentially part of the culture of a group: from the development of a territory or the construction of a dwelling to the way of dealing with sex and age groups or any other groups of individuals, systems of lineage and even ways of walking, of speaking, of expressing and experiencing emotion. In short, it can embrace any event, object, phenomenon or, to borrow a term from psychology, any 'stimulus' originating in our environment or ourselves.

Thus it is evident that delimitation of the cultural dimension cannot be based on, shall we say, what is *contained in it*, as Kroeber, Kluckhohn and many others have attempted to describe and categorize it, but on what *it is contained in*. Is not the reality of culture rather to be found in the structures, configurations, in short, the *forms* which leave their imprint on objects without actually becoming part of them?

There is no lack of authors who have adopted this course (in which the American culturalist school is particularly well represented), generally considered to have originated in the work of Franz Boas (1858-1942) and which, with Ruth Benedict, Margaret Mead, Abram Kardiner and Ralph Linton, flourished in the first half of the present century. By basing themselves on the 'containing' element we have just mentioned, they elaborated the concept of 'pattern'. As S. Clapier-Valladon observed,

it is not useful to search out painstakingly the authors who to some degree or other were part of, or related to, the culturalist school and who contributed to the enrichment and vulgarization of a concept already used by Wiseler between 1923 and 1926.[6]

There is, however, no doubt that it is with Ruth Benedict that the term became part and parcel of the vocabulary of cultural anthropology. Since that time, all approaches to culture have been influenced by it.

What does this term, which nowadays in French is usually translated by 'modèle', mean? The best solution is to examine how the American anthropologists used the concept. They tell us that the Zuñi tribe of the Pueblo Indians of New Mexico value inoffensiveness and sobriety in all matters. Its members are not warlike, and prefer avoiding conflicts or settling them by other means. They do not wear themselves out in contests, rivalries, interpersonal struggles for power or profit. This is not to say that these events never occur, but they could not proliferate, for they are contrary to their way of life. Rather, each member is encouraged to exercise quietly his activity in his place, within a social universe which is as well ordered as his religious world, perpetually re-enacted via a meticulous ritual to which he devotes the better part of his existence. Inwardly, the individual has an obligation to avoid violent emotions, and this is reflected in everyday relationships. Accordingly, anything that reflects violence of any sort is unacceptable: suicide, for example, or scenes between husbands and wives. If a couple wishes to divorce, discreet procedures exist for doing so. Personal assertiveness is the one thing most despised and thus universally avoided, including in the family and in the upbringing of children, who are pampered and not subjected to punishment. Finally, it seems that the idea of personal fault, of *sin*, is unknown to the Zuñis, who base their philosophy on the notion of the absence of conflict, which is justified by the unity of man with the universe.

Anthropologists have criticized this depiction, like the two others given in *Patterns of culture* (1934),[7] for its Utopian character. Without denying the danger of oversimplification, we can see that we are dealing with the presentation of a pattern, the function of which is reminiscent of Max Weber's 'ideal type': that is, an abstract construct of reality representing a kind of limit rarely attained and acting as a type of normative or regulatory mechanism with regard to it.

It was also noted that this model is situated at the terminal level of a philosophy, of a general attitude towards life: in this case, that of the Zuñi tribe. In short, one gradually approaches this level through a feeling of unity which, as we understand it from this model, comes to the fore by the observer highlighting particular behaviours and situations from a multitude of everyday behaviours and situations. These lesser significations are observable in what are usually called cultural subsystems. Yet they must converge sufficiently to be able to be apprehended as part of a more generalized, significant unit presumed to be deeper; otherwise, it would not be possible to identify the terminal model. In other words, a culture only exists insofar as it involves an 'integrated' configuration, that is, more coherence than contradiction, more agreement than conflict.

Yet it is necessary to reach beyond the general characterizations towards the more concrete, towards the effective 'carrier' of culture: the individual. How is it exactly that he is the 'carrier' of these individual significations which lead him to the overall pattern?

The problem is easy to grasp if one crucial fact is borne in mind: the meaning and significations, independent of all cultural considerations, make up the universe in which we are immersed. None of us is directly in contact with the objective event per se, with the 'stimulus', to use a convenient expression. Indeed, no one has ever seen a man or woman in his or herself as an independent 'objective' reality. We see them as integrated into the place we assign to them in nature or, possibly, 'super-nature', in the social universe and its hierarchies and divisions; in what we feel they are entitled to expect from us (their status) and what we believe we are entitled to expect of them (their role). And there are many other parameters still, including the multitude of associations they trigger in our subconscious and our conscious minds because of experiences with them in everyday life. All this makes up the 'unity of meaning' through which we enter into contact with them as with any other stimulus from the outside world or from ourselves, and which determines our behaviour towards them. Let us use another example which has been focused on in studies. We only experience illness through the signification we unfailingly project on to it: as a means of escaping our professional responsibilities, or of making others feel how valuable we are to them because of the negative consequences of our inability to work or of concentrating on reflection, reading, or any other activity we are interested in. On the other hand, we could view it as a very undesirable occurrence because it prevents us from fulfilling roles which enhance our status or justify our existence, etc.[8]

We will agree, therefore, that every individual is permanently locked into a symbolic whole which takes shape and evolves throughout his existence, and in which individual significations dovetail with collective ones, including those which originate in culture. For, we repeat, culture is not to be confused with the entire set of significations presented by the group, to which, as we well know, we owe the better part of our ideologies, opinions and the fashions, fads and various stereotypes we adopt.

Yet, curiously enough, the number of analyses aimed at distinguishing culture from other systems of collective significations is very limited. The reason for this is probably that it appears to be extremely risky, given the current state of progress in cultural anthropology, to differentiate among them using internal criteria. Indeed, it is not clear for what intrinsic reasons a representation simultaneously shared by a part of the population, an image, opinion, fashion or any other form of group conformism, does not enter into our cultural heritage and vice versa. For example, 'avant-garde' democratic ideas about human and civil rights which were defended by small numbers of people when the countries of Europe were ruled by monarchs have for a century been an integral part of the culture of our societies. Conversely, the characteristics defining the organization and life-style of the once predominant patriarchal family have disappeared; but a number of them (omnipotence of the father, parent-child relationship based on fear and respect, constant interference of the former in the lives of the latter, reverence for old age, etc) remained alive for a long time and may still survive in various circles, especially rural.

Of course, we could seek elsewhere those factors responsible for the intrinsic difference we are referring to: for example, in this or that structural property of a culture rather than in the collective *significations* which make it up. At present, it can only be noted that nothing has yet been established in this direction. So, the only criteria currently at our disposal appear to be external: cultural consensuses are those which, synchronically speaking, are diffused furthest throughout the group, above and beyond divisions and oppositions between subgroups and, diachronically speaking, are most lasting through time. The distinction is easy to make in so-called traditional societies in which change occurs slowly and the consensus is deep and far-reaching. In industrial societies, meanwhile, where these characteristics are disappearing, the 'winnowing' of collective, cultural significations from the others is — why not admit it — an empirical interpretation exercise which is often difficult and unsure.

The symbolic characterization of culture, which we elaborate on the basis of the 'patterns' made popular by the culturalists, enables us to integrate elements from other definitions, in particular the heterogeneous data of extensional definitions. Thus, given a specific group, a tool or a poem is not cultural in itself but only insofar as, and under the condition that, it can be integrated into its symbolic system as defined above, via the meaningful unity through which it is perceived by group members. Two further traits commonly mentioned are to be noted: since they are the object of a majority consensus, the elements of a culture will consciously or unconsciously be considered valid or potentially valid by the members of a group, especially unconsciously (for the portion of a culture which is explicitly perceived and formulated is the tip of the iceberg). In this regard, not only is culture potentially transmissible, as we have mentioned, but groups will effectively seek, again, consciously or unconsciously, to make it endure by all means possible and through various modes of transmission. Finally, given the fact that culture only exists as an overall symbolic configuration (its 'holistic' characteristic) it goes without saying that, depending on the type of society, this term can refer to anything from a tightly coherent quasi-system to a relatively loose collection full of contradictions.

Thus our analysis brings us to the following definition: culture is the more or less consistent set of the most enduring and most widely shared acquired significations which the members of a group, because of their affiliation to this group, tend to apply systematically to stimuli from their environment and from themselves, assuming towards these stimuli common, value-attributing attitudes, representations and behaviours of which they try to ensure the reproduction by non-genetic means.

Thus, of the meaningful constructs made by man, cultural patterns are the ones which help structure each group the most extensively, the most profoundly and the most enduringly in a relative sense, and are most apt to maintain the group's unity despite disunifying factors. However, it is clear that terms such as 'the most enduring and most commonly shared' in our definitions unquestionably leave room for doubt between what involves culture per se and what refers to simple sociality. We will not try to deny this, for the simple reason that in our own more rapidly changing, modern societies, this grey area is a reality which appears to be growing more intense. We will see, in the chapter that follows, the problems which result because of this. In any case, ignoring both the question and the debate it has sparked when putting together definitions of culture is not an acceptable alternative.

Academic culture

The definition given above describes what is known as 'anthropological' culture. But in the minds of most people it has a far older and more common meaning: that of culture as the attribute of the 'cultivated' man.

On one hand, the cultivated man is reputed to master the kinds of knowledge which will enable him to learn even more about all aspects of reality, as well as to develop the methods and mental faculties for expanding and deepening that knowledge. On the other, he is regarded as possessing similar abilities in the area of creativity, as being able to, for example, understand and savour works of art which, to others, are inaccessible, as well as to produce his own. Basically, this type of culture refers to a group's stock of privileged information and values to which the individual has access, thanks to a system of individual learning processes which also enable him to add to it. In fact, anthropologists call this a *subculture*, meaning one subgroup as opposed to another. But this one is special. Other subcultures and cultures content themselves with marking differences between groups and individuals on a horizontal plane, that is, without introducing a hierarchy: this is perhaps the most original contribution by contemporary cultural anthropology and is known as *cultural relativism*. Analyses based on this principle have demonstrated that the values of any given human group do not belong to a universal model valid for all mankind, as was believed by those ranked civilizations, but, rather, to plural, self-sufficient configurations of meanings, each independent of the other. How, then, can they be classified according to a common yardstick? Of course, the individuals or societies who need to feel or to proclaim themselves superior to others can attempt to hierarchize these cultural patterns. But a cursory inspection will show that the criteria they use have little to do with science or a sense of objectivity.

On the other hand, the subculture of 'cultivated' people classifies them, usually after comparison and selection, according to a scale of prestige and power based on, or reputedly based on, creative talents and abilities. Here, the difference is, so to speak, defined in a vertical direction. That is why, unlike the others, this subculture is perceived as being promotional and becomes the goal of the various struggles and strategies of which a number of studies have been made. It is also the objective of a process of initiation which in modern times relies heavily on educational institutions. It is, therefore, important to distinguish between these two often confused meanings of the word 'culture'.

Anthropological culture and education: obstacles to convergence

For centuries attention in large, complex societies, which were the most visible makers of history, focused exclusively or primarily on this fundamentally hierarchical, promotional form of culture and, for this very reason, on its increasingly privileged mediator: formal education. The lack of interest in anthropological cultures even continued to persist long after ethnologists had analysed and described them, in Europe in particular.

Two sets of opposing reasons seem to be at the root of this delay in awareness or, more often, this rejection.

One stemmed from all too familiar prejudices and ill-will. The elitist ideology connected with this conception, together with ethnocentrism, having set as the goal of education the attainment of the most elevated, or supposedly most elevated, standards and values in the Western world, led, in the best of cases, to indifference with regard to the values discovered by ethnologists in societies classified as 'primitive' or 'archaic'. In the worst of cases, the view was blatantly racist. Two attitudes thus sprang up. The more 'liberal' one concluded as to the necessity for educators to eradicate these different values and norms in children and pupils from those societies deemed to be backward: for the sake of their own well-being their assimilation to Western culture via the same systems of learning had to be undertaken. The others advocated – or often imposed – policies aimed to some extent or other at denying access by these young people to learning as provided by the ruling societies: either because they were judged to be unfit for it or because Westerners wanted to curtail the risks represented by their assimilation.

These suppositions were considerably reinforced and sustained in time by the great European colonization effort, with obvious political objectives in mind. The concepts 'civilization' or 'culture' in the singular, loaded with evolutionist connotations and consecrating this hierarchical ideology, were predominant at that time. Strong evidence of this is even to be found among American cultural anthropologists.

Paradoxically, this ideological current was reinforced by others whose intentions, at least, were different, if not diametrically opposed. The Cartesian rationalism of the scientific movement which followed, and humanism such as represented by the Enlightenment and the French Revolution, led to the following conclusion: what counts in each individual, no matter what society or subgroup he comes from, is the Universal Man in him. It is this ideal alone that education must help him to attain by abstracting or even completely erasing all differences. Are these differences not purely contingent, devoid of all value in the eyes of Reason, the unifying link between all men?

Thus, the exclusion of anthropological and cultural distinctiveness from the purview of education was the result of two ideologically opposed approaches. On one hand, differences were overemphasized to the point of making it the primary criterion for distinguishing between men, a criterion so fundamental that it made it possible to classify them at different levels of a graduated human scale. It was thus logical to reject those characteristics found responsible for the stagnation of some people at the lower ranks and to retain others. On the other, differences were 'de-realized': only the ladder of pure knowledge was significant and it had to be climbed one rung at a time by means of 'wholesome emulation' in order to attain the rational essence of man. We know the type of education which resulted: intellectualistic and competitive, aiming at atom-like individuals outside of their cultural and socio-economic environment. Many schoolmasters under the French Republic felt it their duty to help their pupils achieve 'equality in knowledge' while making complete abstraction of the 'origins' of these children.

In every country nationalism bent on centralization resulted in a parallel flattening out of ethnocultural diversities as a means of creating the 'national man' via a common, pre-established, educational mould.

The synthesis in the United States

It would take the fusion of diverse political, ideological and scientific movements to change things. We can begin by discussing the advent in the United States of cultural anthropology in education. The United States, as we know, has the historical particularity of being populated by a multitude of immigrant communities emanating from numerous different and assorted cultures. It is because of this, apparently, that cultural anthropology quickly acquired the importance it has and underwent an extraordinary evolution, thanks to the culturalists.

However, the connection with educational concerns was not made immediately, due to the famous ideology of the 'melting pot', which predicted the inevitable fusion of these foreign communities into a single, identical national culture, a theory which was strongly contradicted by the persistent segregation of Indians and blacks, and the marginal status of other particularly underprivileged groups. It took resistance on the part of these communities, some of which acquired political clout and enjoyed the support of a very active intelligentsia, failures in the classrooms and many other dysfunctions caused by racist institutions insensitive to differences which they tried to paste over, the discovery by psychoanalysis of the importance of family and childhood experiences, and the vigorous anti-racist reaction to Nazi activism for education to discover the findings and investigations of ethnologists.

A movement was thus started, based on the realization that 'the melting pot conceptualization is inaccurate and misleading because human cultures are complex and dynamic and don't melt like iron.'[9] G. Spindler is considered to be the main instigator of this operation. According to M. Mauviel,

his article 'Anthropology may be the answer' (1946)[10] marks the start of a process which would lead to the founding, a little more than 20 years later, of the *Council on Anthropology and Education*, a branch of the American Anthropological Association which brought together educators, anthropologists, and linguists. . . . The Council went on to publish a *Newsletter* and, later, a regular, quarterly review. In 1955 Spindler organized at Stanford the first symposium on anthropology and education.[11]

However, according to G.C. Baker, it is Jack Forbes who 'can be credited as being one of the pioneers in the usage of the term "multicultural education"'. His 1969 publication entitled *The education of the culturally different: a multicultural approach* was recognized as one of the most explicit contributions to the concept.[12]

According to the same author, this expression, which until then had been eclipsed by others such as 'education of ethnic minorities', was adopted several years later by institutions such as the *Association for Supervision and Curriculum Development* which described it as follows:

it is a humanistic concept based on the strength of diversity, human rights, social justice, and alternative life choices for all people. It is mandatory for quality education. It includes curricular, instructional, administrative, and environmental efforts to help students avail themselves of as many models, alternatives, and opportunities as possible from the full spectrum of our cultures. This education permits individual development in any culture. Each individual simultaneously becomes aware that every group (ethnic, cultural, social, and racial) exists autonomously as part of an interrelated and interdependent societal whole. Thus, the individual is encouraged to develop social skills that will enable movement among and cooperation with cultural communities and groups.[13]

The scope of this interpretation and the optimism of its outlook are striking. While elaborating these theoretical viewpoints, the authors took care not to neglect the practical aspects: financial assistance and contributions were made possible by State-sponsored initiatives, such as the *Bilingual Education Act*

(1968) and the *Ethnic Heritage Studies Act* (1972). The reconciliation between education and cultural anthropology became official with the symposium held in San Francisco in 1975, the 74th annual meeting of the American Anthropological Association whose theme was 'Towards a definition of multiculturalism in education'.

The underlying, yet powerful, role played by the culturalist school in the bringing together of the two should not be underestimated. It provided the theoretical model which the individual parties needed. Because of it, the many disadvantaged communities acquired the right to be recognized as different without being categorized; better still, they won equal treatment precisely because their differentness was taken into consideration. The ruling groups, who were numerically the minority, were thus able to make a compromise which, by redefining the national community, prevented it from breaking up. In this way, in contrast to what was happening in Europe, ideological prohibitions which could have hindered the complete development of this scientific model and its application in education collapsed.

But, as certain authors observed, if its application was to be genuine and fruitful, a further condition had to be met: that cultural anthropology not be presented as the culturalist movement was wont to present it, as a transcendent reality which takes possession of the members of a society in one fell swoop and for reasons unknown. What conclusion could the educator reach on the basis of such a concept? To draw his interest and provide support for potential action on his part it is necessary to identify the processes through which individuals appropriate the various aspects of their cultural model: that is, to provide him with an analysis, or, if you wish, a theory, of 'acculturation', ie the way in which a subject learns his own culture. In this way, the educator will understand first of all the role culture plays in the making of the personality by 'in-forming' it, that is, by imparting form to it. Moreover, the teacher's knowledge of the operations of pattern interiorization will be a necessary condition for developing his own operations which he can use to foster, modify or replace the original ones.

Finally, whatever the environmental variables which affect acculturation, whether they be economic, social, domestic or educational, they can only, in the final analysis, affect the individual through his subjective self. They thus ultimately involve psychology.

All of these conditions were fulfilled by the culturalist school. Thanks to that school, cultural anthropology became operational for human practice. Its exponents did not stop at introducing the vigorous, new notion of 'cultural learning', strongly reinforced by a conception of culture limited to configurations of significations carried by individuals. They also launched a vast reconnaissance effort to pinpoint the subjective operations which could help better define the content of this kind of learning, and strove especially, with the help of psychoanalysis, to define the operations which are part of the unconscious mind: that discipline thus came to be called upon by cultural anthropology, and though the two have an often stormy relationship, their cooperation has never ceased since. Of course, heated debates have taken, and continue to take, place concerning specific details of culturalist analyses or, more important, their theoretical suppositions: for example, the 'basic personality' of A. Kardiner,[14] that is, the progressive inculcation in the members of a society of a particular, common, psychic configuration produced by the action of the same culture. 'This configuration,' comments M. Dufrenne, 'constitutes the basis of personality for the members of a group, the womb in which character traits develop. In short, it is that by which all Comanches are Comanche, and all Frenchmen are French.'[15] What really matters, in any case, is that the manner in which the culturalists formulated the problem brought us out of philosophy into the science of culture. And, as is unanimously recognized, they added to the latter a new discipline called *psychological anthropology*, which can provide the educator with additional avenues of analysis and new means of action.

Also, under these conditions, the fusion with educational science was so natural that Margaret Mead, for example, spent her life trying to draw from the societies she observed educational lessons for her own country.

The synthesis in other countries

It would take years for the movement to gain some kind of acceptance in Europe. That is, for it to draw the interest of Europeans — who were aware of the work in America and had their own eminent ethnologists — other than as an academic curiosity. People there were far more concerned by developments in sociology, a discipline which, particularly under the impetus of the Durkheimian school in France, was flourishing.

This sociological breakthrough had one important consequence for the subject we are concerned with: it made clear to what extent an individual is indissociable from his group, from his 'origins'. The time had come for educational science, in which Durkheim was keenly interested, to take the full measure of the absurdity mentioned earlier, namely, making the goal of education to be individuals abstracted from their social context.

What is more, common aspects were discovered between 'collective representations', which sociologists regarded as resulting from the influence of society, and the 'patterns' of the culturalists. But as we well know, because of Durkheim's concern to maintain a separation between sociology and psychology in order to ensure its autonomy, he did not attempt to look into the mediations which make it possible to go from one to the other. For him, and even more so for his followers, these representations ultimately became a kind of transcendent reality, no doubt subject to objective, institutional transformations by the environment, but which mysteriously take possession of individual psyches like passive objects, thus considerably diminishing the interest for educators with respect to the possibilities of intervening. In addition, the strictly cultural parameter in the sense it ultimately took on in the history of anthropology, though theoretically understood, was hardly used in collective representations, which only tried to highlight the general influence of the 'social dimension' in general of which sociologists speak.

In reality, to change this situation, it took events of a magnitude to alleviate the burden of censure and overcome ideological inertia, on one hand, and to create insurmountable problems on the other.

It is generally agreed that it was the fall of the colonial empires that deprived the ideology behind their ranking of civilizations and behind hierarchical ethnocentrism in its selectionistic, racist and assimilationist versions of its most formidable objective justification. The simultaneous accession of Third World countries to the status of subjects of history with whom communication in all its forms became necessary and often advantageous gradually generated awareness of the specificity of the cultural variable, in the anthropological sense of the word, in these peoples and of the importance of taking that variable into account when trying to understand these societies. The experience gained through cooperation and assistance to these countries, the failures and inefficacy demonstrated by so many experts involved in technology transfers, due in part to their ignorance of this variable, made its extremely practical value clear. How to acquire 'cultural competence' became a serious concern because it could have definite political and economic repercussions. Acquiring an understanding of cultural knowledge has become an independent branch of learning and the number of institutions in the West which deal in it is multiplying.

But it was the influx of huge masses of immigrants from the Third World, initially invited by industrialized countries and constituting a sort of boomerang effect of the former colonization period, which impressed the 'cultural problem' upon the minds of nationals at a popular level, making it an everyday reality with sometimes painful consequences. Very few of them, especially at an occupational level, have not had to deal at some time or other with these newcomers, with the conflicts and rejection they suffered, and there emerged a strong demand for ways of understanding and managing relations with them in a more rational fashion. In this regard, we need hardly mention the role played by the transformations which European education systems constantly underwent as they were confronted with the massive influx of immigrant children: this was probably the main catalyst for the theoretical and practical fusion of the cultural and educational points of view.

In parallel fashion, similar but far more crucial problems arose in decolonized societies. It was quickly realized in these countries that unless the industrialization effort took into consideration certain subjective factors, the objective means for economic development were rendered useless and, more often than not, undesirable consequences resulted. The discovery of the 'human factors of development' made glaringly evident the reality of cultural configurations and the, again practical, importance of the nuances they add to attitudes and representations. In these circumstances, undertaking a critical analysis of spontaneously used mental models — whether borrowed or original — so as to adapt them to the goals of 'development' came to be regarded as a fundamental task. Designing and setting up an education system for instilling representations in people's minds which were hoped to be better suited to the new, complex cultural situation in these societies became the great challenge.

Concurrently, with these movements, a new consciousness took root and spread in Western societies, which, quite unexpectedly, made culture in the anthropological sense a kind of asset sought after in a big way. To understand this, we must return to the representation of modern society which philosophers, from the Cartesians to Kant, including the encyclopedists of the eighteenth century, had provided: that of a subject stripped of all particularistic links, considered to be alienating and whose autonomy is based on its universal, rational essence.

This, like all great ideologies, produced mixed results. Its negative effects include its contribution to the swallowing up of individuals like ants in vast, anonymous societies which are oblivious to differences and reject the values of former communities, and the exposure of these individuals to highly abstract, bureaucratic institutions. And, of course, 'extra-rational' factors, which an effort had been made to 'de-realize', continued to play a pre-eminent role within the context of the new social relationships that were established. Thus, confirming the assertions of the budding science of sociology, it became clear that the supposedly contingent characteristics linking man to the material universe cannot be detached from his essence, and constitute an integral part of him.

This explains, in part at least, the problem raised by a dissenting movement, which came into existence a few decades ago, against this abstract representation of the individual, accused of giving an incomplete, flimsy and ultimately false picture of reality. The rejection of the 'philosophers' conception of man' led to the championing of his opposite: a flesh-and-blood subject asserting his uniqueness and particularities. At the same time, a campaign was launched to eradicate atomistic individualism by detaching the subject from the anonymous mass and reintegrating him in groups for which he 'feels' he exists and in which he can experience the satisfaction of a personalized type of communication.

It is all this which is meant when the term 'identity' is used, a currently popular concept. Its success is understandable because to it are attributed, either explicitly or implicitly, the objectives and functions we just discussed: the restitution to the individual of his uniqueness and the right to enjoy the recognition and satisfactions of the 'right' group. On top of it all, this concept was immediately adopted and popularized in Third World societies as the ultimate and immediate rampart against the invasion of Western culture and its attempts at domination within the context of an extremely unbalanced 'North-South' relationship.

What is interesting is that, to meet these objectives, the identity used in every case was cultural identity. And the groups chosen in which to implant the 'new subject' were those whose contours were culturally defined. It is on the basis of culture and in no other way (for example, through linguistic differences, economic and technological characteristics, etc) that Third World countries assert their 'authenticity' vis-à-vis the West. Even in European countries, types of ethnic or regionalistic groups were more or less re-invented, again on a cultural basis, prior to those theorized about or constituted by industrial society: nation, social class, generation class, etc, seen as being incapable of serving the purposes described above.

We will not pursue this analysis here. It would suffice to point out the significant result achieved. Thanks to the convergence of these various movements, the notion of culture in the anthropological sense, unknown to the general public until recently or considered to be an exotic curiosity of interest only to specialists, quickly become a matter of universal, practical concern. Not only because of the multiplication of interferences between different societies, but also for reasons internal to them. The effects can only have a direct impact on education in which the 'cultural' variable, for one or other reasons analysed above, can no longer be swept aside.

How can we take it into account? What achievements and what problems result from the introduction of this new parameter? We will try to give an overall, rather than in-depth, view of the situation, drawing upon recent works. That is, although we will not exclude historical developments, we will concentrate on *contemporary* problems resulting from the convergence of current educational concerns and different cultural aspects. In doing this, we hope to show how the analyses to which this phenomenon gave rise can help the educator in two very important ways:

— By identifying educational situations in which the failure to take the cultural dimension into account can have negative effects, as experience has demonstrated. But will this tell us how to achieve positive results? Obviously, such will not always be the case: the answers provided by cultural anthropology may prove partial or even nil. But at least it will have drawn attention to these points and brought new elements to the awareness of the educator: for it must be said, the educator cannot expect ready-made solutions from other disciplines and is never relieved of the responsibility of conducting his own analysis in his 'speciality'.
— By also showing how, in certain cases, the use of culture per se or merely the notion of culture is the source of oppression, myths and alibis: identifying this set of negative aspects is also a valuable service to the educator. Consequently, a critical reading of cultural anthropology is, in our opinion, an integral part of education.

Another point needs to be clarified. It is also a risky undertaking to attempt to provide, in a short document, an exhaustive treatment of a problem in its international diversity. In fact, that objective can never really be attained, if only because of gaps and an unequal distribution of information (we availed ourselves of the data banks of the International Bureau of Education in Geneva and the Centre National de Recherche Scientifique in Paris) which, as we know, are due to factors unrelated to the technical aspect. It would be impossible to discuss everything without giving a superficial patchwork which can be challenged on an informational plane and even more so on an educational plane. That is why, in each chapter, we will discuss the least controversial general problems, perceived as being most genuine by the protagonists and the best depicted by authors. In addition, we will use examples to illustrate the situations we know best. In doing so we hope not to give all the data, but to provide analysis outlines; it will be the reader's task to decide whether these are applicable to cases not mentioned or whether they are in need of modification and to what extent. Our goal, therefore, is to stimulate sufficiently informed *reflection* rather than claim to provide an exhaustive — and impossible — account.

NOTES AND REFERENCES

1. Stoetzel, J. *La psychologie sociale*. Paris, Flammarion, 1963, p. 36.
2. E. Vermeersh. An analysis of the concept of culture. *In*: Bernardi, B., ed. *The concept and dynamics of culture*. The Hague, Mouton, 1977. M. Mauviel. *L'idée de culture et de pluralisme culturel: aspects historiques, conceptuels et comparatifs*. Paris, Université de Paris V, 1983.
3. Herskovits, M.J. *Man and his works*. 1st ed. New York, Knopf, 1949, p. 17.
4. Mauviel, M. *Op. cit.*, p. 297.
5. Kroeber, A.L.; Kluckhohn, C. *Culture: a critical review of concepts and definitions*. Cambridge, MA, Peabody Museum of Archaeology and Ethnology, 1952. (Peabody Museum of Archaeology and Ethnology. Papers, 97.)
6. Clapier-Valladon, Simone. *Panorama du culturalisme*. Paris, EPI, 1976, p. 30.
7. Benedict, Ruth. *Patterns of culture*. Boston, MA, Houghton Mifflin, 1934.
8. Herzlich, Claudine. *Santé et maladie: analyse d'une représentation sociale*. The Hague, Mouton, 1969.
9. Banks, J.A. Shaping the future of multicultural education. *The Journal of Negro education* (Washington, DC, Howard University), vol. 48, no. 3, Summer 1979, p. 247.
10. Spindler, G.D. Anthropology may be the answer. *Journal of education* (Boston, MA), vol. 129, 1946.
11. Mauviel, M. Le multiculturalisme (pluralisme culturel). *Revue française de pédagogie* (Paris, Institut national de recherche pédagogique), no.61, octobre-novembre-décembre 1982, p. 64.
12. Baker, Gwendolyn C. Policy issues in multicultural education in the United States. *The Journal of Negro education* (Washington, DC, Howard University), vol. 48, no.3, Summer 1979, p. 254.
13. *Ibid.*, p. 255.

14. Kardiner, A. *The individual and his society: the psychodynamics of primitive social organisation.* New York, Columbia University Press, 1939.
15. Dufrenne, M. *La personnalité de base: un concept sociologique.* 2e éd. Paris, Presses universitaires de France, 1965, p. 128.

CHAPTER II

From simple societies to complex societies: general approaches to the problems posed

Cultural anthropology's first scientific contributions to education can be easily documented. We owe them to the analyses carried out by American cultural anthropologists and their followers, based on their personal field studies in so-called 'primitive' or 'archaic' societies, and those by a number of ethnologists. To avoid these pejorative terms 'archaic' and 'primitive' invented by Western ethnocentrism, we will use the expression 'simple society' in its technical sense. Indeed, compared to larger societies, which we will call 'complex', they are small in size, exhibit only a slight degree of stratification, and contain relatively non-diverse, non-specialized and non-autonomous subgroups. Moreover, their social processes are simpler and easier to isolate.

Complex societies, meanwhile, are the opposite in every one of these respects and are generally of two types: either traditional (for example, ancient Asiatic, Arabo-Muslim and European societies) or 'industrial'. It should be noted that the adjective 'traditional' has raised frequent objections: because on the one hand, it is becoming more and more difficult to apply it without hesitation to any one contemporary social group; on the other, the term is accused of suggesting an absolute contrast with industrial societies for which there is no justification.

In fact, the use of this term is only legitimate in the case of ancient communities, to the extent that they were left completely untouched by the industrial and technological revolutions. Confronted with infinitely less rapid and fewer discontinuous changes than today's societies, they were able to continue, for a long time, to 'repeat' solutions perfected in the past for problems which likewise evolved slowly. These solutions, therefore, which include patterns and cultural traits, had time to crystallize into traditions. Meanwhile, traditions, while prized for their functional value as an effective means of meeting the challenges of the environment, had the further privilege of being officially consecrated and venerated in themselves. These characteristics, which are to be found in both simple societies and complex, traditional groups, are no longer to be found in a completely intact form anywhere: at present we can only speak, in specific cases, of a traditionalist 'predominance'.

In any case, it was the analysis of traditional groups which furnished the earliest, important lessons for education. A better understanding was achieved not only of how other societies, including industrial or 'industrializing' societies, may experience similar problems, but also of how important their individual educational needs are.

Socialization and acculturation

Ethnology, basing itself on investigations into simple groups, placed strong emphasis on socialization. This has since come to be more distinctly regarded as the under the surface part of education, but whose effects are probably most decisive – given the force and even the primacy of the unconscious or partially unconscious learning process which the individual undergoes from birth. Its influences corroborate or contradict the explicit, normative messages received at the conscious level and institutionalized by education.

Socialization involves first and foremost unconscious mechanisms of transmission which allow the individual to acquire the culture of his group, thus aligning the different aspects of his personality in harmony with the other subjects of his group. This is known as *acculturation* and is to some extent the physical support of socialization.

The common forms which the socializing process imprints on communities, with cultural systems as a point of departure, are what interest the educator.

Indeed the educator, in striving to orient the subject in a certain way, must know how he was previously structured by his cultural environment. The advantage is threefold:

- When the 'form' initially interiorized by the subject is taken into account, his reactions can be understood. In this way a satisfactory, uninterrupted channel of communication is maintained, a prerequisite to success in education.
- Cultural particularities have a determinant impact on the attitudes, aspirations, motivations, representations, skills and behaviour of subjects, heightening some and diminishing others: familiarity with these points is crucial to the proper conduct of the learning process.
- A knowledge of the mechanisms affecting personality is necessary in order to be able to modify them.

We have here, therefore, a parameter of considerable importance, which, together with other 'environmental' factors already known, the educational sciences have been made aware of, thanks to ethnology.

Personality development and acculturation

THE MAIN TRAITS OF THE SOCIAL LEARNING PROCESS

The most representative works within the context of 'modern cross-cultural research', to use W.H. Holtzman's[1] expression, concentrate, as he said, on development during early infancy and family models in different cultures. This contribution was made by M. Mead, B. Malinowski and E. Sapin in the 1930s. But the number of works has continued to multiply ever since, under the impetus of psychological anthropology, and the subject is included in more or less every treatise on social psychology. In view of the importance educators have always attributed to them, let us, with W.J.H. Sprott[2] and J. Stoetzel,[3] recall the traits of the social learning process as conditioned by culture and considered to be an important factor in personality formation from the infant stage onwards. We might add, in this regard, that psychoanalysts have lent considerable support to the culturalist school by insisting on the determinant role of childhood experiences 'in the shaping of outlooks on the outside world'[4] and, later, on the structuring of the individual. The following are the characteristics to which the greatest importance is currently attached.

First, there are the varying degrees of attention of which the child is the object, as determined by the cultural model which establishes his 'distance' with respect to adults: he may be constantly near them and enjoy continuous emotional contact, or he may be left in isolation. There may even be the alternative between cuddling and abandonment as in the case of Balinese infants. Anthropologists and psychoanalysts are debating the permanent adult attitudes which can result.[5] Coherent emotional treatment is generally held to be a necessary condition for personality development.

Akin to this parameter is that of temporal distribution of the satisfaction of the child's needs: anxieties relieved as soon as they manifest themselves and intermittent or irregular satisfaction of needs. Here the entire problem of timing comes into play with respect to feeding, bathing, changing positions, the freeing of movements, etc.

The latter point is related to the practice of swaddling and subsequent unwrapping, which is extremely widespread in the world. Chiefly by means of this practice, the infant undergoes the experience of a constraint–freedom progression. Both the amount of freedom allowed and the attitudes of the people performing the swaddling must be taken into account. The vivid description provided by G. Gorer[6] on a form of swaddling practised in Great Russia, which was so extreme that, even when unwrapped, the babies remained rigid, is classic. What is more, not only are the child's movements restricted, but as soon as he cries a dummy is put into his mouth: this then is one of many examples of integrated practices through which a single trait or even a coherent cultural model is expressed.

Weaning practices have been the topic of a vast body of literature especially following the analyses of M. Mead.[7] It is significant whether this is accomplished progressively, all at once, gently or brusquely. The same applies to toilet training and learning sphincter control and whether this is done at an early or later age includes the obligation to such privacy or involves punishment.

This can result, as J. Stoetzel noted, 'in very different impressions in the child about his body which can affect him for the rest of his life'.[8] It is this last point which is important when we consider these disciplines as a whole. The problem for the investigator is to see how these effects are transmitted and through what avenues they come to shape attitudes in the individual which can be long-lasting, if not permanent. Accordingly, toilet training, which has been extensively studied by psychoanalysts, in our cultures is, as W.J.H. Sprott said, 'a matter of importance in the relationship between parent and child'. It even has symbolic value insofar as 'sphincter control is one of the child's first essays in social responsibility'. An additional factor is 'the heightened emotional atmosphere' surrounding what the child experiences as a debate with his family and his social entourage. Understanding what is at stake, the child's reactions shift levels:

> the response may be one of obstinate refusal to give what is demanded; it may be that an exaggerated regard for cleanliness, tidiness, accuracy is generated as a kind of countermeasure to the primary interest in the abominated thing; it may be that the child, dimly apprehending the sensibilities of adults, realizes that in untimely urination it has a weapon which it can use against them.[9]

Psychologists claim that these types of behaviour tend to become generalized and form components of the personality. We can see how this comes about — the perception of the social stakes within a highly emotionally charged family life. The types of behaviour these disciplines deal with are only the first step towards becoming aware of what is at stake and defining the rules involved. Among these, the most basic are the cultural rules which filter through the specific treatment children receive from their parents.

The kinds of social relationships the child experiences and develops into adult life are also important. First, he will have a different idea of the human environment, depending upon whether or not this environment is differentiated. Beginning with the family, the variety of relationships is determined by the cultural model. The natural parents may take care of their child themselves, the entire group may do so with priority being given to no one, or only the women or only the men. In the three latter cases, in contrast to the first, no one adult will enjoy a more intense or more intimate emotional relationship or have a monopoly on care and protection. These practices exclude disciplinary techniques based on threats. 'If I do this or that, father or mother will give me their affection or withdraw it.' Learning must proceed from other kinds of logic.

Another significant factor is the acuteness of the distinction between ages among siblings and their status according to the place they occupy, resulting in hierarchical relationships of varying degrees to which are attached the notion of 'rank' and special treatment on the part of parents: all of this is by and large of a cultural nature.

When the infant matures, social relationships proper open up to him. Depending on the type of society in which he lives, he will experience extremely different ways of integration into the adult world. The timing at which this takes place varies significantly: early entry into the adult world or a long delay as is the case in Western industrial societies. Above all, the path is signposted to different degrees. In contrast to the specific initiation rites, which in simple societies clearly indicate the stages to be cleared and the rights and obligations the individual must assume, in a good number of contemporary societies, these elements are left unspecified to a significant extent. This lack of clarity coupled with the great number of years necessary to enter into active life and the adult world are held to be determinant factors in the 'adolescent crisis' so frequently spoken of in the West.

However, another important point needs to be considered: the continuity and discontinuity between the roles and statuses assigned to the different age groups throughout life, to which may or may not be attached an obligation to 'unlearn' what had previously been learned. According to Ruth Benedict,[10] in some simple societies, the child is considered to have the same kind of personality as the adult, but not the same capacity of execution. It remains, however, that at a very early age he does, according to his possibilities, the same things he will do as an adult man. Conversely, in Western societies, culture institutes a discontinuity which even creates an opposition between the roles of the child and the adult in at least three areas: irresponsibility and responsibility, submission and domination, and sexuality. In the latter case, the image inculcated at the pre-adult age must simply be reversed at the adult age: this is the source of a good many complications.

THE DEBATE ON THE EXPLANATORY APPROACH

The approaches at observation and analysis efforts whose salient characteristics we have just given are drawn from a large number of monographs in which authors attempted to establish a correspondence between the main adult personality traits and sociocultural conditions of accession to adulthood. They have also attempted to penetrate the socialization 'programme' responsible for the construction of differences in sex-group status in each ethnic group. This was the goal of M. Mead, in particular:

> The underlying purpose of my field studies in New Guinea was to discover to what degree temperamental differences between the sexes were innate and to what extent they were culturally determined, and furthermore to inquire minutely into the educational mechanisms connected with these differences.[11]

Under the influence of behaviourism, however, this approach degenerated into oversimplification. For the psychosociologist J. Dollard,[12] for example, who was extremely influential, acculturation tends to be reduced to ultimately mechanical processes of conditioning and habit acquisition. As P. Erny observed, 'the individual is thus considered to be an organization, albeit complex and extremely specific, of progressively acquired external, material forms of behaviour.'[13] Similarly, the belief which underlies, implicitly at least, this type of analysis is that the malleability of the human being is unlimited: hence, the omnipotence of education. This idea, M. Dufrenne asserts, is typical of American anthropologists (those of the time, at least): 'Everything is possible for whomever has the means. There is no nature which cannot be violated, no past from which we cannot detach ourselves, and no habit which we cannot inculcate.'[14]

The first step was to abandon this exaggerated segmentarist method which tended to make a given individual cultural trait the cause of a given personality trait. As M. Dufrenne pointed out, 'the specific content of education can only be understood in relation to the cultural whole.'[15] At a more concrete level, as M. Mead had already warned us, each learning episode is meaningful only insofar as it is reinforced by other cultural manifestations, by other traits contained in the same subsystems (for example, child-raising techniques) or those contained in other cultural subsystems studied (for example, paternal authority over the child finds expression in sibling relationships, the couple, social stratification, etc). But they are also to be found in the attitudes expressed by the educator while teaching the 'lesson'. 'Brutal weaning using red pepper,' J. Stoetzel observed, commenting on M. Mead, 'will have two different significations depending on whether the mother's attitude is also brutal as shown by her actions and the tone of her voice or whether she cuddles the child and speaks softly to it.' We should add that the child's education is not only a sequential process; it is a process carried out in a cultural world where everything is simultaneous.

A child which is weaned in a violent fashion or frequently subjected to ice-cold baths, as is the case in the Marquesas Islands, will not automatically be predisposed towards witchcraft, but he will nonetheless have seen his mother practise witchcraft, tremble when she sees a neighbour pick up an object she has not seen, and hug her child closely when a stranger passes who may be a witch.[16]

No matter how harsh the effects of learning experiences in the first few years of life, they clearly require the daily, multifold, generalizing reinforcements of the system in which the adult is immersed.

THE DEBATE ON HUMAN NATURE

The second qualification some authors advance with respect to what they consider excessive culturalism is the basic, common, biological constant shared by all men, that is, 'human nature': it marks the limits of change through education.

The debate on this subject was especially important in the confrontation between ethnology and psychoanalysis. From its very origin, psychoanalysis readily accepted variations in personality development under the influence of social factors in general, and cultural factors in particular. Was not the objective of the Freudian approach to reveal the universal avatars of the 'libido' in all human beings resulting from its coming into contact with social norms which prevent it from satisfying itself without hindrance? And may not a culture be considered to be a specific programme for channelling the libido, that is, its expression and repression, a defined system for distributing permissions and frustrations? This explains the interest shown by psychoanalysts in the observations made by ethnologists.

According to Freudianism, however, sociocultural elements belong to the ego, but especially to the superego, the socialized aspect of the personality which is located at the borderline between the subject and his environment. The libido and the unconscious, as the dynamic nucleus of individuality, escape the social dimension because they are suppressed: the drives which are protected from the conscious mind and society are presumed to be identical in everyone.

This position has been challenged by the majority of sociologists and ethnologists.[17] As P. Erny observed, 'this is the crux of the problem'. And he quite rightly adds:

The question is whether the social factor is simply a veneer, or whether it penetrates the living being by stages until it reaches the most intimate, secret layers, whether human society is merely a domesticating and repressive force for instincts which are rigid, immutable and universal, because related to the biological being, or whether it has a genuinely creative capacity and can affect human inclination at its very roots through social processes, cultural change, and historical evolutions. Are complexes, first and foremost the Oedipus complex, cultural, hence contingent, products or the necessary, inescapable manifestations of innate instincts? Does the social context explain psychological diversity or does psychological diversity explain the social context? Should we speak of the 'unconscious' in the singular or the plural?[18]

It is not within the scope of this book to provide a detailed account of the debate. W.H. Holtzman went so far as to assert that 'most early studies of personality development in different cultures were carried out by anthropologists in exotic cultures to test psychoanalytic theory.'[19] Suffice it to say that the second argument discussed above is the most opposed to the Freudian point of view and was at the outset remarkably defended for the first time by B. Malinowski.[20] According to that author, the Oedipus complex corresponds to a well-defined type of family and social organization, the specific traits of which are precisely those which held sway in the patriarchal, sexually repressive Viennese society in which Freud lived. It would not exist in a society such as the one he studied: the Trobriandese, a sexually permissive society which is organized in such a way that the father does not become the son's rival nor is the mother immune to her son's affection. A. Kardiner[21] shares this point of view, as does E. Fromm,[22] who goes so far as to suggest that the libido is capable of socialization. G. Roheim,[23] meanwhile, is convinced of the unity and universality of the libido on to which are grafted cultural differences. Using this argument as a basis, he theorizes that the unchanging libido can simply displace its points of application depending upon the sociocultural organization: on to the maternal uncle, for example, in the case of the Oedipus complex in a matriarchal society. The diversity of cultures is explained by the fact that they play the same role at the group level as defence mechanisms and the various forms of sublimation at the individual level. The complexes are always identical, but the defence mechanisms by means of which social groups overcome them are extremely varied.

The same displacement point of view is defended by M.-C. and E. Ortigues[24] in their treatment of African societies. G. Devereux reverts back to a more orthodox psychoanalytical approach when he asserts that the same unconscious fears, reactions and prohibitions manifest themselves when subjects belonging to different cultures are analysed: he thus concludes that universal principles transcend the individual traits of specific cultures.[25]

The debate has never been definitively decided and it is difficult to see how it can be on the basis of pure reason without field work. On the empirical side, the defenders of these two theories are not on an equal footing. For the exponents of total relativism it would be sufficient to find a single culture contradicting the presumed 'naturalness' of a trait for it to cease being worthy of the qualification 'natural'. Human nature thus becomes, for those who wish to believe in it, a kind of ideal limit: that which has ultimately resisted cultural 'erosion'. But how can we be sure?

This state of affairs cannot but have an influence on practitioners, and educators, especially: culturalism broadens their potential scope of activity without predetermined boundaries, encourages them to distance themselves from current practices, to accept nothing as absolute, and not to shrink from innovation. Does it follow that there are no more obstacles to voluntarism in education, which would consider man to be capable of submission to no matter what scheme?

Whereas this conclusion may leave some people optimistic, it inspires extreme distrust towards cultural relativism on the part of others: by enabling us to consider that everything in education is possible and relative, and thus eliminating all possibility of establishing a hierarchy of educational standards, this system can only lead to complete scepticism and laxity. One proof of this is the liberalization of educational practices in the United States following the publication of the observations of Margaret Mead and other anthropologists (the fact that one followed the other being held to be a causal relationship).

The state of affairs is based on a misunderstanding. By making known the educational options offered by human reality (rather than 'nature'), the culturalists are only striving to inform: for it is not their role to make any recommendations whatsoever, nor to establish a hierarchy of any kind. Like physical scientists they provide or would like to provide lists of established sequences: educating in a certain way, in a given context, obtains a certain result. The rest is to choose, but the criterion for the choice of any human act is not to be found in anthropology any more than in any other science. Once this fact is accepted, a more specific criticism can be voiced: this school of researchers discarded an excellent principle by destroying, in actual practice if not in theory, the concept of a universal human nature. We can counter by asking, how do we determine the point in time at which human beings, on the basis of this 'nature', decide on a system of morals, the ultimate authority which determines their educational choices? Every time men have attempted to do so, the point of departure has been a particular idea of 'nature', thus remaining within the realm of ideology, upon which moral systems are dependent. And as we know, in the overwhelming majority of cases, it is precisely in opposition to their nature (ie its image) that they have constructed these systems.

The culturalist contribution, therefore, has changed nothing with respect to the basic conditions of renewal in education. They cannot be accused of leaving the door open to educational voluntarism because, taken in its broader sense, we have never got away from it, given the fact that educational standards have always preceded systems of representation and conceptualization produced by the human mind. It still remains that these systems did not come out of nowhere: in putting them together, groups and individuals are influenced by, or take into account, their overall environment and the challenges it poses. All the data and analyses provided by the social sciences are extremely valuable, in particular those provided by cultural anthropology which brushes a vast panorama of educational experiences as related to real-life situations. The only other discipline to offer something similar is comparative education.[26] Like any new source of information, these branches do not determine our choices but, in an initial phase, render more complicated the *conditions* in which these choices are made. For they upset ready-made stereotypes, reveal the simplistic character of former solutions, and expose illusions (and often generate nostalgia on their behalf). In the long run, however, they made more refined alternatives *possible*.

In the final analysis, a distinction needs to be made within voluntarism itself between 'gratuitous' and enlightened voluntarism. It is the latter variety which cultural science helps to establish, provided we ask of it only what can legitimately be asked of a science.

NEW TYPES OF INVESTIGATION

The well-known studies we have just cited were monographs on small, simple groups. This traditional type of research has not run dry as J. Rabain's study[27] on the Wolof child in Senegal, considered a classic of its kind, and others demonstrate. These mainly involved case studies, rather than cross-cultural research, because they were not conducted explicitly for the purposes of comparison. The comparison was made later, often by people other than the authors, with the flaws associated with this kind of procedure: as each author conducted his study in his own way, how can we compare something which is sometimes far from being comparable, and make valid interpretations and conclusions?

An attempt was subsequently made to design research projects which avoided these drawbacks and to incorporate into them a comparative blueprint which would make it possible to question cultures on identical points, decided upon in advance, and in identical methodological conditions. These projects made it possible to deal with several societies at a time, including complex societies or subgroups within them, and made use of modern, large-scale techniques of investigation and exploitation. A typical example of this new approach is the vast programme launched by Whiting.[28] This investigator undertook the comparison of six cultures, based on a sample of 100-odd societies, ranging from a New England village to an African tribe in Kenya. Survey teams conducted an intensive study of 24 mother-child groups. But, faced with limited material means, they decided to concentrate on a number of aspects of personality development defined in advance: in this case, patterns of aggression, dependence, the interiorization of various mechanisms of behaviour control. As W.H. Holtzman[29] noted, we have here a model which is well known to modern psychologists: an investigation of correlations between several variables (as, in another survey by the same investigator, the correlation between the amount of permissiveness allowed the child and the type of family structure), using whole societies as sample units and statistical calculations as the basis for generalization.

This type of approach is likewise not without imperfections: as Holtzman remarked,

the data came from observation and interview, leaving still unsettled the problem of calibrating the human observer. The number of cases in each sample remains uncomfortably small because of the great expense of collecting such intensive data. And the level of quantification generally falls considerably short.

And he concludes, 'From a psychologist's point of view, the pancultural approach is severely limited in what can be added to our present knowledge of personality development.'[30]

Accordingly, it was considered more realistic to concentrate on a very limited sampling of cultures, selected in such a way as to multiply the number of variations on a dimension deemed to be of special interest and making it possible to increase the number of subjects surveyed. This was the case with the study conducted by H. and G. Anderson[31] on the development of moral values in children from nine countries in Western Europe and America. They used a questionnaire to gather data and the story completion technique to evaluate the dimensions of honesty, responsibility, anxiety and guilt, based on the imaginative material obtained. An evaluation was made of the correlation between these traits and the nine countries, which were classified according to a scale of political and social structures ranging from authoritarianism to democracy.

Unfortunately, this study contained a flaw which most frequently affects pluricultural studies: the societies selected differed with respect to a good many other independent variables. It thus remains to be seen whether the differences noted are in fact due to the cultural variable being considered, which needs to be extracted from its package ('packaged variables').

W.H. Holtzman himself conducted one of the few studies in which the variables of culture, socio-economic status, sex and age were separated.[32] The objective was to compare representative samples of young people from 6 to 17 years old in the United States and Mexico on the basis of personality development. This study, which lasted 12 years, had the rare advantage of being longitudinal: a barrage of cognitive, perceptive and personality tests were given to each subject each year.

We will not relate here the various special results of the cognitive part of this study. In the case of personality development, meanwhile, a few interesting points may be highlighted in illustration of what this type of modern approach can achieve, a far cry from traditional ethnological methods:

— In both groups of young people, the degree of consistency in measurements increased with age. However, where there were cultural differences between individuals, they were less persistent with Mexicans than with Americans: cultural 'standardization' seems to be more intense with the former.
— In many cases, sets of intercorrelations proved to be remarkably similar in both cultures.
— Clear, uniform differences between the two cultures were to be observed, independent of sex, age and socio-economic status. Several uniformly significant differences, from the cultural point of view, emerged. Class-related differences in performance were noted in the case of Mexicans, but not their American counterparts. In some cases, the difference between the two groups was reversed with age. Girls were shown to be more field-dependent than boys, and Mexican girls more so than American girls.

The author concludes,

The many significant differences found between Mexican and American children led to several broad generalizations dealing with the cognitive abilities and intellectual stimulation of the child, active versus passive coping styles, and the way in which field dependence or psychological differentiation is related to socialization practices in the two cultures.[33]

Studies carried out by other researchers seem to agree with the results he obtained with respect to several general hypotheses:

— Americans tend to be more active than Mexicans in their style of coping with life's problems and challenges. Americans tend to be more technological, dynamic and external than Mexicans in the meaning of activity within subjective culture. Americans tend to be more complex and differentiated in cognitive structure than Mexicans.[34]
— Mexicans tend to be more family-centred, while Americans are more individual-centred. Mexicans tend to be more cooperative in interpersonal activities, while Americans are more competitive. Mexicans tend to be more fatalistic and pessimistic in outlook on life than Americans.

We thus have a typical portrayal of attitudes and values assembled by anthropologists on the basis of investigations, not all of which are as sophisticated as the one we just described. We have, however, come a long way from traditional ethnological studies, but are still relatively close to the syntheses made by the founders of culturalism in their effort to find the ultimate model which would reveal the 'hard core' of a culture (in the previous chapter we gave the example of the Zuñi model described by R. Benedict).

The danger of this approach is still the same, however: these composite pictures are always the result of generalization, logical systemization and rationalized interpretation based upon a set of localized, specific, contingent facts. The extrapolation will be even greater if, given the current cultural fad and the resultant popularization effect, actual research is replaced by somewhat hasty 'observations'. In the final conclusions, the truth is likely to be seriously tainted with stereotypes.

In all investigations of this type, we cannot be over-vigilant about the adjectives used, for they are par excellence the unconscious, insidious means of penetration of ethnocentric references. For example, great care must be taken in presenting *behaviour* patterns for which pairs of qualifiers such as 'optimistic-pessimistic', 'dynamic-fatalistic', 'active-passive', 'competitive-cooperative', etc are used. And, as we have seen, these types of behaviour must be situated within the overall cultural context of which the actors are a part: it is based on this condition that an investigator often finds himself obliged to reconsider the adjectives which came spontaneously to mind.

Functions, aptitudes and acculturation

Cultural factors have not only been studied in relation to personality development, but also to their impact on the psyche and its confrontation with the environment.

The basic, guiding principle behind this approach is obvious. Although it may be that individuals, because of their membership of the human race, are endowed with the same psychic apparatus and are potentially capable of the same operations, they do not necessarily use them in the same way. This is due to a number of reasons, some of which involve cultural patterns. Indeed, these patterns help designate systems of typical situations in the environment: for example, in how we deal with aspects of the physical universe, animals, production, consumption, work, time, birth, death, relations between the sexes and between generations, etc. There is a limited number of possibilities in dealing with these. Accordingly, no matter how men and women approach each other, individual variations in a given society are part of a pre-established scheme which they anticipate. This coherent set of models, of 'codes', which by and large make individual adaptive improvisation unnecessary, ensures smooth 'social circulation' for subjects belonging to the same culture and governed by the same system of typical situations.

An interplay of attitudes and motivations develops around these situations, concentrates on them and favours them, while brushing all others aside. The exercise of functions and aptitudes in this way takes specific directions, stimulates learning experiences and channels everyday efforts and behaviour towards specific points of application. At the same time, the repetition of the same types of conduct in the same types of situation leads to their reinforcement and refinement. Thus, in every culture, individuals choose a set of effective, differentiating *performances* from within the field of their theoretical possibilities.

If such is the case, we posit that the various social and cultural groups have at their disposal an equivalent capital of aptitudes: the difference is due to the fact that some are implemented and others not. What also varies from group to group are the stimuli which trigger these capabilities.[35] Obviously the consequences for cross-cultural education are considerable. Indeed, the inability to achieve a certain performance in a Western school has every chance of being interpreted, by the uninformed teacher, as a 'deficit'. But, as M. Mauviel commented,

if the deficit involves the interaction of a specific situation and a specific kind of behaviour which does not adjust to it, the teacher's problem is to identify the conditions which stimulate cognitive capacities and motivations, to reproduce these conditions in the classroom, and then to facilitate the incorporation of these capacities into a broad, representative assortment. . . . Thus, taking situations and interaction with them into account is extremely important.[36]

To define the way in which each group perceives its milieu, H.C. Triandis coined the expression *subjective culture:* 'Subjective culture is a cultural group's characteristic way of perceiving the man-made part of its environment. The perception of rules and the group's norms, roles, and values are aspects of subjective culture.'[37]

Cultural variations of this type affect all aspects of the psyche, as was amply demonstrated as soon as cultural anthropology stimulated research in this direction.

Affective behaviour types, generally held to be most 'natural' and including basic emotions such as fear, anger, joy, sadness, desire, etc, change culturally in their individual parameters, particularly with respect to the mechanism which triggers them (what generates passionate jealousy in one case in another causes indifference or amusement); their degree of intensity; the circumstances in which expressing them is permitted or required; the way in which they are expressed (mimics, gestures, attitudes); their social accompaniment (in private, in the presence of a large or small group, in an informal or institutional way); the social characteristics demanded of their agents (manifestation permitted, recommended or required depending on sex, age, status, etc) and many other things as well. If the educator is aware of these, he can avoid certain abrupt, harsh reactions, such as those described by V. Masemann:[38]

One is reminded of King's description of a residential school in the Canadian Yukon where Indian children who have been socialized at home in 'affective learning' are admonished by the teachers to 'stop pawing' them when they reach out in gestures of affection...

Thus, all these variations, which are commonly thought to belong to a domain where spontaneity reigns, in fact answer to a minutely detailed code. For these types of behaviour are not only instances of self-expression, but are also signs for others; as a result, given the importance of affective energy and its potential consequences, the group is extremely intent on converting this spontaneous language into an institutionalized one, making it possible to interpret exactly what is at stake and to control its manifestation and satisfaction.[39]

Perception is intimately 'in-formed' by culture, so much so that individuals from different cultural groups, when confronted with stimuli which are thought to be objectively identical, do not perceive the same things. They 'manipulate' the spectrum of colours and visual, olfactory, auditory and rhythmic scales differently. Numerous surveys have been conducted showing how people perceive the things in their environment to which they have been sensitized. This translates into an amazing sharpening of the senses with respect to these aspects of reality and a no less amazing diversification of language (the classical examples of nuances on snow in Eskimo, camel position in the case of desert tribes, etc). In contrast, there is the absence of words from the vocabulary of other groups which seems to indicate that their indifference to certain aspects of the environment goes so far as to 'cloud' their perception. Analysis of colour vision also sheds light on universal and cultural nuances through study of linguistic encoding.[40]

With respect to how people handle *time* and *space*, ethnological — and sociological — studies over the past 50 years have revealed an amazing degree of variety. For example, numerous studies have demonstrated differences in sensitivity to optico-geometrical 'illusions' among populations living in spatial environments structured according to specific dominant shapes: for example, environments which are 'saturated' with right angles (cube-shaped architectural forms), vertical lines (cities, tropical forests) or horizontal lines (flatlands and open spaces).[41] As P. Dasen noted:

The stimuli projected on to our retina are always ambiguous; we often interpret them automatically, that is, unconsciously, as emanating from a given object according to previous experience with like configurations in a functional manner. Optico-geometric illusions make use of generally functional processes, but lead to wrong interpretations in a specific case.[42]

This does not mean that automatic conclusions can be drawn: according to the same author, cultural differences notwithstanding, 'the universals are often surprising'. He cites a study on sensori-motor intelligence in Baoulé children of the Ivory Coast[43] in which researchers were 'amazed to find that adaptation of equipment (choosing objects from the environment rather than unfamiliar objects such as rakes, plastic tubes, small casts, etc) in no way changed the results'.[44] As N. Warren stated, differences are only recognized on the basis of a common stockpile.[45]

Finally, again with respect to the subject of space, a new discipline is currently being developed known as proxemics, which analyses interpersonal space and the different ways in which people structure and occupy space: generally speaking, the objective is to explore the relationship between space and communication. As the work of E.T. Hall[46] has demonstrated, cross-cultural comparison in this area is particularly stimulating. Much has been learned about how contacts between individuals from different cultural backgrounds are structured.

Time also undergoes various 'manipulations'. For example, to cite just a few conclusions, the linear organization of time and the activities for which it serves as a support, with a before, a during and an after, and the expectation of a certain order and a conclusion, are not universal.[47]

For the Hopi Indians of Arizona, time and space are in a way truncated and mingled with other more basic categories. The attitude towards them in general and the way they are used may change according to the social group or subgroup.

Thus, in the United States, great emphasis has been placed on the differences between subjects of Anglo-Saxon culture and Hispanic culture and the importance they attribute to time, to how precise it is, to the commitments it gives rise to, to planning and to the meaning of 'future'. Surveys conducted in France by A. Vasquez[48] using immigrant Lusitanian children and Spanish-speaking South American children registered the words most frequently used by them in speech. The word pronounced most often is *vite* (quickly). According to the author, this word 'characterizes time in France for these subjects. They find that speaking about time and acting in time are synonymous with speed: *"faire vite"* (hurry up), then, becomes the definition of school. A subject from the older group of children gave an illustration of this with respect to the natural sciences teacher who told the class the first day that the curriculum was a "race against the clock". Another subject reported that he asked his physics teacher for further explanation and the teacher refused because "there was no time".' Following this word in frequency of appearance is '*être ou arriver en retard*' (to be or to arrive late). At the same time, '*lent* and *bien* (slow, well) and *lent* and *réfléchir* (slow, reflect) appear to be used as counter-values, representing the organization of time over there, particularly in opposition to the classroom where "quickly and well" are generally associated.'[49]

To conclude on the question of perception, we might add that 'distortions' can be institutionalized depending on sociocultural demands, as B. Malinowski demonstrated: in the Trobriand Islands, it is understood that a person never resembles his mother, or her brothers and sisters, or his own brothers and sisters.[50] As J. Stoetzel comments, 'perception gives us "reality".' That is what we mean when we speak of institutionalization of perception.[51]

The *memory* has also been extensively written about in ethnology and sociology. It was found that we memorize according to what is meaningful to us and our activities. As we know, culture contributes enormously to the selection and assignment of value to significations while at the same time relativizing them, because they only appear as such within a defined group. In the early part of the century, the sociologist M. Halbwachs produced an extensive theoretical study on the social aspects of this faculty,[52] and in his discussion on the memory of social classes and of religious groups he shed light on the relationship between memory and subcultures. Later on, F.C. Bartlett made his now classic observation concerning the Swazis of South Africa.[53] He showed how faithfulness and precision of recollection and the way in which events are remembered and formulated were all directly related to the importance of the social and cultural interests at stake.

But the meaning assigned to objects depends also on attitudes towards them. Accordingly, the influence of attitude towards other communities and ethnic groups can be evaluated. During a study, V. Seeleman[54] presented photographs of black students and white students and found that subjects who were hostile towards blacks were less able to identify them when shown the pictures a second time: racial stereotypes have as strong an influence on memory as on perception.

Among contemporary works, we might dwell on an approach shared by a great many researchers. Leaving aside all considerations of general mental faculties, this approach attempts to identify the specific ways in which groups and individuals function, whether with respect to perception or to the different aspects of reasoning. The investigations of D.A. Wagner[55] and M. Cole applied their outlook to memory. Cole, who was a teacher in Liberia, sought to understand the processes of acquisition of mathematical concepts among the local people, the Kpelle. He was thus one of the founders of cognitive anthropology. He conducted a series of tests comparing conditions of free recall of lists of words by sample groups of people: illiterate subjects, on one hand, and subjects schooled in the Western style, on the other. Unlike the second group, the first proved unable to perform, whereas they had no difficulty with recollection in normal life situations.

The difference, according to the author, was due to the experimental nature of the situation in which, contrary to the more common recall situations, 'grammatically disconnected'[56] material was used: subjects who had not had Western-type school experience could not fit them into any pre-existing scheme of things, 'a ready-made organization that is habitually evoked by certain situations and used to structure recall'. In Bartlett's terminology, these structures correspond to 'persistent social tendencies' which act in such a way that 'things are remembered because their natural contexts are organized in ways which are socially real for the individual'. What is more, in these experiments, the objects named were familiar but 'the motivation to remember them comes from an arbitrary source, such as the desire to earn money or to appear clever. Recall is requested almost immediately.' The aptitude for structuring the arbitrary, meanwhile, which American pupils seemed to master best, appears to be acquired through learning, thus proving two things: one, that 'the skills necessary for effective short-term recall differ among cultures',[57] and two, there is little justification for speaking of differences in psychological structure, because learning makes the acquisition of similar skills possible.

Intellectual operations are of interest to cultural investigation for several reasons. First of all, it is evident that the term 'intelligence' is applied by social groups according to their needs and their own criteria. As J. Stoetzel said, 'certificates of intelligence or stupidity are conferred for very different reasons in the country or in towns, by young people or by middle-aged people, in the factory, in the shop, in universities. . . . Each group defines intelligence in its own way.'[58] Among the Kpelle people, studied by M. Cole,

the adjective *clever* does not apply to such technological operations as rice farming, house building and car repairing. A farmer may be considered lazy or hard-working, but the term *clever* is restricted to the social sphere. A related fact is that the same kinds of people who found it difficult to explain the principles of good house building found it easy to tell us how their children should be raised.[59]

Mundy-Castle corroborates this observation[60] when saying that because of differences in the stimuli to which they are exposed, Africans acquire an intelligence which is more oriented towards social knowledge and Europeans towards technical knowledge. Among social factors involved in the granting of 'certificates of intelligence', an analysis has no difficulty in identifying those which are cultural in nature.

But differences can also affect the way in which intelligence functions, that is, 'reasoning'. For example, M. Granet, at the beginning of this century, characterized the process of traditional Chinese thought as being based on 'analogical intuition' and gave the following example:

Close relatives are treated like close relatives, that is why ancestors are honoured. Ancestors are honoured, that is why the elder branch is respected. The elder branch is respected, that is why the unity of the family group is maintained. The unity of the family group is maintained, that is why the temple of ancestors is venerated. The temple of ancestors is venerated, that is why the altar of the earth and the harvest are considered strong, etc...[61]

In general, as M. Cole states, observations have 'led to the widespread belief that different cultures produced different psychological (in the present case, cognitive) processes'.[62] Thus, numerous references can be found to the 'concrete' character of traditional African thinking, to the distaste of unschooled Africans for abstract thinking,[63] and to cultural differences affecting psychological differentiations.[64]

What conclusions can we draw from these variations in the way judgments are connected? Can we go so far as to deduce that, depending upon the culture, the basic mechanisms of thought themselves are liable to vary? Lévy-Bruhl,[65] we know, was famous for using this point of view in his theory about the 'primitive mentality' as opposed to our own (a hypothesis he ultimately abandoned). According to this author, our intelligence is governed by the principles of identity and determinism. However, the mentality of the primitive, he believes, functions according to a 'principle of participation', the possibility for entities and realities to be both themselves and something else at the same time, a notion totally foreign to our logic. In addition, seen from the point of view of the content of representations, this way of thinking he qualified as 'mystical'.

Two major objectives were opposed to this theory, preshadowing the types of arguments which would systematically come up. First, it was shown that in many circumstances (especially in the case of practical actions necessary for survival) 'primitive society's' man knew how to use the principles of identity and of objective causality. And 'civilized' people have been known to 'participate' in emotional, passionate states when affectivity takes over. Franz Boas[66] concludes from this debate that no judgment about the way of thinking of a group's members can be made based on its everyday beliefs.

M. Gluckman, summing up the position of a great number of anthropologists, stated that these processes are 'more complex' in the 'primitive society' now and that 'neither his character nor the type of mind he possesses, nor his *Weltanschauung* can be extrapolated from beliefs belonging to his culture, especially myths and mystical beliefs'.[67]

These arguments, however, did not bring the debate to a close. From the empirical evidence of the differences presented by cultures, we could conclude that there are not two, but an infinite number of structures of thought. At the same time, there is a certain resurgence of interest in dichotomies analogous to that advanced by Lévy-Bruhl.[68]

M. Cole concentrated specifically on this point of view in his work in Liberia. He proved that subjects educated in Western schools had acquired specific attitudes: like Americans of the same age, they possessed the 'ability to treat the individual stimulus presentations as subproblems (or examples) from which the solution to *the* problem can be derived';[69] they also demonstrated an ability to make use of general, abstractly isolated dimensions such as the colour or size of objects in solving these problems. In short, these subjects showed a marked aptitude for thinking in terms of general ideas and abstract concepts. Must we, therefore, oppose them as different 'in nature' to their non-educated counterparts? The originator of this research does not think so: 'We cannot conclude from these data that the observed differences in performance reflect differences in the cognitive skills possessed by the two groups,' for 'our data also indicate that (1) under some conditions non-literate subjects will combine subproblems, and (2) under some conditions non-literate subjects use a common stimulus dimension to guide their responding.'[70] For example, he adds, if we had to base our generalizations on the results they obtained in discrimination transfer operations, we could conclude that they are only capable of rote processes.

However, 'we found concept-based learning in the transposition and reversal-shift studies.'[71]

Thus he concludes that cultural differences reflect changes in the situations to which different cognitive skills apply, rather than in general thought processes. And he formulates some heuristic rules on this basis, which to us appears to bring the logical side of the debate to a definite close. The first is that we should never conclude on the basis of research or observations of any kind, 'that one group "has a process" while another does not. . . . It is always possible that further experimentation would turn up evidence of the hypothetical process under the proper circumstances.'[72] Second, however decisive the situational factor may appear to be (the very one commanded, inter alia, by cultures), before commencing an experiment prior ethnographic analysis is needed 'in order to identify the kinds of activities that people often engage in and hence ought to be skilful at dealing with'.[73]

Note that for his hypothesis on the relativity of intellectual processes to the typical situations most often confronted, Cole quotes A.R. Luria. This scientist, a student of Lev Vigotsky, elaborated this point of view following research in the USSR in the 1930s on the effect of the Soviet socialist revolution on ancient Islamic culture.[74]

No discussion on cross-cultural research in cognitive psychology, a particularly attractive field for contemporary experts, can take place without speaking about the numerous works which, to test Piaget's theory of the stages of the development of intelligence, bring in the cultural parameter by focusing on the most diverse societies. The Geneva psychologist believed that the order of these stages is universal and that cultural factors only affect the age at which they are reached. Is this really so? The question has been intelligently analysed by Lautrey and Rodriguez-Tomé,[75] Dasen[76] (1979) and Dasen and Heron.[77] According to the latter, the majority of research until now centred on concrete operations and the problem of retention, but none dealt with the theory as a whole.

These authors drew several lessons from their work: both universal elements and cultural variations are involved and there is a tendency towards developmental diversification as age progresses, due to differences in the typical environmental situations as determined by culture and other factors. Thus, according to an investigation by P.R. Dasen, Eskimos are observed to be precocious in understanding the concept of horizontality (this facility in grasping spatial notions being characteristic of nomadic peoples), whereas in agricultural societies the concepts of conservation of quantity, weight and volume, due to experience with the conservation and bartering of foodstuffs at markets, dominate.

There is little doubt as to the universality of the first stage, but a great deal more with respect to the latter. Significant cultural variations have an impact on the quantitative side, namely, rate and speed of progress through the various stages, and at the ages at which they are achieved. But the influence of the cultural factor seems to be more significant than Piaget believed.

In particular, Piaget's concept of 'holistic structure' and all general notions such as 'developmental level' and 'intellectual level' need to be re-examined. Not infrequently, a curve is obtained showing development restricted to a certain asymptotic level in the case of one notion, and different curves, indicating developmental leads or lags, in other cases.

Thus, as Dasen and Heron conclude, 'a development curve never reflects an "operational level" or any other such global construct, but is limited to the concept being studied and to the particular experimental setting in which the measures are obtained.'[78]

The implications of this statement are all the more far-reaching when one considers the fact that, as strongly suggested by contemporary research on acculturation as discussed above, a similar kind of reassessment seems to be under way with respect to cognitive functions as a whole: perception, memory, reasoning, etc. In each case, the objective is to identify the specific solutions adopted by each group and subgroup, as demanded by the specificity of the situation with which they are confronted, and as determined by, inter alia, cultural factors. Even in Western industrialized culture, the diversity in the actual acquisition of mental operations is far greater than was expected and only levels off towards the end of this stage. Then, when the development of formal operations begins, significant individual variations reappear.[79]

Others go even further. Brossard,[80] for example, distinguishes between 'several systems of representation upon which the subject acts simultaneously'. Consequently, 'the subject can overcome difficulties encountered with one system of representation, if he has recourse to other systems of representation'. The important educational perspectives thus opened up are obvious: 'this means that educational situations have to be imagined in which the child can work by using a number of different procedures.'[81]

However that may be, several lessons can be drawn. First, that the functional relationship between cognitive processes and specific situations renders potential value judgments meaningless. Especially in view of the fact that learning opportunities (schooling, in particular) contradict the existence of different mind structures and basic psychological mechanisms. Second, a new way of analysing and evaluating the development of the individual is called for: one which takes into account the nature of cognitive orientations, and the ease or difficulty in achieving the performances as defined by what are called 'emic' development criteria, that is, those defined by the individual's own *milieu*.[82]

Given these considerations and to conclude, the rationale behind the questions W.S. Longstreet suggested schoolmasters ask themselves when dealing with 'non-standard' groups becomes clear: How do they approach the fact of learning? What types of questions do they ask during the learning act? How do they approach the question? Upon which intellectual abilities do they lay emphasis? To which do they grant lesser importance? Is the exercise of some skills made easier by specific contexts or types of activity?[83]

Put another way, based on the great majority of anthropological experience, the following recommendation can be made to the educator: whenever an assigned performance results in failure, rather than attribute the cause to innate shortcomings, it would be an operative solution to identify the context in which the assigned performance is situated and to look for another situation which could replace it to good advantage. Cultural anthropology practises this kind of situational analysis.

The educational process as a comprehensive system

Another lesson can be drawn from simple societies: the educational process is, and must be understood as, a comprehensive system, involving the entire community, comprising all the agents and institutions which claim to be educational, but also many others which do not have that explicit vocation. It is through this variously systematic whole that the circular cause and effect relationship between culture and education results; the second is 'in-formed' by the first; but since models and cultural signification are instilled in individuals mainly through education, culture is in a sense an effect of education.

We thus come to the necessity of identifying what in fact functions as an educational entity, groups and institutions in particular, and to analyse the conscious and unconscious messages they pass on and to evaluate the extent to which they make up a coherent whole or are disparate or even contradictory.

These groups are already present in simple societies. They become more complicated in traditional, complex societies. But in both cases there is a high degree of coherence because of the holistic character of culture, which changes very slowly. Thus, educational agencies disseminate messages which to a significant degree reinforce each other so that the individual's 'social circulation' confirms his beliefs, representations and attitudes.

In industrial societies, meanwhile, these groups not only abound, but they have greater autonomy on a representative basis: this is why the subcultures they spawn are susceptible of diverging from the national culture on a number of important points. The national culture tends to become the lowest common denominator of the subcultures rather than the structure which integrates them into a unified whole. Because of this, the concept of culture, which in traditional societies is operative, here becomes problematical. It only becomes functional once again if it ceases to be regarded as a system, but rather as a relatively loose collection of elements, the actual force, reciprocal compatibility and evolution of which must be measured. Use of this approach has shown that in cities in the West, variations among subcultures can exceed cultural differences between nations.

Educational agents and institutions, the smaller groups involved in this subcultural diversity, will thus need to become the object of special attention and analysis on the part of the educator. Hence the trend away from studies on the 'national character' in favour of studies on formation within it. This is particularly the case with small groups. Psychoanalysis and ethno-psychoanalysis have attributed to the family, in what we might call 'loose' cultures, a very significant role in filtering and channelling the entire surrounding culture and this role needs to be better understood. But, for the same structural reason, the educator will also be interested in the village, the neighbourhood, the apartment block, youth movements, recreational and professional groups, etc.

The smaller groups in turn fall within larger, more abstract formations whose influence is such that they have come to be regarded as classical variables in social science research: socioeconomic groups, more commonly referred to as 'social classes', groups based on sex, age, urban or rural environment, etc. Within their structures are to be found complex elements, one of which is a characteristic subculture. Each of them has been the object of analyses which are of direct interest to the educational sciences. We will discuss the results of these studies when we take up the subject most written about, namely the manner in which these groups interfere with another privileged formation, that is, the classroom subculture, and their impact on the school curriculum.

We thus already have an insight into how the particular type of segmentation of industrialized societies, the intensity and conflicting disparities it involves, reinforced by a high degree of formalization and institutionalization, create a great number of teaching problems which are unheard of in simple societies. The educational functioning of these societies as described by ethnologists arouses a sense of nostalgia and can easily be regarded as a model which modern complex societies should try to emulate on a number of scores.

This type of segmentation has one other theoretical and practical consequence. On the theoretical side, we were forced to rethink the oversimplified ideas about the mechanics of cultural transmission which had been handed down by ethnologists from their early observations on so-called 'archaic' societies. As M. Mauviel commented, 'with respect to the process of acculturation, the child is no longer considered to be someone who learns his culture more or less passively in the course of the training processes described in earlier texts: rearing practices, the effects of gratification, frustration, and reinforcement... all of which constituted weapons in the debate on socialization.'[84] To the extent that he will mingle with groups acting as vehicles of different subcultures — and sometimes cultures — he will have the opportunity of distancing himself from one or the other, to compile for himself a kind of differentiated 'cultural pool' representing a certain personal assortment of the influences received. As W.H. Goodenough[85] pointed out, as societies grow more complex and interpenetrate one another, cultural reality becomes more relative: it becomes less and less a total entity attached to a specific group, whether ethnic or otherwise, and even less an essence which takes possession of individuals. When speaking about the learning of a culture, emphasis is now placed on the activities of subjects within the actual scope of their interrelationships. For no individual actually comes into contact with culture per se, but rather other 'culture carriers' who never carry intact the totality of the culture attributed to the group, but out of which each has carved his own mixture.

On the practical side, the implications for educational strategy take two specific directions:

- The 'personalization' of education, which tends to be a sort of negotiation between educational agents and the subject's cultural 'montage'. This factor will come up again when we discuss the question of education as reproductive.
- Cultural competence: 'The process of learning a society's culture,' W.H. Goodenough states, 'or macro-culture as I would rather call it, is one of learning a number of different or partially different micro-cultures and their subcultural variants, and how to discern the situations in which they are appropriate and the kinds of others to whom to attribute them'; and he concludes, 'All human beings, then, live in what for them is a multicultural world.'[86]

'Learning' these cultures and reacting appropriately is a variable-degree skill. The same author states that in our complex societies especially, culture plays an increasingly important role in the conduct of business and the attainment of various forms of power. It is interesting to note that, presented in this light, culture is not a transcendent entity which takes possession of individuals: it emerges in the natural course of everyday learning, within the context of social interaction, so that each person's cultural 'reservoir' or 'pool' depends on the manner in which he directs that interaction. We will discuss this further when we take up intercultural educational science.

The anthropological method in practice

The use in simple societies of what the authors call the anthropological, ethnological or ethnographic method has enjoyed great popularity in the United States among educators and all others who are concerned with methods of observation in the area of education, but educational institutions in particular.

This is the name generally given to a point of view, which, rather than constituting a set of precise, methodological recipes, is a dual approach to the dynamic class of social processes, which has its own inherent unity and is linked to social dynamism as a whole together with its many facets including the cultural.

This method's conceptual characteristics include a comparative orientation, reappraisal of situational variations (eg the status of minorities) and intensive analysis of the 'field'. Its success is presumably due to the dissatisfaction with the quantitative, experimental methods of the social sciences, directly borrowed from the natural sciences[87] and which removed man from the 'central stage', and 'objectified' his subjectivity. They were consequently dealing with an abstract model, cut off from reality and dissociated with the actual situation encountered by educators.[88] For instance, these studies have shown, and made it possible to predict, that school careers are related to socio-economic status, to urban-rural differences, ethnic origin, etc. But how can we explain the actual process by which these structural variables are linked to scholastic performance?[89] As F. Ianni observed, 'It is no longer enough to say that John can't read; what is now being asked is why can't he and what will make him learn?'[90]

This is how the anthropological approach, using observation, participation in daily class life, recording and analysis of behaviour in the field, can bridge the gap. Monographs describe processes and types of action and interaction which never appear in large-scale statistical studies or comparative studies. They enable us to get away from the decision-making processes of systems and to describe how these systems actually operate in various cultural contexts, above and beyond the normative, stereotyped images institutions always convey.

From the point of view of teaching, in contrast to the traditional approach, those who use the anthropological method are less interested in the school's outputs (eg ranking of performances, results of competitions...) than in the internal processes which precede them and the representations and significations by which they are conditioned. For example, as V. Masemann commented, we might have been surprised by the fact that a school in West Africa was highly esteemed by both parents and pupils (girls), despite the poor results at examinations. But the ethnological method made it possible to discover the 'hidden curriculum' which they expected from this school and because of which the studies appeared meaningful to them in an unexpected way. These girls were learning how to live a 'modern life' as their milieu saw it, that is, the essential things the wife of a distinguished man must know about running a household; how to make fashionable clothes in European and African styles; a smattering of history and business; how to move among other members of the cultivated elite; knowledge of how to deal with administrations and bureaucratic institutions; an adequate conception of time, how to use it wisely, kill it, waste it, etc; the proper way of using their personal status in relation to figures of authority, and many other things. This achieved, they were recognized as cultivated young women, in spite of the statistics.[91]

In this direction of analysis, the anthropological method also relies on history (the past of subgroups, minorities) and genetics: it goes back to childhood experiences to study the pupil's present.

On a research level, it gives precedence to field work and 'free' observation with respect to pre-established theories. It is particularly attached to the synthetic, globalistic dimension, refuses to limit itself to segmental analysis, and takes into consideration the overall learning situation. Finally, it is interested in qualitative or even clinical components. This is why it is often confused, in the minds of researchers and practitioners, with the phenomenological approach or some other qualitative process with no direct connection with the cultural dimension.

One criticism was to be expected: unlike classical methods which require solid technical training, the 'nebulousness' of the anthropological method may give the illusion that anyone with the right flair and intuition could use it, leaving the door wide open to any number of 'amateurs'. As far as the effort to involve total situations is concerned, it can result in globalized views of complex situations which are left unanalysed, making comparisons impossible. Finally, too frequently it happens that overgeneralizations at the national level have been made, which the inherent limitations of monographs and case studies should have prohibited.

At the same time as they advise that a critical examination of the conditions required for the proper application of the anthropological method be made, some authors also suggest some other ways of combining or complementing various approaches.[92]

NOTES AND REFERENCES

1. Holtzman, W.H. Concepts and methods in the cross-cultural study of personality development. *Human development* (Basel, Switzerland), vol. 22, no. 5, 1979, pp. 281-95.
2. Sprott, W.J.H. *Social psychology.* London, Methuen, 1952. 268 p.
3. Stoetzel, J. *La psychologie sociale.* Paris, Flammarion, 1963. 320 p.
4. *Ibid.*, p. 73.
5. For example: Mead, Margaret. *Male and female: a study of the sexes in a changing world.* New York, Morrow, 1949.
6. Gorer, G.; Rickman, J. *The people of Great Russia: a psychological study.* London, Gresset, 1949.
7. Mead, Margaret. *Sex and temperament in three primitive societies.* New York, Morrow, 1935, 1963. 335 p.
8. Stoetzel, J. *Op. cit.*, p. 75.
9. Sprott, W.J.H. *Op. cit.*, pp. 161-2.
10. Benedict, Ruth. Continuities and discontinuities in cultural conditioning. *Psychiatry* (Washington, DC, William Alanson White Psychiatric Foundation), vol. 2, no. 1, 1938, pp. 161-7.
11. Mead, Margaret. *Sex and temperament in three primitive societies. Op. cit.*, p. 164.
12. Dollard, J., et al. *Frustration and aggression.* New Haven, CT, Yale University Press, 1939.
13. Erny, P. *L'ethnologie de l'éducation.* Paris, Presses universitaires de France, 1981, p. 104.
14. Dufrenne, M. *La personnalité de base: un concept sociologique.* 2e éd. Paris, Presses universitaires de France, 1965, p. 111.
15. *Ibid.*, p. 113.
16. Stoetzel, J. *Op. cit.*, p. 81.
17. Cf. Bastide, R. *Sociologie et psychanalyse.* Paris, Presses universitaires de France, 1950.
18. Erny, P. *Op. cit.*, p. 113.

19. Holtzman, W.H. *Op. cit.*, p. 281.
20. Malinowski, B. *Sex and repression in savage society.* London, Routledge and Kegan Paul, 1927. xiv, 285 p.
21. Kardiner, A. *The individual and his society: the psychodynamics of primitive social organisation.* New York, Columbia University Press, 1939. xxvi, 503 p.
22. Fromm, E. *Escape from freedom.* New York, Holt, Rinehart and Winston, 1941.
23. Roheim, G. *Psychoanalysis and anthropology.* New York, International Universities Press, 1950.
24. Ortigues, Marie-Cécile; Ortigues, E. *Œdipe africain.* Paris, Plon, 1966. 336 p.
25. Devereux, G. *Essais d'ethnopsychiatrie générale.* Paris, Gallimard, 1970. 424 p.
26. Cf. Lê Thanh Khôi. *L'éducation comparée.* Paris, Colin, 1981. 315 p.
27. Rabain, Jacqueline. *L'enfant du lignage: du sevrage à la classe d'âge chez les Wolof du Sénégal.* Paris, Payot, 1979. 240 p.
28. Whiting, J.W.M.; Child, I.L. *Child training and personality: a cross cultural study.* New Haven, CT, Yale University Press, 1953; Whiting, B.B., et al. *Children of six cultures: a psycho-cultural analysis.* Cambridge, MA, Harvard University Press, 1975. 237 p.
29. Holtzman, W.H. *Op. cit.*, pp. 286-7.
30. *Ibid.*, p. 282.
31. Anderson, H.H.; Anderson, G.L. Image of the teacher by adolescent children in seven countries. *American journal of orthopsychiatry* (Menasha, WI), vol. 31, July 1961, pp. 481-92.
32. Holtzman, W.H.; Diaz-Guerrero, R.; Swartz, J.D. *Personality development in two cultures: a cross-cultural longitudinal study of school children in Mexico and the United States.* Austin, TX, University of Texas Press, 1975. 447 p.
33. Holtzman, W.H. Concepts and methods in the cross-cultural study of personality development. *Op. cit.*, p. 290.
34. *Ibid.*, pp. 290-1.
35. Lee, P.C.; Gropper, Nancy, B. Sex-role culture and educational practice. *Harvard educational review* (Cambridge, MA, Harvard University), vol. 44, no. 3, August 1974, pp. 369-410.
36. Mauviel, M. Le multiculturalisme (pluralisme culturel). *Revue française de pédagogie* Paris, Institut national de recherche pédagogique), no. 61, octobre-novembre-décembre 1982, p. 69.
37. Triandis, H.C., ed. *The analysis of subjective culture.* New York, Wiley, 1972, p. 4.
38. Masemann, Vaudra. Anthropological approaches to comparative education. *Comparative education review* (Madison, WI, Comparative and International Education Society), vol. 20, no. 3, October 1976, p. 372.
39. Cf. Klineberg, O. *Social psychology.* 2nd ed. New York, Holt, Rinehart and Winston, 1954.
40. Bornstein, M.H. The psychophysiological component of cultural difference in color naming and illusion susceptibility. *Behavior science notes* (New Haven, CT), vol. 8, no. 1, 1973, pp. 41-101; Bornstein, M.H. The influence of visual perception on culture. *American anthropologist* (Washington, DC, American Anthropological Association), vol. 77, no. 4, December 1975, pp. 774-98; Berlin, B.; Berlin, Elois Ann. Aguaruna color categories. *American ethnologist* (Washington, DC, American Anthropological Association), vol. 2, no. 1, February 1975, pp. 61-87; Witkowski, S.R.; Brown, C.B. An explanation of color nomenclature universals. *American anthropologist* (Washington, DC, American Anthropological Association), vol. 79, no. 1, March 1977, pp. 50-7; Deregowsky, J.B. Perception. *In*: Triandis, H.C.; Lonner, W.J., eds. *Handbook of cross-cultural psychology. Vol. 3.* Boston, MA, Allyn and Bacon, 1980, pp. 21-116.
41. Segall, M.H.; Campbell, D.T.; Herskowits, M.J. *The influence of culture on visual perception.* Indianapolis, IN, Bobbs-Merril, 1966; Dasen, P.R. Apports de la psychologie

à la compréhension interethnique. *In*: Société suisse des sciences humaines. Colloque, 5e, Sigriswil, Suisse, 1980. *L'ethnologie dans le dialogue interculturel*, ed. par G. Baer et P. Centlivres. Fribourg, Suisse, Editions universitaires, Fribourg, 1983, pp. 47-66.
42. Dasen, P.R., Apports de la psychologie à la compréhension interethnique, *Op. cit.*, 1980, p. 53.
43. Dasen, P.R.; Lavallée, Margot; Retschitzki, J. Training conservation of quantity (liquids) in West African (Baoulé) children. *International journal of psychology/Journal international de psychologie* (Paris, International Union of Psychological Science), vol. 14, no. 1, 1979, pp. 57-68.
44. Dasen, P.R. Apports de la psychologie à la compréhension interethnique. *Op. cit.*, p.56.
45. Warren, N. Universality and plasticity, ontogeny and phylogeny: the resonance between culture and cognitive development. *In*: Sants, J., ed. *Developmental psychology and society*. London, Macmillan, 1980, pp. 290-326.
46. Hall, E.T. *Hidden dimension*, New York, Doubleday, 1966.
47. Bateson, G.; Mead, Margaret. *The Balinese character: a photographic analysis*. New York, New York Academy of Sciences, 1942; Lee, Dorothy, D. Lineal and nonlineal codifications of reality. *Psychosomatic medicine* (New York), vol. 12, 1950, pp. 89-97.
48. Vasquez, Ana. Temps social/temps culturel. *Enfance* (Paris), no. 5, novembre-décembre 1982, pp. 335-50; Vasquez, Ana; Proux, Michelle B. 'La maîtresse dit que je suis lent': représentation de l'école française dans le discours d'élèves immigrés. *International review of education* (The Hague), vol. 30, no. 2, 1984, pp. 155-70.
49. *Ibid.*, pp. 160-1.
50. Malinowski, B. *Op. cit.*
51. Stoetzel, J. *Op. cit.*, p. 104.
52. Halbwachs, M. *Les cadres sociaux de la mémoire*. Paris, Alcan, 1925.
53. Bartlett, F.C. *Remembering: a study in experimental and social psychology*. New York, Cambridge University Press, 1932.
54. Seeleman, V. The influence of attitude upon the remembering of pictorial material. *Archives of psychology* (New York), no. 253, 1940, p. 69.
55. Wagner, D.A. Culture and mnemonics. *In*: Gruneberg, M.M.; Morris, P.E.; Sykes, R.N., eds. London, Academic Press, 1978, pp. 180-8, Wagner, D.A. Culture and memory development. *In*: Triandis, H.C.; Heron, A., eds. *Handbook of cross-cultural psychology*. Vol. 4. Boston, MA, Allyn and Bacon, 1981, pp. 187-232.
56. Cole, M., et al. *The cultural context of learning and thinking: an exploration in experimental anthropology*. London, Methuen, 1971; New York, Basic Books, p. 229.
57. *Ibid.*, pp. 229-30.
58. Stoetzel, J. *Op. cit.*, p. 125.
59. Cole, M., et al. *Op. cit.*, p. 220.
60. Mundy-Castle, A.C. Social and technological intelligence in Western and non-Western cultures. *Universitas* (Legon, University of Ghana), vol. 4, no. 1, 1974, pp. 46-52.
61. Granet, M. Quelques particularités de la langue et de la pensée chinoise. *Revue philosophique de la France et de l'étranger* (Paris), 45e année, t. 89, janvier-février 1920, pp. 98-128; mars-avril 1920, pp. 161-95, repris dans Granet, M. *Etudes sociologiques sur la Chine*. Paris, Presses universitaires de France, 1953, p. 142.
62. Cole, M., et al. *Op. cit.*, p. 215.
63. Greenfield, Patricia M.; Bruner, J.S. Culture and cognitive growth. *In*: Goslin, D.A., ed. *Handbook of socialization theory and research*. New York, Rand McNally, 1969, pp. 633-57.
64. Witkin, H.A.; Berry, J.W. Psychological differentiation in cross-cultural perspective. *Journal of cross-cultural psychology* (Beverly Hills, CA), vol. 6, no. 1, March 1975, pp. 4-87.
65. Lévy-Bruhl, L. *Les fonctions mentales dans les sociétés primitives*. Paris, Alcan, 1910.
66. Boas, F. *Primitive culture*. New York, Macmillan, 1915.

67. Gluckman, M. Social beliefs and individual thinking in tribal society. *Memoirs of the Manchester Literary society* (Manchester, UK), no. 91, 1949-50, pp. 73-98.
68. Hallpike, C.R. Is there a primitive mentality? *Man* (London, Royal Anthropological Institute), vol. 11, no. 2, June 1976, pp. 253-70; Mangan, J. Piaget's theory and cultural differences: the case for value-based modes of cognition. *Human development* (Basel, Switzerland), vol. 21, no. 3, 1978, pp. 170-89; Tulviste, P. On the origin of theoretic syllogistic reasoning in culture and in the child. *Acta et commentationes Universitatis Tartuensis* (Tartu, Republic of Estonia), no. 474, 1978, pp. 3-22
69. Cole, M., et al. *Op. cit.*, p. 224.
70. *Ibid.*, pp. 224-5.
71. *Ibid.*, p. 228.
72. *Ibid.*
73. *Ibid.*, p. 217.
74. Luria, A.R. *Cognitive development: its cultural and social foundations*, ed. by M. Cole. Cambridge, MA, Harvard University Press, 1976. 175 p.
75. Lautrey, J.; Rodriguez-Tomé, H. Etudes interculturelles de la notion de conservation. *In*: Reuchlin, M., éd. *Cultures et conduites*. Paris, Presses universitaires de France, 1976, pp. 247-81.
76. Dasen, P.R.; Ngini, L.; Lavallée, M. Cross-cultural training studies of concrete operations. *In*: International Association for Cross-Cultural Psychology. International Congress, 4th, Munich, Federal Republic of Germany, 1978. *Cross-cultural contributions to psychology*, ed. by L.M. Eckensberger, Y. Poortinga, W. Lonner. Amsterdam, Swets and Zeitlinger, 1979, pp. 94-104.
77. Dasen, P.R.; Heron, A. Cross-cultural tests of Piaget's theory. *In*: Triandis, H.C.; Heron, A., eds. *Handbook of cross-cultural psychology. Vol. 4*. Boston, MA, Allyn and Bacon, 1981, pp. 295-341.
78. *Ibid.*, p. 312.
79. Modgil, S.; Modgil, Celia. *Piagetian research: compilation and commentary. Vol. 3: The growth of logic: concrete and formal operations*. Windsor, UK, National Foundation for Educational Research, 1976. 313 p.
80. Brossard, M. *Conduites verbales, activités cognitives et origine sociale*. Bordeaux, France, Université de Bordeaux II, s.d. [Thesis].
81. *Ibid.*, p. 792.
82. Irwin, M., et al. The problem of establishing validity in cross-cultural measurement. *Annals of the New York Academy of Sciences* (New York), no. 285, 1977, pp. 308-25; Serpell, R. Estimates of intelligence in a rural community of Eastern Zambia. *In*: Pan-African Conference on Psychology, 2nd, Nairobi, 1975-6. *Modern psychology and cultural adaptation: proceedings...*, ed. by F.M. Okatcha, Nairobi, Swahili Language Consultants and Publishers, 1977, pp. 179-216; Guindo, B. *Eléments pour une appréciation du développement intellectuel au Mali: contribution à l'étude analytique et expérimentale du banangolo*. Bordeaux, France, Université de Bordeaux II, 1979 [Thesis].
83. Longstreet, Wilma, S. *Aspects of ethnicity: understanding differences in pluralistic classrooms*. New York, Teachers College Press, 1978.
84. Mauviel, M. *L'idée de culture et de pluralisme culturel: aspects historiques, conceptuels et comparatifs*. Paris, Université de Paris V, 1983, p. 11 [Thesis].
85. Goodenough, W.H. Multi-culturalism as the normal human experience. *Anthropology and education quarterly* (Washington, DC, Council on Anthropology and Education), vol. 7, no. 4, November 1976, pp. 4-7.
86. *Ibid.*, p. 5.
87. Foley, D.E. Anthropological studies of schooling in developing countries: some recent findings and trends. *Comparative education review* (Madison, WI, Comparative and International Education Society), vol. 21, nos. 2/3, June/October 1977, pp. 311-28.

88. Ianni, F.A.J. Anthropology and educational research: a report on Federal Agency programs. *Anthropology and education quarterly* (Washington, DC, Council on Anthropology and Education), vol. 7, no. 3, August 1976, pp. 3-11.
89. Masemann, V. *Op. cit.*
90. Ianni, F.A.J. *Op. cit.*, p. 4.
91. Masemann, V. *Op. cit.*
92. For example: Casserly, M.D.; Garrett, J.R. Beyond the victim: new avenues for research on racism in education. *Educational theory* (Urbana, IL, University of Illinois), vol. 27, no. 3, Summer 1977, pp. 196-204.

CHAPTER III

Schools and national culture problems in the West

In addition to their contributions on the subject of acculturation and its effects on the individual of which we have just given a glimpse, the majority of studies in contemporary cultural anthropology situate learning problems in relation to the educational institution. The latter, for reasons familiar to us, has acquired a role of such paramount importance that the 'child' has been replaced by the 'pupil'. This is especially true in the West. The situation in the Third World will be discussed in a later chapter.

It can be said at once that the very structure of this institution incorporates the essential characteristics of what is commonly referred to as Western industrialized culture. As a result, pupils are likely to experience a genuine cultural shock upon their very first contact with it. Beyond this, however, the schools with which they are involved, at least in the so-called 'liberal democracies', claim to be 'neutral', that is, to disseminate culture without reference to the ideologico-cultural content of various subgroups, and especially without showing preference to any one of them.

Yet, all the studies conducted in the past half-century in Western countries show this to be false. The studies' conclusions were based on different scholastic achievement profiles of pupils including rates of failure.

Failures at first appeared to be 'blameless', that is, distributed according to individual 'merits' for which the pupil alone was responsible, independent of all environmental factors. The functionalists[1] considered them to be the beneficial effects of a useful selection process necessary for the proper functioning of society.

Then, during the 1950s and 1960s, the neo-functionalist theory,[2] which viewed education as 'productive investment' in an expanding industrial society and demanded the development and generalization of skills, lamented their waste due to failures and scholastic 'inachievement'. This theory echoed the concern on the part of Marxist theoreticians of the 'scientific and technical revolution'.[3] Hence, the existence of a large number of studies on disparateness in scholastic success using the extensional methods introduced by the natural sciences.

One inescapable fact became apparent from these studies: far from being unrelated to the 'milieu', the distribution of inequalities revealed itself to be strongly linked to the nature of the social subgroups from which the youngsters come. The relationship established between educational handicaps and socio-economic subgroups, commonly called 'social class', especially aroused interest because of its distinctness and because of its conflict with ideological concerns and the ideal of social justice. Thus was launched the 'conflictualist' approach which we will discuss below.

Initially, in the old Marxist tradition, efforts focused on the objective ('material') environmental factors deemed responsible for these negative effects and those related to insufficiencies and injustices in the distribution of education and 'promotional culture'. Neo-Weberian criticism[4] complemented this explanation by introducing the factor of attitudes and representations, or the 'ethico-attitudinal' parameters of the personality, to borrow the expression J.-C. Forquin used in one of his invaluable syntheses on these problems.[5] Thus, the way was paved for the analysis of factors originating in cultural anthropology. In Collins' view, already, 'education transmits something else besides "objective" knowledge, develops something else besides culturally "neutral" operative skills: it imposes a particular culture (system of manners, style of behaviour, values), the culture of the groups currently in control of the education systems, and by that very fact, elevated to the status of a "legitimate", universal culture.'[6] Hence, the selection process of the classroom and the classification of pupils according to what Parsons claimed was an 'axis of achievement' are only the tangible expressions of social cooptation. And competition eliminates favouritism. This idea was taken up and brilliantly developed in the neo-Marxist thesis of educational stratification, concurrently represented in the United States by Bowles and Gintis[7] and in France by Bourdieu, Passeron, Althusser, Baudelot and Establet, etc. The 'conflictualist' school centres its analyses around a conception of the school as an instrument of ideological and social transmission, guided by the standards of the ruling subgroup, which disputes the thesis of ideological and cultural neutrality.

We will take a closer look at these topics, beginning with an examination of the relationships between educational subgroups and social classes. We will then take a look at the relationship with other national subcultures which are also conflictive to some degree, but about which far less has been written.

The educational subculture and social class subcultures

THE FACTS

Numerous and varied results in diverse countries attest to the reality of the relationships in question, and always with the same thrust: as a general trend, the quantitative decrease in educational level and its qualitative decline become more and more pronounced as we descend the socio-economic ladder. To only give a few examples, Bowles and Gintis,[8] based on a mixture of statistical data in the United States, calculated the differential probability of attaining various levels of socio-economic success according to three variables: social origin, childhood and adult IQ, and level of education. They concluded that IQ and cognitive factors in general had relatively little importance. Education, however, played a major role, but for reasons relatively unrelated to cognitive ability. According to another comparative study conducted in the United States,[9] the differentiating factor of social origin proved to have a greater impact on scholastic performance than differences between teachers, teaching methods or variations in class size. Statistics quoted by R. Girod[10] show how the group of the 'undereducated' recruits its members primarily from the most disadvantaged segments of popular urban classes and rural people. They give an insight into how this deterioration in both Europe and the United States is connected, not only with social classes as a whole, but also with segments of these. Similar studies reveal the same pattern in failed exams, the relationships between IQ and the professional scale, and between cognitive development and socio-economic category. The result of a large-scale review of questions by J. Pelnard-Considère was

the revelation of a pattern difficult to ignore: each time a systematic variation factor linked to differences in socio-economic or cultural status was brought to bear on a variable linked to intelligence, the averages of social classes varied directly with class status, even when attempts were made to avoid this result.[11]

These data demonstrate the need for analysis of the 'background' variable and of 'social affiliation' especially. A theoretical outline for interpreting the effect of social structures (milieu in general) on cognitive ability was provided by J.-F Le Ny:

The best theoretical solution to the problem one can provide is to say that on one hand there is a causal relationship between the cognitive abilities observed in a given group and a set of unknown factors determining C — which we may call cognitive conditions — and a second relationship between the social structure of a society and the distribution of C. But there is no direct cause-and-effect relationship between social structure and the distribution of cognitive abilities. It is not apparent how, from an epistemological point of view, the two concepts can in any justifiable way be seen to be directly related outside of these two areas.[12]

It thus became necessary to look for 'intermediate' variables: the family, in particular, appears to be the prime mediator. It is also necessary to rigorously elucidate the distinction between the various causal factors at play. The first step, begun a long time ago, was to isolate a series of objective factors which act overwhelmingly in favour of well-to-do groups to the detriment of the disfavoured: the distribution of learning establishments, geographical distances, the length of study cycles, the obligation or not to enter active life at an early age, the way in which schools are equipped, their academic level, the degrees possessed by teachers and their possibilities of advancement, programme levels, the level of financing, the cost per student, physical and psychological handicaps.[13] All of these factors need to be evaluated in each case if one is to avoid falling into the 'panculturalist' myth which consists in attributing more importance to cultural factors than is actually justified and putting them where they do not belong, for doing so is one of the best means of discrediting them. The correct identification of where this variable's proper place is, its points of application and its precise mode of intervention are the best means of ensuring it is seriously taken into account by educators.

It is also necessary to isolate the advantages and drawbacks inherent in promotional culture: the educational level of parents and the family environment; the degree of maturity of logo-syntactic structures (in a Piagetian or quasi-Piagetian sense) according to the development possibilities offered by the milieu and tied in with the linguistic instruments it makes available;[14] sensorimotor and intellectual stimuli in general; the presence and quality of documents in general; learning aids; unequal availability of information on schools, studies, branches and career opportunities; the socio-professional spectrum, etc.[15] On the subject of tests, we might mention the current debate on genetic and hereditary factors. If we bear this series of precautions in mind, we should be able to distinguish, as far as their relationship to scholastic expectations is concerned, the different factors originating in anthropology: making an inventory of this scope is, for the present, at least, the most original undertaking ever which is directly related to our subject. Already a broad consensus among researchers seems to be forming around a few theses.

First of all, there exists an anthropological subculture of economically privileged classes, the so-called 'upper' and 'middle classes' of the United States. It has been shown that in the US, as in France and the United Kingdom, for children with equivalent IQs and levels of scholastic achievement, the demand for education is lower among the working class.[16] In addition to the objective causes which explain this phenomenon authors, especially in traditional American sociology, see cultural attitudes as playing a role.[17] To the credit of the affluent, they denote an 'ascetic' rationalism, fostering a sustained kind of 'deferment behaviour' which sacrifices immediate gratifications for long-term objectives, the fundamental concern with success, voluntarism and competitive effort. To the disadvantage of the underprivileged classes, meanwhile, they denote what they termed passivity, fatalism or even 'irresponsibility'. They also laid lesser importance on formal education or university studies as factors of success in life and gave precedence to security and immediate economic advantages. Their expectations, aspirations, and goals in general appeared to be more limited.[18]

According to these studies, one variable is shown to be decisive – attitudes towards time. Attitudes towards the future are significantly linked to scholastic motivation and achievement.

The middle classes, meanwhile, look 'far ahead': according to B. Bernstein,[19] their conception of the world is that of a rational universe within which long-term projects can be formulated.

But for the working classes, who are obliged to confront the difficulties of life on a day-by-day basis, the future is vague and depends more on luck than on coherent planning. They are accordingly more oriented towards the present.[20] In a more general way, the middle class, in contrast to the others, regard the present as integrated into a system of relationships which make it meaningful: extremely general principles are used to account for the here and now. Correlatively, the 'world is spoken', that is, organized by language: immediate experience is signposted by discourse whose purpose is to give it structure.[21]

The discovery of further elements is the result of the investigations of Kohn in the United States. In a study on discipline, analysing the results of polls carried out among a representative national sample, he found that manual workers made greater use of corporal punishment on children. The affluent classes rely on reasoning and feelings of guilt. The former wish primarily to transmit to their progeny the values of obedience and order, whereas the middle class emphasize the values of initiative and self-control.[22] In one case, socialization is dominated by the idea of conforming to rules imposed from the outside, in the other, by greater emphasis on the child's personal dynamism. For the former, the sanction is justified by the materiality and actual consequences of the offence, for the latter, by the presumed incriminating intention. The interpretation would be as follows: in the privileged classes, the child is perceived primarily in terms of the future and his future; hence the desire to socialize him in such a way that he can 'function independently', that is, on his own. Accordingly, parents strive to instil in him principles which make actions legitimate, to communicate to him a sense of individual responsibility and autonomy, the form of activity which Bernstein calls 'personal appeal':[23] this brings us back to the puritan ethic of interiorization and self-command.

It is thus true, and Bronfenbrenner[24] confirmed it in the United Kingdom, that the middle and upper classes show themselves to be more 'tolerant' and more 'liberal'. But as J.-C. Forquin noted, what is important

is not so much the degree of authoritarianism or tolerance (notions which are vague and rather ambiguous) as the means by which cultural norms are inculcated, the degree to which this process relies on verbalization, rationalization and culpabilization, and whether it aims at some measure of interiorization of the faculty of control.[25]

Bernstein took over these notions and contributed tremendously to the identification of the 'cultural ethos' connected with social classes, based on his analyses of their language: we will treat this subject in more detail in Chapter VI.

As this analysis advanced, a most striking fact became apparent: this subculture, that is, the set of attitudes and representations of the middle and upper classes, is favoured by the school. A style of education which 'strives to produce "inner-directed men" in Riesman's sense, must also produce,' J.-C. Forquin concludes, 'pupils who are more studious, more inclined to "self-discipline" and better adapted to the "stringent" expectations and demands of the school (no matter what may have been said about school "regimentation") rather than more direct and more rigorous forms of conformation'.[26]

Simultaneously, the 'working-class' subculture is in the process of making a counter-adaptation to the educational universe. Other characteristics, in addition to those discussed above, have been brought to light in the course of research.

Thus, various sources have underscored the varying significance of failure in school, depending on how failure in life is represented. The pupil whose scholastic career is lacking will be inclined to accept the situation if he belongs to a milieu in which success as defined by the ruling classes is not an essential value. He is not compromising his future because it does not imply advanced studies. 'What is more,' Girod quite rightly observed, 'his family does not become overly disturbed about it and his comrades will convince him not to worry. They place the emphasis on other activities: after-school jobs which earn a bit of money, mass entertainment, sports, possibly delinquency or semi-delinquency.'[27] So much so that a good number of them wait to be out of school to accede to the status of young workers; that, for them and their milieu, is 'real' success, which makes the success promised by the school only relative.

These considerations and many others place the emphasis on the role of the family. The family is one of the subgroups which acts as a mediator between the subject and the culture of the society, and its action is ever so much more effective because it means more to the individual. The main syntheses on this point were due to Reuchlin[28] and Marcos.[29] The family environment itself is a 'package of variables' from which may be isolated: parental authority (along an authoritarianism-liberalism axis, according to Reuchlin), the degree of structuring of family life, attitudes towards child autonomy and dependence, the manner in which parents express affection, attitudes and behaviour towards schoolwork (stimulation, participation, encouragement, indifference, etc).

What interests us is the relationship between parental attitudes of significance to the child's schooling and the subculture of which the family is a member. In 'positional' type families, authority is based on status and roles are prescribed, independently of the person himself, and rigorously defined. In 'personal orientation' type families, individual characteristics are of greater significance to roles, which are prescribed to a lesser extent and have a larger recognition component, as well as to decisions. Behaviour control is achieved to a greater extent through verbal explanation, arbitration, and adaptation: the margin of independence people enjoy with respect to the formalized rules of the sociocultural model encourages autonomy. This second type of family is more prevalent in the middle and upper classes than in the working class and favours, it would seem, schooling. Yet, the 'permissiveness' must not go too far: according to part of the research of J. Lautrey,[30] based on a Piagetian scheme, the success level in certain cognitive tests is higher among children whose family environment is structured in a flexible way than those whose backgrounds are 'rigidly structured' (hyper-constraining), or too loosely structured (anarchistic). This flexible form of structuring, which fosters an optional degree of 'field-dependence', or the ability to stand at a distance with respect to organized configurations of stimuli, has been shown to be more frequently encountered in the privileged classes.

Likewise, we cannot consider positive the notion widespread among the popular segments of the population which regards failure as fate ('It's not everyone's lot to succeed') and success as luck. As E. Tedesco commented, families from the disfavoured strata of society rarely emphasize the sociocultural gap between their milieu and the milieu which facilitates scholastic achievement. And subjects appear to be resigned rather than prepared to reflect on the effects of their condition.[31]

Finally, the handicap is not only due to the 'internal' characteristics of these families, but also to dysfunctions in their contact with the educational institution. Among these, one is particularly culture-related: the differences in communication codes. At the most superficial level, this implies the inability to understand the teacher ('He doesn't talk like we do'), an unfamiliar style of relationship which could lead to teachers being judged as intimidating, haughty or disdainful. At a deeper level, these parents are obviously less capable of dealing with the organizational code of institutions than members of the upper classes. Consequently, they are little able to understand, much less question, decisions made by the 'administration' with regard to their children.

As research in the area grows, still other parameters become evident. E. Plaisance,[32] based on the analysis of inspection reports from the Paris region, speaks of a shift, which began taking place in 1975 in nursery schools, from a 'productive' model consisting basically in using the qualities of perfection or success to characterize what children produce, towards an 'expressive' model in which, on the contrary, it is the child's personality itself which is evaluated. This evolution coincides with the extension to middle-class districts of nursery schools traditionally established in working-class neighbourhoods. And this researcher contends that the shift has been to the disadvantage of the popular classes to the extent that the former productive model corresponded to some of their expectations, by analogy with the workshop in which a person is judged and evaluated in terms of the products of his activity. The expressive model, meanwhile, enters into complicity with the values of families from the 'cultivated' classes and no doubt more from the middle class in particular.

More commonplace are the ideas developed by Bernstein on 'invisible' education which in schools competes with 'visible' education. The items explicitly dealt with are accompanied by a multitude of subliminal information based on the culture which is only known to the privileged strata. In this sense, as Bourdieu and Passeron demonstrated, the best teaching method to reduce inequalities due to social backgrounds would be the one which is most explicit, ie the most didactic. And the autonomy granted the child in his classroom activities, reliance on diffuse and not very explicit methods of evaluation and monitoring, better correspond to the cultural expectations and presuppositions of the 'new middle class' (Bernstein) than to those of the working class, which is more at ease with traditional didacticism.

The 'gaps' in visible teaching systems do not only consist in implicit, factual references. According to Bourdieu, they also encompass the life-style and attitudes of the ruling classes and the code of their *savoir-faire* and *savoir-être* which represent the hard core of their anthropological subculture. It is apparent through the 'elegance', the 'ease', the 'panache' and the 'charisma' of the model lecture course, and many other qualities supposed to transcend 'learned' knowledge and of which the school cannot provide the code because it can only be infused by the family environment.

It is thus understandable why working-class children create in the educational institutions they attend an 'anti-school' culture which has been remarkably analysed by P. Willis based on a British example. Virile and tough, it reflects workshop culture; the take-over of the class by these pupils who substitute their own schedule for the official one and organize their own life-style; opposition to the official authority, organized within the informal group of 'mates' to the exclusion of conformists and 'tattlers'; cultivation of a 'working-class' sense of humour in which intimidation has an extensive role; rejection of schoolwork, feeling of 'knowing better', pre-eminence of practical abilities with a proliferation of apocryphal stories about the 'stupidity' of theoretical knowledge; blockage or reinterpretation of information disseminated by the school, especially concerning work; filtering of the message handed down by teachers and guidance personnel and an attitude of scepticism with regard to it; choice of a career based on the tradition of the 'gang'; permanent creation of a set of 'semi-official' criteria. In such an arrangement the 'us' is opposed to 'them' via the separation into 'mates vs. bootlickers' and 'white collar vs. blue collar'. Basically, in contrast to the official model, an alternative, an overall vision is developed of what the future holds and according to which human gratification in communion with the 'workshop culture' and the 'in' group is more important than the rest; thus the transition from the school to the factory is experienced as a 'liberation'. Lastly, 'the anti-school culture', P. Willis says,

Proceeds from an appreciation by young people of working-class origin of chances of success and of the advantages of the conformism and obedience the school expects of them. This implies deep scepticism as to the value of what the school has to offer in relation to the sacrifices this demands: ultimately the sacrifices involved mean not simply biding time, but the qualities of action, involvement, and independence. What would have to be sacrificed is not only immediate gratification, but a permanent life-style. Becoming a 'bootlicker' now and acquiring qualifications of dubious value would destroy forever the elements which permit and produce immediate gratification.[33]

The conflictualist interpretation

Not only did the interpretation of these results add fuel to the case of educators against the educational establishment, but it also reinforced the tendency to turn the debate into an ideological campaign. The defective structure of society is attacked, and the school as the means of its perpetuation.

For, according to the conflictualist school, especially its exponents in France, the facts brought to light by these analyses are neither fortuitous nor 'blameless'. To the educational institution, the egalitarianism it officially affects is absolute. The 'indifference to differences', upon which its neutrality is based, 'disguises something which only becomes apparent after a second reading' (Snyders[34]): to wit, the active complicity between the school and the ruling classes. This complicity is based on, among other things, the culture they both share, which implicitly conditions classroom activities and scholastic achievement and which they agree to keep out of the reach of the common people. Thus the charismatic character of the curriculum is not accidental. It has an effective role of social discrimination. Analysis of exams and the judgments made by teachers reveal that they serve the same objective. Even the definition of the excellence of a pupil is highly significant. As Bourdieu and de Saint-Martin observed,[35] 'Are not the "overly scholastic" qualities of the pupil who owes the brunt of his culture and his social ascent more to the school than to his family, viewed with condescension or even contempt?'

In the final analysis, underneath what appears to be competition lies *co-optation*. We are thus indeed dealing with an ideology in the Marxist sense: an overt meaning disguising a concealed meaning and making it possible to transmit it insidiously; production of an apparently universal, rational item whose objective is to satisfy class needs surreptitiously. This ideology takes on other forms, such as the 'ideology of giftedness', in all areas which justify scholastic failure of the uninitiated to the dominant subculture in such a way as to draw attention away from the real reasons.

In the case of the disfavoured classes, meanwhile, analysis of the characteristics of their subculture has shown these characteristics to be functional and the negative aspects attributed to them are actually an 'objectification' ('rationalization' psychologists would say) of these people's difficulty in succeeding through study, given the many handicaps related to their social condition. Here, as elsewhere, culture is not the primary factor, but is rooted in objective social causality. In fact, groups define what they hold to be success according to strategies based on an overall, realistic evaluation of their actual possibilities.[36]

This explains the lack of value attached to education, the lack of interest at the bottom of the social scale in the future, in preparing and organizing it, the lack of concern for training the child to face it successfully by himself, the absence of 'deferment' behaviour, the concentration on immediate satisfaction, etc. From this point of view, the 'class ethos', to use Bourdieu's expression, which includes educational demands and expectations, is to be considered the product of the 'interiorization of objective possibilities into subjective aspirations'.[37]

It is thus clear why an anti-school culture is generated by the working-class culture, which, once properly decoded, shows what the real situation is as opposed to the 'myths about reality the educational institution spreads'. And to the class which creates this culture 'the educational scale and the stratification of functions do not give an indication of their abilities, but of the immutable domination to which they are subjected.'[38] Thus, when pupils succeed in maintaining among themselves a 'workshop culture' felt to be valid and attractive, this constitutes a 'subjective success within an objective failure'.[39]

This vast movement of ideological and educational anti-school protest, to which cultural anthropology made a considerable contribution in the form of data and possibilities for new types of analysis, has in the past few years revolutionized the institution's image and that of its actors. It should not be surprising that it sparked the re-evaluation currently under way, the main elements of which we will discuss. First, however, one point needs to be made. Whether we consider the conflictualist explanation to be accurate or not, it helps bring out an ever-present aspect of culture: cultural anthropology, as created by society, can be taken over and manipulated by it to various ends, particularly for the purpose of domination. In this specific case, indeed, it appears that national subcultures, which are connected to the subgroups we have just spoken about, are implicitly involved in the conflicts and alliances of these subgroups via the avatars of social dynamism which they undergo. Hence their fundamentally dualistic nature: culture as a means of expression, as an emancipation and authentication can be transformed into a means of oppression, of alienation and denaturalization. That is why it has been suggested that culture can function as an ideology. All cultural education or all use of culture in the area of education must take into account this dual aspect.

Criticism against the conflictualist theory

But, obviously, the conflictualist conception provoked many reactions. Indeed, if taken literally, the demobilizing, nihilistic effects it had in the educational sector became quickly apparent. They aroused protests on the part of 'progressive' theoreticians themselves, including those by and large in agreement with the overall scheme.[40] The version of this theory given by certain authors, especially the followers of Bourdieu, culminated in such a radical form of opposition (in the tradition of the leftist movement of May 1968 in France) that it came close to being a choice between 'social revolution or nothing'. And as we know, in this kind of situation it is usually the second alternative which is achieved. Thus, the critics generally did not reject the conflictualist thesis, but attempted to modify it in various ways. To do this, they began with a more 'concrete' examination of the facts.

In the first place, new research has revealed a high degree of diversity in social classes in the West which had been readily presented as monolithic. Within these classes themselves there exists a certain amount of latitude, for classes do not determine, as we have known for a long time, attitudes and representations in an absolute way. Consequently, cultural differences are far from being mechanically aligned with divisions of the population into socio-economic categories based on income brackets.[41] With respect to the relationship between cognitive development and professional class, for example, M. Reuchlin discovered on the basis of existing data that the categories partly overlapped.[42] In some working-class families, the parents' way of life, their way of thinking, their vocabulary, their aspirations for their children, the quality of their pastimes, their trade union and parish responsibilities, and their relations with non-working-class groups make possible the satisfactory scholastic performance of their progeny. For another important element comes into play: the reference group, which complicates and diversifies the otherwise merely intermediary effects of the membership group.[43]

Also the educational milieu's rigid representation by the conflictualists seems an abstract, reductive presupposition. In opposition to Baudelot and Establet, who were accused of oversimplification, some authors[44] began by emphasizing the internal heterogeneousness of the primary-professional (P-P) and secondary-superior (S-S) networks, which the former believed to represent the top and the bottom of the scale respectively. They asserted that there were upper and lower branches within each network. This situation arises due to an inherent contradiction: the ruling classes, while desirous of preserving their privileges, need to guarantee their technological well-being and so must diversify and enhance the quality of labour.

While still relative, the diversification of social representations does not stop at the classroom door. In France, for example, curricula and school textbooks have for two centuries included authors and movements opposed to the ruling classes as part of the country's historical and cultural tradition. Although teachers are essentially recruited from among the upper and middle classes and their basic attitudes reflect this fact, they do, at least in 'liberal democracies', espouse different ideologies, including those opposed to the group from which they originate. And, quite obviously, they do not all conduct their courses or base their educational methods on the dominant academic 'mandarin' model or the practice-teaching lessons of the literary disciplines.

In short, we need hardly be surprised to realize that school walls are not hermetically sealed to plurality, to disagreement, to the objective and subjective contradictions present in these countries. They infiltrate among all educational protagonists, but with one important difference, namely that the social class pyramid there is the inverse of that in society itself. This led one American writer to comment:

Despite our observation that we are not optimistic about school reform, we are fully cognizant of the contradictory nature of the American educational system. In spite of the role it plays in reproducing and justifying inequality, the educational system has not been a mechanistic reproduction institution.[45]

Lastly, it is just as inaccurate to assume that pupils are imprisoned within their subculture and incapable of comprehending anything but the code in which they were socialized. We need only recall the observations of W.H. Goodenough concerning the 'cultural competence' which everyone must necessarily acquire in contemporary complex societies, the possibility of distancing oneself from his membership culture and the necessity of becoming familiar with the code of other groups. Modern mass media, in fact, help a great deal, so that, except in a few cases which do exist, the invisible significations of the education of the ruling classes are not totally impenetrable by the uninitiated and, especially, do not remain so indefinitely. However, it is true that the isolation of an underprivileged subculture has every likelihood of becoming real in the case of the 'ghetto' of the special education classes in which a good number of young people from the working class end up.

In the end, these considerations do not reflect the thesis of an educational system which favours the upper and middle classes, and consequently, treats the underprivileged more unfairly, the further down they are on the social-economic scale. But by pointing out the gaps revealed by observation, they rescue us from 'educational despair' and the blameworthy passiveness which can result.

Other avenues of investigation

Another outlook tends to reduce the role of the school in determining success or failure, by placing the emphasis on social institutions. The comparative study of pupil stratification and the social mobility of their parents (data reported by M. Reuchlin)[46] show that social processes, to a greater extent than scholastic structures, lead to rigidness in the social hierarchy. Yet other studies examining social careers and school curriculum ascribe a smaller role to schools in the adult's ultimate success or failure.[47] These analyses, which opened new vistas in the sociology of educational inequality, have been taken up and re-examined by numerous authors whose articles were published in the United States in the *Harvard educational review*, 1973; *Sociology of education*, 1973; *American journal of sociology*, 1973; and the *American educational research journal*, 1974. The exponents of this point of view in Europe are Girod and Gaussen.[48]

Lastly, conflictualist themes in Europe sparked a debate on the intrinsic value of underprivileged or disregarded cultures, beginning with the 'working-class culture'. The first impulse here, as in ethnic cultures which we shall see later, is to 'make up' for the handicap due to the gap between working-class culture and that transmitted by schools. Even if never openly admitted, this reaction implies a very marked value judgment: the culture of the economically privileged is the proper one; any other culture needs to be rooted out of the subjects who are its carriers. Hence, a series of educational measures for bridging the 'gap' are organized in the context of 'remedial' or 'compensatory' courses.

This position, with the rebirth of anthropological cultures and the emergence of cultural relativism, is currently being called into question. The accent is placed on the positive character of the popular subculture and we are even witnessing a reversal of the concept of a handicap;[49] working-class children ultimately are the inheritors of a vaster culture which education can destroy, or at least jeopardize. Hence, there arises the legitimization and even idealization of anti-school behaviour; so-called underprivileged children will realize that, in actual fact, tests and other classroom activities are artificial, or even idiotic exercises, and will refuse to become part of that gratuitous universe. Systematically, they will dislike 'talking to the walls', reject meaningless speech, artificial manipulation of the language in contrast to the children of white-collar parents who respond 'mindlessly' to the teacher's questions.

It is clear how easily cultural considerations can be grafted on to ideological and political stances concerning the working class. One obstacle to this position is the assertion that the cultural handicap of the working classes is not purely fictitious; an intensive weakness can be distinguished, one which is not merely relative to the bourgeois model.[50] Ignoring this fact would mean precisely perpetuating the negative status of underprivileged groups; thus, schools must remedy this weakness, this incomplete redistribution of the legacy of mankind and the achievements of history to all individuals.

This controversy lies at the heart of an important debate within the branch we are interested in: the interpretation of cultural relativism and the content and modes of multicultural education. We will resume this topic in our final chapter.

Classroom subcultures and national subcultures

THE SCHOOL AND 'REGIONAL CULTURES'

The demand that these cultures be taken into consideration is recent and we have seen its causes. Its impact on educational institutions for the time being is minimal and gives rise to symbolic measures at most. At the practical level, the more insistent demand is for the teaching of the mother tongues of children in state schools for reasons which we will discuss in Chapter VI.

SCHOOLS AND SEX-GROUP CULTURES

This is the oldest debate in the West directly related to our subject. The demands of feminists have received the decisive support of cultural anthropology. The impetus was provided by Margaret Mead with her book entitled *Sex and temperament in three primitive societies*, published in 1935, containing her observations on three small peoples in Oceania. As she said in her introduction,

I shared the general belief of our society that there was a natural sex-temperament which could at the most only be distorted or diverted from normal expression. I was innocent of any suspicion that the temperaments which we regard as native to one sex might instead be mere variations of human temperament, to which the members of either or both sexes may, with more or less success in the case of different individuals, be educated to approximate.[51]

She discovered that two of these societies were, so to speak, 'unisexual' at least from the point of view of the ideal personality model, but in opposite directions:

> Whereas the Arapesh have standardized the personality of both men and women in a mould that, out of our traditional bias, we should describe as maternal, womanly, unmasculine, the Mundugumor have gone to the opposite extreme and, again ignoring sex as a basis for the establishment of personality differences, have standardized the behaviour of both men and women as actively masculine, virile, and without any of the softening and mellowing characteristics that we are accustomed to believe are inalienably womanly.[52]

With the Tshambuli people, meanwhile, sexual differentiation, which permeates all aspects of reality, even the earth, is the very principle upon which the dichotomy of social life is based, according to a pattern familiar to us. But, contrary to what we might expect in this patrilinear society, men, who are treated with benevolent condescension, perform activities and have roles which we relegate to women and vice versa. Thus, in her conclusion, M. Mead feels she can safely deduce that 'many, if not all, of the personality traits which we have called masculine or feminine are as lightly linked to sex as are the clothing, the manners, and the form of headdress that a society at a given period assigns to either sex.'[53]

In other words, once ethnological investigations were able to demonstrate that, from one society to another, traits which had been presumed to belong to 'feminine nature' were contingent and that they could even characterize men or vice versa, the extent to which these 'natures' were 'prescribed' identities was measured experimentally, using as a reference sex subcultures presenting a variety of normative characteristics.

This brings us to another aspect of the ambivalence of culture. The cultural traits of the working classes, which place them in difficulty vis-à-vis the bourgeois culture of which schools are the vehicle, have at least the merit of being elaborated in their own midst and thus of having their own consistency and objective existence. On the other hand, ethnological studies and the considerable evolution of the status and role of women and the 'feminine model' in our own societies indicate that the traits of sex cultures are, by and large, attributed from the outside and exist only because these prescriptions were interiorized. We know to what extent cultures imposed upon men and women in the majority of past societies have favoured the former, and restricted and disadvantaged the latter with respect to roles, recognized attitudes, accepted attitudes and activities, legitimate models of personal achievement. We also know the segregations, inequalities and limitations in which this resulted in the area of education generally, and elementary schools in particular: women were considered not to need schooling; either they were incapable of learning or were inept in certain fields (mathematics, science) supposedly 'contrary' to their nature which was believed to abhor abstraction, etc; assertions which have all been disproved by the facts.

Currently, the situation is generally as follows, even in societies reputedly most committed to the principle of equality of the sexes: on one hand, there is hardly an area of study in which women are not present, thus proving that it is not contrary to their nature; on the other hand, however, they are often under-represented in comparison to boys (an example of this is given by the situation in the United Kingdom described in 'The education of women').[54] The problem therefore, above and beyond the objective causes of this phenomenon which do not concern us here, is to determine the specific effect of interiorization of images of the woman such as transmitted by the family, the environment, popular or even intellectual literature, textbooks, advertising, the media, and by women themselves. There is no doubt that the assimilation of these representations by the group concerned is to a large degree responsible for barriers and handicaps in their advancement.

THE SCHOOL AND HABITAT CULTURES

The literature on this subject, unlike that on socio-economic groups, is not abundant. What does exist, however, emphasizes the problems rural people experience with respect to educational institutions deemed to be biased in favour of city dwellers. The basic understanding is that farm children are those who are most often eliminated or demoted, although some escape this fate. For, we must be careful not to oversimplify matters by speaking of a monolithic body of farmers without subdivision into categories. However, it might be that this group is, in general, educationally disadvantaged; all the inequalities present are not identical and do not have the same consequences, as Jegouzo and Brangeon[55] showed in France, distinguishing between small, medium and large-scale farming families.

Here again, the line must be drawn between objective factors of the mean educational handicap in rural areas (the city tending, for example, to monopolize assets of all sorts with regard to school utilization, the number of different types of institution, the quality of teacher recruitment, etc) and the factors we are concerned with here: the cultural factors.

From this point of view, according to the authors we have just cited, whereas farm people prove to be totally heterogeneous on the material and social plane, their reactions and practices vis-à-vis cultural phenomena and the school appear to be less differentiated which may justify the standard table produced by earlier authors.

As an example, we can use the table drawn up by P. Rambaud[56] at a time when the crisis of rural change in France was still acute. We feel it is sufficiently applicable to the remaining European countries to the extent that a mainly traditional, small and medium-scale farming society still exists.

This author explores the ambiguities and contradictions in rural residents, their desire to move to the city, to leave the country, at the same time as their dislike for the urban educational institution. Apart from certain reasons of a methodological nature, for example the relative unsuitability of education to further the career objectives of these young people, he identifies 'problems resulting from cultural divergencies, such as two forms of expressing intelligence, one mainly practical the other mainly verbal, the practical form being more prevalent in the country than the verbal'.[57]

Culturally, the school is a place of words, of speaking and reading skills, and this constitutes one form of domination over matter; the rural world is culturally a place of work, of 'action' skills, which constitutes another. The rural person's intelligence functions more on intuition than on reasoning or definition, 'it thinks and immediately acts upon its thoughts, rather than speaking before asking.'[58] A. Rambaud comments: 'The scarcity of verbal expression is a sort of dissolving of reflection into action, which is in no way an absence of reflection, and vocabulary is poorer as a result.'[59] Hence the reticence towards intensive schooling, which some would describe as atrophied, in verbal forms of expression. Need we add that the same could be said for a good many categories of working-class people in cities?

This characteristic is most likely linked to the high regard in rural society for manual labour, the crucible of all culture. What is more, its conception of work 'implies an attitude towards nature which... is still oftentimes simple submission without a genuinely technical dimension'.[60]

The school requires yet two other changes imposed by urban culture. First of all, with respect to time: 'Working at age 14 and tilling the earth signify that the future is sacrificed for the present; wanting to learn a trade, on the other hand, means situating the present as the time of learning something new, rather than engaging in repetition.' Thus, the new culture implies wanting 'to no longer search the past for the clues of what is to come',[61] the 'predominance of the future and the call for innovation over past time in which everything was handed down'. But it also requires, to comply with the urban model, interiorization of a new concept of space. 'The space within which the future can become reality is a set of trades having its own internal order, facilitating mobility, depending upon the qualifications acquired.' The relationship of each person with it 'is not the original, the one born into or inherited from the family past or the place of residence, but that created by a multi-form vocational potential. The undefined field of social relations, coextensive with the influence of the city, supplants or becomes superimposed upon agrarian space, which is a limited surface and an institution of isolation.'[62] Like the new concept of time, with which it combines to form a space-time continuum, the new space concept is characterized by its diversity and complexity, and is subordinated to the logic of the constant evolution of needs and desires.

It can thus be understood how the traditional young country boy will find himself handicapped by, among other things, his subculture, and that this will cost him a number of failures vis-à-vis an educational institution which he nonetheless fervently wishes to become part of. The failure itself is interpreted in the light of representation by which the failure is made even more serious. Like the urban proletarian, the rural boy need only turn to his fellows to find 'reinforcement' of his ideas: school is useless, education compensates for an immediate ineptitude to work and is a means of escaping agricultural work; to succeed at school requires 'being made for it' and the pupil bears the sole responsibility for his failure. Given this frame of mind, a conception of educational culture is cultivated which perceives the latter as a content within a containing element and of schools as 'an intangible reality, valid in itself, and which one "enters into" or abandons, without questioning its goals or methods'.[63] Now that this inventory of specific points of incompatibility between rural children and classroom culture has been made we can complete our analysis of the latter in relation to working-class children. It helps us to understand better, by way of contrast, what is meant by urban culture.

Here again, accusations of ideological manipulation are not absent. Jegouzo and Brangeon suspect the school of wanting to divert rural children from the condition of farmer to orient them towards the condition of worker, in other words, to convert them from one minority subculture, deemed to have become useless, to another considered to be useful.

'YOUTH' CULTURE

Can we speak of a set of attitudes, representations and values which are specific to all young people, despite the fact that they belong to different social groups and subgroups? Long before speaking about their 'culture' we began by admitting that they occupied a separate place within societies because of the 'adolescent crisis' which all young people experience. Initially, however, this condition was considered, despite its dysfunctional aspect, to be a necessary psychological phase before attaining adulthood. It was cultural anthropology which relativized the phenomenon by showing, as we have already seen, that it was related to certain objective, educational characteristics of contemporary Western industrial societies. Even though it was thus recognized that this crisis placed young adolescents in a position of relative marginalization with respect to adults, they were not considered to be the originators of an individual subculture.

It took time to come to this realization, thanks to a number of authors in the 1960s such as Eisenstadt, Coleman, Campbell and Alexander and Sugarman.[64] The incidents of May 1968 in France, which had a resounding ideological and cultural impact, gave rise to a considerable volume of literature which coined the expression 'empire of youth'. Even M. Mead, after describing the transmission of culture from one generation to another,[65] developed a theory on the relationships between them in a vision of mankind in which she distinguished three types of culture:[66] 'past-figurative', in which children are essentially educated by their parents; 'cofigurative', in which children and parents learn from their peers; and 'prefigurative', in which adults also learn from their children.

Cofiguration has become extensively formalized in industrial society, giving use to the phenomenon of juvenile or 'teenage' culture, which does not necessarily exclude adult dominance. It comes about when technological change, which in turn generates other transformations, occurs at such a pace that the models of the older generation can no longer serve the younger generation. The result is an interruption of cultural transmission: grandparents and even parents become 'obsolete' and witness the disappearance of the educational value of their message. Sometimes role reversal results and children become susceptible of teaching their elders (prefigurative type). Indeed, the three types of transmission currently coexist, depending on the field and, no doubt, the social subgroup. This unquestionably complicates the task of educators who are ill-equipped to make these minute distinctions and more often than not do not know in which direction to turn. Misunderstandings, rifts and conflicts are even further multiplied in a situation of overlapping codes.

With this theory, based on the analysis of the evolution of social dynamism in the broadest sense of the term, the 'conflict of generations' becomes burdened down with a notional content quite different from that with which it was laden at the time when we spoke of an 'adolescent crisis', implying a 'crisis of opposition' due to contingent, transient, psychological factors. As we shall see, this new point of view merits further study. But first, we would look at what youth culture might be.

Campbell, summarizing numerous studies, distinguishes various traits: hedonism and insistence on the immediate gratification of desires, fondness for new experiences, a preference for 'horizontal' types of power structure in opposition to hierarchical social structures, and constant preoccupation with demarcating the separation between youth and adults. The latter objective translates into extreme anti-conformism with regard to social norms, coupled with a high degree of internal conformism, and into the pursuit of anything which can strengthen the consciousness of 'us' in opposition to 'them'.[67] Consequently,

any attempt at *rapprochement* on the part of adults most of the time causes a reaction of alienation in young people. Inevitable alienation, for by adopting their jeans and hairstyle, adults deprive young people of their means of identity and thus condemn them to beat a retreat to preserve their difference.[68]

F. Ferrarotti, following a long line of other authors, took this analysis further in his conclusion to a series of articles on young people in different parts of the world published in a Unesco document.[69] Speaking of young people in the West based on various studies and noting their lack of involvement in organizations and parties created by adults, after having dreamed of a revolution (in 1968) in their own style, he observed in their way of life a predominance of 'expressive' types of behaviour as opposed to 'instrumental' types, which are entirely justified by the goals to be achieved. These forms of conduct

> have no value in relation to...goals determined *a priori*, but only insofar as...they give rise to a group mood. They thus help to generate a collective consciousness that, although too fluid and often too spontaneous to crystallize in an articulate pattern of behaviour, ultimately creates a sense of identity, that is, enables a human group to feel united in the gestures, shibboleths, and reactions it has in common.[70]

Hence the absence of

> rationally thought-out programmes, the superiority of the realm of instinct, something closely akin to the captivating, unpredictable mobility of the child, considered to possess a capacity to 'live on self-demand'. On the practical level, we may note a relative irresponsibility in attitudes to duty, a reluctance to make specific commitments that can be evaluated in terms of achievements, a tendency to make indictments of society while at the same time expecting to be supported by it, a chronic state of indecision — which, however, is presented and seen as a state of openness and responsiveness to all occurrences, to the most disparate or seemingly contradictory experiences, and to the inspiration of the moment. 'What is gained on the swings of expression is lost on the roundabouts of reflection.'[71]

However, the youth culture thesis has been the object of a number of criticisms, or at least attenuations, on various planes. One adjustment consists in diminishing the importance, if not denying the existence, of such a culture, by regarding it merely as reactional movement, in contrast to M. Mead's organic conception. This is the point of view adopted by F. Ferrarotti for whom the phenomenon is linked to the marginalization of young people in industrial societies, which, to varying degrees, are a source of frustration and incapable not only of satisfying the needs and aspirations they create, but also of guaranteeing basic rights especially the right to work in the case of the present recession. Other authors before Ferrarotti restricted the reality of subculture even further, reducing it, as did Delooz in 1970,[72] to a mere product of the school; by separating the young person from the adult world more completely and for an increasingly longer period, the school confines him with his peers, creating a microsociety which ends up becoming at one and the same time his point of reference and of affiliation.

Actually, these points of view are not all incompatible. We are dealing with a complex reality whereby the intrinsic cultural valorization of young people, because of the accelerated obsolescence of contributions from the past, can very well coexist with the relative social 'minoritization' and marginalization of part of them in crisis-afflicted structures maintained by elders... or, at least, by the 'less young' (for we should perhaps come to an understanding about age in this connection). An item-by-item analysis of the manifestations of juvenile culture should enable us to distinguish between that which is due to its 'organic' aspect, that is, that which is the positive expression of evolutionary, social dynamism, and that which constitutes a reaction to its dysfunctional aspects. The school, for its part, is not only the main factor in the creation and preservation of groups of children and adolescents, but also, because of the marked sociocultural character of its organization, its activities, and its messages, understandably — as this entire chapter shows — it provokes reactions and reinforces counter-cultures which are constantly challenging it. We find here a rather new idea with respect to earlier considerations: not only does the school present a subculture different from that of a large number of pupils, but the realization by pupils of these differences leads them to accentuate the difference, by consolidating their original patterns and even by creating traits specifically directed against the educational institution. In fact, Sugarman,[73] followed by Polk and Pink,[74] established a positive correlation between the anti-school attitude (poor conduct, poor results, reduction of academic aspirations) and participation in youth culture.

Another set of observations helped attenuate the radical aspect this concept may have acquired. Not only do they relativize it by showing to what extent this phenomenon concerns specific types of societies (it is by and large unheard of in Third World societies) and within these societies, they concern specific age groups and subgroups, but emphasis is placed on the multiplicity of links and points in common indicative of adolescent participation in 'adult' structures. First, the manipulation of this concept by adults for purely ideological motives had to be denounced: 'Reverting to the accents of a kind of new Rousseauistic messianism,' we once wrote, 'in the wake of the events of 1968, they went so far as to transform young people into the support of an anti-society identified with the rediscovery of "nature", which is inherently good and a source of salvation.'[75] Thus, rejecting the concept of an autonomous 'empire of youth' with its own specific causality, empirical studies, when finally undertaken, showed how social conditioning spares no one. Following an investigation of this type among pupils and students we concluded:

The basic social subgroups of which young people are a part by the same token as their elders, also have an undisputable effect on them, and in a direction generally verifiable by adults. Such is the case, in particular, of the social class and economic interests in general, of sex status and even family milieu.[76]

Moreover, as far as the comparative contents of models from various age groups are concerned, studies on young people in the West[77] came to the same realization. Even if the results reveal an amount of distance-taking, criticism and repetition, they show them to be intertwined just as frequently, if not more so, with attitudes and themes of social participation and linked up with explicit or implicit acceptance of a number of 'adult' values and representations.

Since the 'content' evolves over the years, so to speak as a matter of principle, in the case of youth groups, let us, using the criteria established at the beginning of the present work, look into which elements are 'cultural'. The term certainly seems to be inappropriate for the majority of representations and even values.

But we can probably isolate a nucleus of attitudes which seem to hold up much better. In any case, one point appears to be certain. On one hand, the juvenile connotation in every group and every situation from now on will weigh more heavily and be the vehicle of an undeniable specificity, even if it changes significantly in time and space. On the other hand, and more importantly, the young person no longer challenges adult values as a matter of fact but with a guilty conscience as is the case of a purely post-figurative situation: he becomes susceptible of rejecting them in principle, based on peer models, and to 'do what he feels like' in perfectly good conscience thanks to this parallel source of legitimacy. This fact cannot be ignored in education.

In conclusion, based on given considerations on the positioning of the educational institution in the cultural domain, we discover a far more complex and fluid situation than is usually presented. Accordingly, the real task at school, for which the anthropological method is especially indicated, is to establish how opposing cultural patterns are transmitted, when they are localized and how they evolve, to describe their different degrees of penetration, the waves generated because of their coexistence, and the configurations of models which result. Certainly, all these currents are not juxtaposed, but we will see that to some degree or another they reorganize themselves into a *field* reflecting the specific subculture of each school. It translates into an image — perhaps the image of the school — and reliance on distinguishing representations and even rituals.[78]

Nonetheless, no amount of 'psychologizing' will eliminate the sociological realities: primary schools without a doubt favour and serve as a vehicle for some specific subcultures rather than others. The overall picture merely shows that the problem is posed in terms of trends and dominant characteristics, not barriers and strings, leaving room for diversification of analysis and providing a support, at the same time as a direction, for educational action.[79]

NOTES AND REFERENCES

1. Durkheim, E. *Education et sociologie*. 2e éd. Paris, Presses universitaires de France, 1968; Davis, K.; Moore, W.E. Some principles of stratification. *American sociological review* (New York, American Sociological Association), vol. 10, April 1945, pp. 242-9; Parsons, T. The school class as a social system: some of its functions in American society. *Harvard educational review* (Cambridge, MA, Harvard University), vol. 29, Fall 1959, pp. 297-318.
2. Kerr, C., et al. *Industrialism and industrial man: the problem of labor and management in economic growth*. Cambridge, MA, Harvard University Press, 1960; Clark, B.R. *Educating the expert society*. San Francisco, Chandler, 1962.
3. Richta, R. *La civilisation au carrefour*. Paris, Seuil, 1974. 352 p; Kotásek, J. The idea of continuing education in the current reform of educational systems and teacher training. *In*: Unesco. *The school and continuing education: four studies*. Paris, 1972, pp. 169-224.
4. Collins, R. Where are educational requirements for employment highest? *Sociology of education* (Albany, NY, American Sociological Association), vol. 47, no. 4, Fall 1974, pp. 419-42.

5. Forquin, J.-C. La sociologie des inégalités d'éducation : principales orientations, principaux résultats depuis 1965. *Revue française de pédagogie* (Paris, Institut national de recherche pédagogique), no. 48, juillet-août-septembre 1979, pp. 90-100; no. 49, octobre-novembre-décembre 1979, pp. 87-99; no. 51, avril-mai-juin 1980, pp. 77-92; Forquin, J.-C. L'approche sociologique de la réussite et de l'échec scolaires : inégalités de réussite scolaire et appartenance sociale. *Revue française de pédagogie* (Paris, Institut national de recherche pédagogique), no. 59, avril-mai-juin 1982, pp. 52-75; no. 60, juillet-août-septembre 1982, pp. 51-70.
6. Forquin, J.-C. La sociologie des inégalités d'éducation. *Op. cit.*, no. 51, 1980, p. 80.
7. Bowles, S. Unequal education and the reproduction of the social division of labour. *Review of radical political economics* (Ann Arbor, MI, Union for Radical Political Economics), vol. 3, no. 4, September 1971, pp. 1-30; Bowles, S.; Gintis, H. I.Q. in the U.S. class structure. *Social policy* (White Plains, NY), vol. 3, no. 4, November-December 1972; no. 5, January-February 1973, pp. 65-96; Bowles, S.; Gintis, H. *Schooling in capitalist America: educational reform and the contradiction of economic life.* New York, Basic Books, 1976. 340 p.
8. Bowles, S.; Gintis, H. I.Q. in the U.S. class structure. *Op. cit.*
9. Averch, M.A., et al. *How effective is schooling? A critical review and synthesis of research findings.* Santa Monica, CA, Rand Corporation, 1971. 249 p.
10. Girod, R. Les adolescents sous-instruits dans les sociétés industrielles de l'Ouest. *Revue française de pédagogie* (Paris, Institut national de recherche et de documentation pédagogiques), no. 22, janvier-février-mars 1973, pp. 21-35.
11. Aubret-Bény, F.; Pelnard-Considère, Jacqueline. La liaison entre appartenance socio-économique et développement. *In*: Reuchlin, M., éd. *Cultures et conduites.* Paris, Presses universitaires de France, 1976, p. 58.
12. Le Ny, J.-F. Capacités cognitives et différenciation de classe. *La Pensée* (Paris), no. 190, 1976, p. 22
13. Girod, R. *Op. cit.*; Willis, P. L'école des ouvriers. *Actes de la recherche en sciences sociales* (Paris), no. 24, 1978, pp. 51-61; Léger, A. *Enseignants du secondaire.* Paris, Presses universitaires de France, 1983. 256 p.
14. Perrenoud, P. *Stratification socio-culturelle et réussite scolaire: les défaillances de l'explication causale.* Genève, Librairie Droz, 1970. 77 p.
15. Chan, K.S.; Rueda, R. Poverty and culture in education: separative but equal. *Exceptional children* (Reston, VA, Council for Exceptional Children), vol. 45, no. 6, March 1979, pp. 422-8; Tedesco, Emmy. *Des familles parlent de l'école.* Paris, Casterman, 1979. 188 p.
16. Kahl, J.A. Educational and occupational aspirations of «common man» boys. *Harvard educational review* (Cambridge, MA, Harvard University), vol. 23, no. 3, 1953, pp. 186-203; Boudon, R. *Education, opportunity and social inequality: changing prospects in Western society.* New York, Wiley, 1974. 220 p.
17. Cf. Forquin, J.-C. *Op. cit.*
18. Hyman, H. The values systems of different classes: a social psychological contribution to the analysis of stratification. *In*: Bendix, R.; Lipset, S.M., eds. *Class, status and power: a reader in social stratification.* Glencoe, IL, Free Press, 1953, pp. 426-42; Miller, S.M. Dropouts: a political problem. *In*: Schreiber, D., ed. *Profile of the school dropout: a reader on America's major educational problem.* New York, Vintage Books, 1968, pp. 184-97.
19. Bernstein, B. Social class and linguistic development: a theory of social learning. *In*: Halsey, A.H.; Floud, Jean; Anderson, C.A., eds. *Education, economy and society: a reader in the sociology of education.* Glencoe, IL, Free Press, 1961, pp. 288-314.
20. Coser, L.A.; Coser, Rose L. Time perspective and social structure. *In*: Gouldner, A.W.; Gouldner, H.P., eds. *Modern sociology.* New York, Harcourt, Brace and World, 1963, pp. 638-50; Bourdieu, P. L'école conservatrice: les inégalités devant l'école et devant

la culture. *Revue française de sociologie* (Paris, Centre national de la recherche scientifique), vol. 7, 1966, pp. 325-47.
21. Brossard, M. *Conduites verbales, activités cognitives et origine sociale.* Bordeaux, France, Université de Bordeaux II, s.d., p. 96. [Thesis]
22. Kohn, M.L. Social class and the exercise of parental authority. *American sociological review* (New York, American Sociological Association), vol. 24, no. 3, June 1959, pp. 352-66; Kohn, M.L. Social class and parent-child relationships: an interpretation. *American journal of sociology* (Chicago, IL), vol. 68. no 4, January 1963, pp. 471-80.
23. Bernstein, B., et al. *Class, codes and control*, vol. 1, London, Routledge and Kegan Paul, 1971, 238 p.
24. Bronfenbrenner, U. Socialization and social class through time and space. *In*: Maccoby, Eleanor E.; Newcamb, T.M.; Hartley, E.L., eds. *Readings in social psychology*. New York, Holt, Rinehart and Winston, 1958, pp. 400-25.
25. Forquin, J.-C. La sociologie des inégalités d'éducation. *Op. cit.*, no. 49, 1979, p. 90.
26. *Ibid.*, p. 90.
27. Girod, R. *Op. cit.*, p. 29.
28. Reuchlin, M. Les facteurs socio-économiques du développement cognitif. *In*: Duyckaerts, F., et al. *Milieu et développement*. Paris, Presses universitaires de France, 1972, pp. 69-136.
29. Marcos, H. Climat familial et réussite scolaire. *In*: Reuchlin, M., éd. *Cultures et conduites*. Paris, Presses universitaires de France, 1976, pp. 285-312.
30. Lautrey, J. *Classe sociale, milieu familial, intelligence.* Paris, Presses universitaires de France, 1980. 288 p.
31. Tedesco, E. *Op. cit.*
32. Plaisance, E. *L'école maternelle en France depuis la fin de la seconde guerre mondiale: étude sociologique.* Paris, Université de Paris V, 1984. [Thesis]
33. Willis, P. *Op. cit.*, p. 58.
34. Snyders, G. Est-ce le maître d'école qui a perdu la bataille contre les inégalités sociales? *Enfance* (Paris, Laboratoire de psycho-biologie de l'enfant), no. 1, janvier-avril 1970, pp. 1-22; Snyders, G. *Ecole, classe et lutte de classes*. Paris, Presses universitaires de France, 1976, 384 p.
35. Bourdieu, P.; Saint-Martin, Monique de. L'excellence scolaire et les valeurs du système d'enseignement français. *Annales* (Paris, Centre de sociologie européenne), no. 1, janvier 1969; Bourdieu, P.; Saint-Martin, Monique de. Les catégories de l'entendement professoral. *Actes de la recherche en sciences sociales* (Paris), no. 3, 1975, pp. 68-93.
36. Klein, Josephine. *Samples from English cultures*. London, Routledge and Kegan Paul, 1965. 2 v.
37. Bourdieu, P. Avenir de classe et causalité du probable. *Revue française de sociologie* (Paris, Centre national de la recherche scientifique), vol. 15, no. 1, janvier-mars 1974, pp. 3-42.
38. Willis, P. *Op. cit.*, p. 59.
39. *Ibid.*
40. Baudelot, C.; Establet, R. *L'école capitaliste en France*. Paris, Maspero, 1971. 324 p; Snyders, G. Est-ce le maître d'école qui a perdu la bataille contre les inégalités sociales? *Op. cit.*; Snyders, G. Ecole, classe et lutte de classes. *Op. cit.*
41. Girod, R. *Op. cit.*
42. Reuchlin, M. *Op. cit.*
43. Sauvy, A.; Girard, A. Les diverses classes sociales devant l'enseignement. *Population* (Paris, Institut national d'études démographiques), no. 2, mars-avril 1965, pp. 205-32; Girod, R.; Tofigh, R. Family background and income: school career and social mobility of young males of working-class origin. A Geneva survey. *Acta sociologica* (Copenhagen), vol. 9, fasc. 1-2, 1965, pp. 94-109.

44. Bernard, R. *Ecole, culture et langue française: éléments pour une approche sociologique.* Paris, Tema Formation, 1972. 311 p.
45. Cheng, C.W.; Brizendine, Emily; Oakes, Jeannie. What is «an equal chance» for minority children? *The Journal of negro education* (Washington, DC, Howard University), vol. 48, no. 3, Summer 1979, p. 285.
46. Reuchlin, M., éd. *Cultures et conduites.* Paris, Presses universitaires de France, 1976. 360 p.
47. Jencks, C., et al. *Inequality: a reassessment of the effect of family and schooling in America.* New York, Basic Books, 1972; Boudon, R. La sociologie des inégalités dans l'impasse? *Analyse et prévision* (Paris), no. 17, 1974, pp. 83-95.
48. Jackson, P.W., et al. Perspectives on inequality, *Harvard educational review* (Cambridge, MA, Harvard University), vol. 42, no. 1, 1973, pp. 37-164; Symposium review: Inequality, Jencks et al. *Sociology of education* (Albany, NY, American Sociological Association), vol. 46, no. 4, Fall 1973, pp. 427-70; Coleman, J.S., et al. Review symposium: *Inequality: a reassessment of the effect of family and schooling in America,* by C. Jencks, et al. . . . *American journal of sociology* (Chigago, IL, University of Chicago), vol. 78, no. 6, May 1973, pp. 1523-44; Symposium review of Jencks, et al., *Inequality, American educational research journal* (Washington, DC, American Educational Research Association), vol. 11, no. 2, Spring 1974, pp. 149-75; Girod, R., et al. *Inégalité, inégalités: analyse de la mobilité sociale.* Paris, Presses universitaires de France, 1977. 183 p.; Gaussen, F. Non, l'égalité des chances n'existe pas... *Le Monde de l'éducation* (Paris), no. 1. décembre 1974. pp. 14-19.
49. Colloque sur les handicaps socio-culturels, Paris, 1975. *Le handicap socio-culturel en question.* Paris, Les Editions ESF, 1978. 213 p.
50. Snyders, G. *Ecole, classe et lutte de classes. Op. cit.*
51. Mead, Margaret. *Sex and temperament in three primitive societies.* New York, Morrow, 1935, 1963, p. xiv.
52. *Ibid.*, p. 165
53. *Ibid.*, p. 280.
54. The education of women. *Trends in education* (London, Department of Education and Science), no. 4, Winter 1978, pp. 3-10.
55. Jegouzo, Guenhael; Brangeon, J.-L. *Les paysans et l'école.* Paris, Cujas, 1976. 287 p.
56. Rambaud, P. *Société rurale et urbanisation.* Paris, Seuil, 1969. 320 p.
57. *Ibid.*, p. 107.
58. Circular of 30 June 1952 concerning the curricula of technical colleges, quoted by Léon, A. *Formation générale et apprentissage du métier.* Paris, Presses universitaires de France, 1965, p. 97.
59. Rambaud, P. *Op. cit.*, p. 108.
60. *Ibid.*, p. 107.
61. *Ibid.*, p. 114.
62. *Ibid.*, p. 115.
63. *Ibid.*, p. 110.
64. Eisenstadt, S.N. *From generation to generation: New age groups and social structure.* New York, Free Press, 1956: Coleman, J.S. *The adolescent society: the social life of the teenager and its impact on education.* New York, Free Press; London, Collier-Macmillan, 1961. 368 p.; Campbell, E.Q.; Alexander, C.N. Structural effects and interpersonal relationships. *American journal of sociology* (Chicago, IL), vol. 71, no. 3, November 1965, pp. 284-9; Sugarman, B. Involvement in youth culture, academic achievement and conformity in school: an empirical study of London schoolboys. *British journal of sociology* (London), vol. 18, no. 2, June 1967, pp. 151-64.
65. Book review of current anthropology: continuities in cultural evolution, by Margaret Mead. *Current anthropology* (Chicago, IL), vol. 7, no. 1, February 1966, pp. 67-82.

66. Mead, Margaret. *Culture and commitment: a study of the generation gap.* New York, Doubleday, 1970.
67. Campbell, E.Q.; Alexander, C.N. *Op. cit.*
68. Héry, G. La transmission des modèles culturels par l'école. *Recherches anglaises et américaines* (Strasbourg, France), vol. 14, 1981, p. 122.
69. Ferrarotti, F. Youth in search of a new social identity. *In*: Unesco. *Youth in the 1980s.* Paris, The Unesco Press, 1981, pp. 305-20.
70. *Ibid.*, p. 315.
71. *Ibid.*, pp. 315-16.
72. Delooz, P. La jeunesse occidentale: un état de la question. *Revue nouvelle* (Bruxelles), vol. 26, t. 51, no. 5-6, mai-juin 170, pp. 454-63.
73. Sugarman, B. *Op. cit.*
74. Polk, K.; Pink, W. Youth culture and the school: a replication. *British journal of sociology* (London), vol. 22, no. 2, June 1971, pp. 160-71.
75. Camilleri, C.; Tapia, C. *Jeunesse française et groupes sociaux après mai 1968: enquête sur des populations universitaires et scolaires de Paris et de province.* Paris, Centre national de la recherche scientifique, 1974, p. 173.
76. *Ibid.*, p. 174.
77. Fletcher, R. *The family and marriage in Britain: an analysis and moral assessment.* 3rd. ed. Harmondsworth, Penguin, 1973. 282 p.; Bachy, J.-P.; Bachy, Claudine. *Les étudiants et la politique.* Paris, Colin, 1973. 240 p.; Camilleri, C.; Tapia, C. *Op. cit.*; Camilleri, C.; Tapia, C. *Les nouveaux jeunes: la politique ou le bonheur. Jeunesse de France, d'Europe et du tiers monde.* Toulouse, France, Privat, 1983: Francès, R. *L'idéologie dans l'université: structure et déterminants des attitudes sociales des étudiants.* Paris, Presses universitaires de France, 1980. 232 p.
78. King, R. *Values and involvement in a grammar school.* London, Routledge and Kegan Paul, 1969. 194 p.; Holland, Patricia. School imagery. *New society* (London), vol. 43, no. 800, 2 February 1978, pp. 261-2.
79. Cf. Héry, G. *Op. cit.*

CHAPTER IV

Educational problems raised by ethnic minorities

The groups treated in the preceding chapter belong to the same ethnic group but to different cultures. In this chapter we will take a look at other groups whose cultural differences within a given society are due to an ethnic origin which is foreign or which has become foreign (eg the case of the American Indian). Thus, distinctions cannot, as a rule, be reduced to differences between subcultures within a given whole: they exist between cultures and are thus more profound and give rise to more serious reactions and problems. Generally, these individuals of foreign origin are immigrants to the society under consideration, or their descendants.

For reasons already mentioned, the significant analyses carried out in North America deal with these groups. In Europe, the vast majority of research undertaken for many years dealt with the problems discussed in the preceding chapter, but the waves of immigrants from developing countries following World War II have given rise to a considerable body of literature.

Problems of adaptation in Western industrialized countries

Integration and, more generally, the life of these immigrants in societies which are culturally different and sometimes extremely different are the sources of much tension and psychological problems related to difficulties with adaptation. Europe currently enjoys ideal conditions for identifying these difficulties because the massive influx of foreigners is recent and the 'integration crisis' is current and intense. It is necessary to present the main characteristics of this crisis, for the educator must be aware of what goes on in the personalities of subjects. This is the necessary, if not sufficient, condition for adapting his behaviour. First, a distinction must be made between the influx of what might be called 'unskilled' workers and those with a high social standing (white-collar workers, intellectuals, diplomats, etc) for whom the consequences of their immigration, it is unanimously agreed, are minor or even nonexistent. Their financial situation obviously enables them to overcome all objective shortcomings which are a major source of handicaps and maladjustments. But, to our view, the overriding reason is to be found elsewhere, namely participation in the promotional subculture as defined in Chapter I, whose principal means of transmission is the school and which is characteristic of 'cultivated' people. As R. Berthelier[1] quite rightly observed,

the intellectual level (in the university or academic sense of the term) of the family group explains their greater mastery of the second language and minimizes the risk of failure in school; in addition, 'culture' and academic knowledge are, as Almeida said, a passport, because they provide universally recognized and utilizable defences, and represent an international code.

Moreover, a distinction must be made between the so-called 'first generation', who immigrated, and their descendants, the 'second generation' whose socialization took place entirely or essentially in the host country: they constitute the crux of the educational problem and it is of them we wish to speak. While their parents already suffer from the vagueness of reference points in their existence, at least for them their personalities are already formed and do not add to the confusion. However, their descendants are affected during the very process of personality formation. These problems acquired a specific psychological and educational character when families came in great numbers to join the individual workers, bringing with them children already born and procreating in the host country. Of the vast literature on the subject, we will cite just a few publications: an abstract on *Native culture and migrant cultures* by the Council of Europe[2] with analyses by B. Ducoli, A.J. F. Köbben, A. Gokalp, H. Esser, M. Alaluf dealing with several European countries; another on *Socialization and deviance among young immigrants in France, Switzerland, West Germany and Italy* (Acta of the Syracuse Colloquium of 1982);[3] a comparative study carried out in Paris comparing young immigrant delinquents and nondelinquents from the Iberian Peninsula and the Maghreb to nationals in order to study the relationship between identity crises and deviance, with contributions by I. Taboada-Leonetti, M. Zaleska and H. Malewska-Peyre;[4] finally, a special edition of the magazine *Les temps modernes*[5] on immigration from the Maghreb.

The difficulties increase with the disparity between the culture of the society of origin and that of the host country. They reach their culmination with Africans, Turks and immigrants from the Maghreb. The latter, who are especially numerous, have been the object of special attention. The problems they encounter and the analyses which have been devoted to them seem to be particularly revealing of immigrants from ex-colonies in the Third World. Tensions flaring up in relations between young people of the second generation and their families, their community of origin, the host society. The studies have revealed several dominant characteristics which are generally common to other groups of foreigners in similar situations and which we have attempted to summarize.[6]

In addition to divergence between the content of the systems present, which makes negotiating change more delicate, a further complication comes into play, namely, the difficulty of grasping the patterns to be linked up. Even though they are born in Europe, immigrants lack the necessary means of understanding the Western code. They also have a poor knowledge of their own culture, to which they are exposed by a group of immigrants, a family which is separated from a society which continues to evolve. What is more, the parental relationship to the culture is not without defects. Parents often claim to preserve it, but in so doing, rigidify it, a common reflex among people who feel lost or threatened. They are thus prompted to impose it upon their children as a set of incomprehensible constraints, wrapped in tautological catch phrases: 'That's the way it is in our country', 'Our religion says so', 'We are not French, Swiss, etc'.

When they adopt Western traits, they rarely try to achieve a coherent synthesis with the original system. Most often the result is a syncretic construction brought about by the juxtaposition of representations borrowed from the two antagonistic systems, as circumstances dictate and according to an irrational logic. A number of convergent investigations show that, given the weakening of structures of ancestral control, subjects do not shrink from performing 'corrupting manipulations' on the traditional code. We may thus term these 'strategies of advantage maximization': for example, improper interpretation of the code, normally oriented towards the good of the community, in the sole interest of the individual and often to the detriment of the young (in arranged marriages, determination of the dowry, etc); a tendency to exploit the advantages of both systems, but without assuming the corresponding responsibilities; obstinate maintenance of purely symbolic observances and abandonment of other important values, eg rigorous observance of Ramadan while other religious prescriptions are not respected; unequal application of codes based on sex, allowing boys to adopt modern mores but denying them to girls; invention of frustrating compromises to make partial enjoyment of modern privileges possible, while at the same time trying to preserve traditional values.

It is thus clear that these young immigrants as a whole are dealing mainly with by-products of their cultures. The spectacle of these incoherencies and 'cultural tinkering' by their elders does not encourage them to take an interest in the original, which they 'only accept according to the way in which their parents will transmit it'.[7]

Moreover, even though the change appears to be quite similar in the country of origin and the country of immigration, at home it takes place within a national context which is better controlled and more in conformity with the desires of the protagonists, whereas in the host country it constitutes a form of impotence in the face of a foreign, intimidating environment, which affords young people the possibility of relying on antagonistic institutions and even to use laws against the family community.[8] The latter, as a result, undergoes many exogenously imposed changes. Of course, the tensions between generations thus created will lead to efforts at moderation which at a practical level may be successful, but which are not always justified at the level of educational philosophy. For example, tacit contrast of coexistence will be concluded within the family in exchange for the unexpressed tolerance on the part of parents for various violations of their original values, provided the child respects, or pretends to respect, certain traditional dictates. In this way, peace is restored to the family group, especially when the mother knows how to play her role as mediator, but we might wonder what the psychological effects of this masquerade, which takes the place of conflict, of the dissociation of two types of behaviour, one at home, and the other elsewhere, might be.

In one type of behaviour abscribed by observers there is neither revolt nor masquerade: conceived not to hinder the adaptation to the new environment and extremely desirous of advancement in the new society, some parents believe they are doing the right thing by not interfering in the lives and 'modern' evolution of their children, to the extent of effacing themselves in front of them. Some attempt to hide their world of origin, satisfying themselves with presenting it in a playful or superannuated way via naive stories and by speaking the ancestral language 'to amuse them'. Happy about the progress in school of their sons and daughters, they listen to them willingly when everything is well; but when their children bring home problems of conflicts with teachers or classmates, or tell them about racism, they become gloomy, upset or go away without a word. Here again, immediate tensions are skirted, but more serious problems can spring up in the long run and the impact of this behaviour with respect to the young person's satisfactory personality development is not to be underestimated.

Thus, the conditions are frequently achieved for the inadequate interiorization of the framework of both foreign and native values. The situation is not improved, observers insist, by the visible contradiction, a major one in the case of highly patriarchal cultures, between the status of superiority conferred by the culture, ie the authority of the father and the extreme inferiority of his socio-economic status; social reality thus makes a mockery of the cultural model.

Given these facts, the temptation arises to reject the ancestral culture. However, attempts in this direction run into obstacles. In the first place, there is the fear of being deprived of the support of one's compatriots, of harming the family, which studies have shown, even for young people, still remains an important focal point in immigrant circles. But there is yet another problem: the attitude of the host country in Western Europe. Certainly young foreigners by and large integrate themselves at the objective level. To a large extent they abandon the native language, read the publications of the new country, listen to its music, progressively become involved in recreational structures, trade unions and comradeship, friendship and sentimental relationships with their European peers. Systematic study of sociometric networks at school, even for children from the

Maghreb, does not allow us to make categorical, dualistic representations:[9] instances of immigrant-national intermixing are numerous, especially with girls. But even if objective relationships with the host society grow, subjective ties do not follow. If any increase is to be noted in this respect, it is in complexity, ambiguousness and their conflictive character. For immigrants and nationals are separated by their respective groups, with the reciprocal action of their images and behaviour. Host groups are ill-disposed to judge and behave in accordance with the actual personality of each foreigner. They project on to the immigrant communities as a whole a collective image which, especially in the present recession, mainly implies rejection since it focuses on the socially disadvantaged with whom the problems of coexistence with nationals have not yet been solved.

The young immigrant of this type, of which the North African is a prototype, is thus made aware of the ineffectiveness of his efforts against the group image of which he is a prisoner: 'Since I am a foreigner, I will always be a foreigner.' We were told by a student during a recent survey, 'I am forced to remain Algerian because I am not accepted by others.' He discovered, in fact, the prescribed identity (imposed by others) which, for him, becomes an identity prison.

The final obstacle to attempts at social assimilation or, at least, integration, for this young foreigner is the fear that rejection of his native identity will be interpreted as a betrayal. This fear is reinforced by the fact that he perceives his community in a position of inequality with respect to this society, in a 'dominator-dominated' relationship. The accusation of traitor and the subsequent feeling of culpability are made all the more acute by the fact that the community betrayed is disfavoured and subject to rejection or persecution.

One consequence of this is obvious: in questions of identity related to immigration situations a great deal of importance is attached to social stratification. We might perhaps even venture to say that most of the problems being discussed here would be significantly attenuated or eliminated altogether if inter-group relationships were felt to be equal, as between natives of Western industrialized societies.[10] Another consequence of this observation needs to be emphasized: the symbolic role which any identity construct acquires becomes, in the case we are discussing, extremely important. The desire to give it a non-guilt-generating significance can lead to paradoxical behaviour on the part of young immigrants; however many values they borrow from the host society, and even if they embrace its entire culture, many continue to lay claim to their original culture. This becomes an 'identity of principle' based on a dissociation: a tendency to practise the values of a group with which they do not want to be a member (the host society) and yet asserting affiliation to a group the patterns of which (the society of origin) they reject. There is consequently a kind of malfunctioning of the usual mechanisms. The implementation of social and moral values is more often than not linked to a feeling of affiliation to community from which one fears being excluded. The 'jamming' of this feeling, in the case at hand, is susceptible of rendering moral consciousness even more fragile.

We can thus comprehend the difficulties in identifying themselves and surviving experienced by this 'second generation' who often have the impression of fighting with their backs to the wall, since the alternative of returning home and being accepted by the native culture poses problems. It is interesting to note that the young immigrant easily formulates eclectic wishes with respect to that society. To its pleasant climate and natural beauty he would like to add the structures, the national 'disciplined' organization and various scientific achievements (including birth control) which are the fruits of industrialization. Often he also hopes to find freedom of expression and the right to privacy, the values of social activism: equality, social justice, improvement in the status of women, elimination of privileges. He would like to combine the advantages of the pre-industrial and industrial eras.

To escape the difficult situation in which they find themselves, some of these young people toy with the idea of a third culture or a 'transculture'. Until these formulae receive an identifiable content, we can indicate, on the basis of observations at our disposal, a few principles to help attenuate this 'existential anguish'. Whatever decision he may make in the future, it is important that the young immigrant has the impression that he has a choice, that he is not forced to leave or stay against his will. Moreover, his conflicts with the host society become relative if he feels he can go home without that decision being disastrous for him; he thus requires a vantage point from which his present difficulties appear less dramatic. But, if the return home is to represent a serious alternative and not a mere compensatory dream, two conditions must be met.

He must first have what is needed to reintegrate himself comfortably into the country of origin, namely, good professional training and satisfactory schooling from the host country; an appropriate educational system, among other things, is thus implicitly required for the attainment of this goal. But something else is needed: whatever the position adopted by the subject vis-à-vis his culture, it must appear respectable to him and he must not be ashamed of it. For, even if he does not adhere to it, it is on the basis of this equilibrating feeling, which restores his dignity, that his sociocultural evolution becomes genuinely free and thus wholesome.

That will also depend, of course, on factors out of the educator's control: for example, the reduction of inequalities in relations between the two societies from which the protagonists come or between individual statuses or roles. In this connection, studies have revealed the positive impact of the access on the part of the immigrant father to a skilled profession:[11] this diminishes the child's feeling of inferiority and increases his esteem for the ancestral culture. But for the teacher, and the institutions of which he is a part, as we will see in several chapters of this book, there are many opportunities he should not overlook.

Immigrants and the host society's school

Already experiencing personality disturbances because of the kind of exposure they have with the foreign society, these young people run into the same problems in the classroom subculture. A subculture which, on top of it all, is a reflection in the West of the privileged classes of which they are definitely not part. Hence, there arise a number of specific handicaps and problems sharing many common traits with those mentioned in connection with disfavoured nationals; their academic careers are on average poor or mediocre, with disturbing rates of failure and repetition.

These difficulties were first focused on in the United States. This has resulted in a general movement to analyse the values, beliefs and life-styles of various large immigrant communities, as well as of blacks and Indians. These studies differ from those of ethnologists, for they concern themselves with traits, which, with respect to their representations and attitudes, contrast with those of the school, which are impregnated with the 'Yankee' culture of the privileged classes. For example, they analyse representations of success and failure in comparison to Passon's notion of 'achievement', and the way in which they are accepted and interpreted; representations of the role and usefulness of formal Western schooling, the notion of time, the value of books, reading, etc.

From the abundant literature in the United States on black children, we will simply borrow, for the sake of illustration, a table summarizing the results of various studies:[12] from their African cultural legacy which favours a holistic view of the world, young African-Americans draw a globalizing perception of their environment and respond to it as a totality — hence, for them, the artificiality of the separation between behaviour and learning. Moreover, mental, emotional and physical nature are of equal importance. Consequently, intellectual stimulation, the teacher-pupil relationships and a proper functioning of the personal, physical and environmental aspects are all considered as factors to bear in mind to guarantee the best possible learning situation. For example, African-American children

> seem to learn better when the whole context for the information being covered is presented versus information in isolation for the purpose of memorization. Therefore, presenting underlying assumptions, integrating information, and ensuring cumulative consistency are keys to successful teaching.[13]

Thus, Euro-Americans are 'monochromic', meaning they learn better when they concentrate on only one register of sensory stimuli at a time. Afro-Americans, meanwhile, are 'polychromic': their performances are better when they are presented with multiple stimuli at one time:

> For example, learning exercises incorporating visual and auditory stimuli and involving motor activity would be preferable for African-American students, while sitting quietly working on math problems or reading may be more appropriate for Euro-American children.[14]

Much attention has also been devoted, again in the United States, to the case of minorities of Hispanic origin. We have already discussed some of the conclusions on the subject drawn by W.H. Holtzman.[15] Another author, A. Castañeda,[16] asked teachers several years back to take the following traits into consideration when dealing with Mexican Americans: identification with the family and the ethnic community, definitions of status and roles based on membership in these two groups, personalization of interpersonal relationships and Catholic ideology.

We could also cite a number of other analyses of Indians at school. C.B. Cazden et al. provided a brief, yet revealing, summary report on the United States.[17] The question reviewed by Cazden et al. is composed of five parts and can be applied to all communities of immigrants: presentation of tests given before school admission; learning styles; conflicts of values; patterns of socialization; a discussion on learning styles, learning values and the education of Indians. The conclusions made on the basis of the studies cited have the advantage of showing that caution must be exercised when making generalizations, and that a degree of diversity among the different tribes studies must be taken into account.

Again on the subject of Indians, but this time in Venezuela (the Guajiros and Calinatas), L.C. Watson wrote an article which by and large can be generalized to the sometimes sharply defined representations and expectations of 'culturally marginal' ethnic groups.[18] For example, we discover in this work the importance of what is considered to be the pattern of personality completion. In this particular tribe, girls are often taken out of school at puberty to receive the traditional education which will make them accomplished women. This training can only be carried out at home, when they are subjected to rigorous discipline.

Representations of scholastic aptitude are similar to those we have already seen with respect to working-class people and farmers in Europe: a pupil is 'good' or 'bad'. A 'bad' pupil will not learn anything in school and so it is useless to send him; in fact, it is best to keep him under as close surveillance as possible because he is not worth much more when it comes to traditional learning. The good pupil, on the other hand, can be improved through school training in the same manner as through training at home 'because he will know how to use properly what he learns'. The conception of learning is passive all the same: most Guajiro children in Calinatá simply come to school and sit passively in the classroom. When class is over they return to a way of life that is almost totally unrelated to what they are taught in school. They are not made aware of the importance of doing lessons at home nor are they encouraged to apply the little they do learn in other contexts.

It is only to the extent that some Guajiros are aware of the adaptive value of classroom education that they grant it secondary importance. They then appreciate the ability to speak Spanish, to read and write, to do elementary calculations for business transactions or their purchases in town. They also see the advantages their compatriots draw from it when they leave the community to live among white people. At that moment, their idea of school as something mysterious, the secrets of which are not easily revealed, begins to change. They even learn that certain children were 'miraculously transformed by the experience'. A parent reasoned that 'the same would happen to his son or daughter and weighed the advantages of sparing the child from domestic chores a few hours a day so that he could go to school'[19] but within reason....

Thus, it is by understanding the intrinsic benefits in situations of change that the value of the educational institution begins to be appreciated. But ignorance of, or even a lack of interest in, what goes on inside and in the avenues of learning it provides, means that the family environment is of absolutely no help to the pupil. Worse yet, more often than not the pupil, by interiorizing his parents' attitudes, remains at the surface of learning activities, thus perpetuating the wall of misunderstanding which makes him and the school strangers to each other, despite years of physical attendance. School attendance becomes a parenthetic episode with no lasting effect. This analysis has the advantage of being applicable in varying degrees to a good many disfavoured ethnic minorities who find themselves in an environment in which culture, and consequently, school are extremely remote entities. This is doubtless the most valuable lesson to be learned, and the crux of the problem.

To bring these considerations to a close, we might mention that studies of this kind are still rare in Europe. A great deal of attention has been devoted to the educational and cultural difficulties encountered by the immigrant in the host society and his child's failure at school, in particular. But studies such as that conducted by A. Vasquez[20] which isolated the learning difficulties due specifically to the disparate cultural representations at work, are only a beginning.

However that may be, the realization of the differences between the pupil's original culture and the culture he must confront (the term is appropriate) at school led to two series of observations. One group of authors attempted to demonstrate the extent to which it is the child's native culture which is central to his personality, that is, his 'mother' culture in the true sense of the word, because it is acquired through the child-mother relationship in early infancy.[21] References to psychoanalysis and ethno-psychoanalysis are used to show to what extent the infant is emotionally conditioned by his surroundings, including the cultural environment.[22] Hence the role of the 'hidden curriculum' (made up of childhood experiences as influenced by both structural and cultural aspects of the family circle) on the cognitive skills demanded in the classroom, on learning motivation, mastery of the 'correct' language and the willingness to adopt the 'good student' model.[23] Considerable functional value is thus attached to this initial education and, because of it, to the stamp of native culture. The conclusion is, implicitly or explicitly, that the role of the school is necessarily secondary.[24]

With these conclusions in mind, one should, the authors feel, design an educational institution which pays greater attention to the cultural baggage the pupil has acquired via the family environment. Theoretically, the necessity of preserving the cultural identity of the pupil in school and the beneficial effects this will have is generally accepted.[25] Yet, a look at schools in general reveals that the situation just is not so. Everything is subordinated to the school's own demands, which everyone knows are linked to specific ethnocentric and sociocultural factors. This brings us to the second line of reflection. The authors begin by underscoring the antagonistic character of representations which are determinant for a good educational profile, and go on to expose the inappropriateness for ethnocultural minorities of curricula, programmes, equipment and books, teaching methods, teachers, language requirements, and tests used for selection, aptitude evaluation, and orientation. We are thus still caught at the 'two-culture stories' level with respect to the current situation. We will explore these points in greater depth in this and in subsequent chapters.

Participation and specific aspects of the scholastic world

PARENTS

Often analyses of ethnic minority cultures take special interest in parents as the privileged partners of schools. Did not the Plowden Report in the United Kingdom[26] assert that success at school was less dependent on specifically scholastic variables than the attitudes and behaviour of parents towards study? The subject of parents raises a number of questions.

To begin with, it is important to know by means of what mechanisms parents draw their information about schools. A study by R. de Villa Nova[27] on intragroup information circuits in the Portuguese immigrant community in the Paris area provides a number of indications which can apply generally to other immigrant groups. For this author — and this observation applies to other Western countries which import manpower — 'France is characterized by the existence of a stable administrative system and a body of labour legislation which functions through specialized agencies each with its standardized forms.' But the

situation in Portugal is very unlike this world of bureaucratic public services. In that country, achieving effective results depends more on the particular pressures exerted, on personal contacts, or simply on circumstances at a level below written formulations, legislation, administrative procedure, and planning. (p. E/9)

The Portuguese belong to an oral culture in which 'bureaucratic (administrative) language in its official forms is stagnant, closed, and non-actualizable because it does without interlocutors. It gives rise to a state of dependence...'[28]

The messages transmitted, therefore, by host societies to immigrants are not received or are extremely distorted when they are received, for

the postulate underlying informative discourse and the public services which use it is the effectiveness of purely objective information, independent of any actualization (ie adoption or elaboration) on the part of the subjects concerned. For the Portuguese, it must be understood that the effectiveness of a system is subject to the unpredictability of particular, loosely defined attitudes, and of the contexts determined by the community's customs and ethics.

It is thus necessary — and this observation can apply to all immigrant groups alien to the rational, written culture of industrial societies — that this information be incorporated into 'an oral or verbal system' which in this case 'happens to be modelled after the family structure', with relationships of a 'feudalistic' type. The same might be said about the information disseminated by and about educational institutions. Immigrants will expect a reinterpretation (with the inevitable manipulations that this implies) of the family model, more specifically, of the roles of 'mistress' (for whom the Portuguese woman works as a servant), master, and the staff of a small 'family' business employing unskilled or 'underemployed' foreign manpower. This set-up alone will be fully understood because it is based on a structure of communication imbued with a degree of 'paternalism, well in harmony with the customs of a community for whom affective parental structures determine the division of labour and hierarchies'.[29]

This, then, is one of the major reasons for the gap between the family concept of ethnic minorities and that of educators. There are other causes: authors point to the different expectations of ethnic parents and educators with respect to the goals of schooling, the image parents have of the teacher and their expectations of him and his style of teaching, their relationship to him and with the administration. Add to all this the handicaps which make them incapable of helping their children with school work.

To give a brief example, we have the observations formulated by M. Laferrière[30] with respect to Haitian and Indian pupils in Quebec. Parents and children in the country of origin were accustomed to instructors with unlimited authority, who gave lessons orally and expected them to be scrupulously memorized, accepted questions only if permission had been given, and tended to use corporal punishment. In comparison 'Quebec schools seemed anarchic to them'. Likewise, at home, technical or vocational training corresponding to individual needs was rare. Instead, its function was 'To maintain the status of the elite and the social mobility of a select minority of the middle class', so that its ultimate purpose was to 'consolidate the position of leading families'.[31] Because of this, what the Canadian school asked for was not understood, and judged to be 'without dignity and not really respectable'. Thus, as is often the case with teachers in the West, we are not surprised by the lack of participation by Haitian and Indian parents in school life. Indeed, for them, the teacher holds the reins of authority. According to the system of education they have 'interiorized, those in authority have complete control and it is considered rude to question their educational competence'.[32] Also, in this case as in others, the difference in culture between the teacher and parents has an intimidating and inhibiting effect on the latter. We might simply add that these comments could easily be applied to a number of immigrant communities, particularly from Mediterranean countries.

Finally, an observation made by Gallimore, quoted by K.S. Chan, is worth commenting on, because ethnologists feel it is valid for a number of societies, especially simple societies: for Hawaiians living in the United States, both the siblings and the parents are to look after the well-being of individuals in a system of co-responsibility. As a result, individuals are oriented towards their peers to the same extent as towards their elders. But 'Hawaiian children were often thought to be cheating when they consulted other children for help or to be noncommittal to schooling when they rarely paid attention to the teacher or sought the teacher's help.'[33] These are just a few examples and many more can be given.

TEACHERS

A large volume of anthropologically-oriented literature has been devoted to the teacher: he is cast as the central figure whose actual behaviour can dominate all other factors, whatever the quality of the institution. It is thus essential to understand how his impressions with regard to the pupil are formed. According to M. Gilly,[34] who undertook such a study, the way in which the teacher perceives each pupil depends on general, normative conditions in conjunction with several other parameters: his reference values (man, child and behaviour models); the education objectives set by the school; his personal past; and his experience with the pupil in specific situations. In this way, a normative system influenced by the frame of reference peculiar to his profession takes shape in his mind and, collecting indications furnished by the pupil's behaviour, he codes, sorts and organizes them.

This to say that this construct has its own past and dynamism, very often moving the teacher to reject the directives of social and educational authorities in the form of school regulations, circulars and recommendations which incorporate the latest educational ideology. A study conducted in a region of France[35] brought out the image primary school teachers had of the pupil. It gravitated around two poles: the child as 'need' (who has various needs, penchants and wrong tendencies) and as 'lack' (suffering from various lacunae placing him in a marked situation of inferiority and subject to the guardianship of adults): need to be sanctioned, need for adult authority and encouragement, blame-worthy tendencies, particularly that of despising weak adults and of giving in to laziness. What is more, the qualities he might possess do not exclude the use of punishment.

The focus in this representation on the part of teachers is the fact that the child is not fully developed (quantitative aspect) rather than on the fact that he is different (qualitative aspect), consistent with historical and traditional attitudes... presenting us with an archaic stereotype which completely disregards over half a century of scientific progress in psychology.[36]

Put differently, a particular past form of culture used at school may remain ingrained in the minds of many teachers for a long time underneath new cultural currents to which they give mere lip service with no effect on their actual behaviour. The problem, therefore, is the use of two educational philosophies by the teacher, one which is officially recognized and one which is hidden, unconscious and operating implicitly.

It is thus important to identify consciously the 'unadmitted' curriculum which effectively penetrates the fibre of the classroom relationship and because of which Rosenthal and Jacobson[37] attributed to the teacher a 'Pygmalion effect', referring to how his positive attitudes have a favourable effect on the child and his expectations of failure help to bring it about. This is the 'labelling theory' whereby the labelling or stigmatization of the pupil will help create in him types of behaviour contributing to his failure.[38] Without indulging in misleading exaggerations, we can see that this theory is not entirely unreal. Labelling infiltrates the teacher's actions, his recommendations, prescriptions and predictions and is all the more effective (and dangerous) because it is unconscious.

How is the teacher to react when confronted with pupils from a subculture quite different from his own (a different social class) or from a different culture (foreign)? Failure to adapt teaching behaviour may be due to two factors. The first factor, as we said in the discussion on the conflictualists, is negative and concerns the communication distortion due to an objective gap in the cultural codes of the protagonists involved in the school situation. To this we might add the active influence of stereotypes and prejudices which the teacher shares with his compatriots and which are nurtured by ignorance and even xenophobic and racist attitudes. The resultant behaviours, which the pupil sees as being discriminatory and aggressive, lead to negative behaviours on his part compounding the teacher's own negative *a priori* attitudes, providing him with the justification for his way of acting, his diagnosis, his predictions, etc. Deficient teaching, in many cases, ends up creating or reinforcing the circumstances which serve as its justification.

Research, therefore, should focus on the various components of this vicious circle. Teachers, like other ordinary citizens, are not likely to be led to admit openly to xenophobia and racism. Even when some of them, as Laferrière observed in the case of Quebec, forbid Haitian pupils to speak 'black language', that is Creole, this attitude is justified at the conscious level on educational, practical, etc grounds. It is still interesting to analyse some of the expressions they use. For example, J.-P. Zirotti[39] studied the comments made by teachers of one *département* in the educational orientation files of foreign students and nationals. This led to the recommendation by Bourdieu and Saint-Martin that 'the taxonomies which reflect the ritualistic phrases teachers employ based on their expectations and judgments'[40] be identified and 'the categories of assumptions on the part of teachers' which these expressions hide. It was found that teachers gave standard replies to requests for a detailed evaluation showing little diversity and applied without distinction to both immigrants and French children. The particular circumstances which apply to the education of immigrant children are completely overlooked.

Several interpretations are possible. For example, we might be led to think of the ideology of formal egalitarianism which, in France and all countries claiming to be democratic, is part and parcel of the cultural legacy which the school puts at the disposal of teachers. Its main characteristic is

> to avoid all references to elements which might contradict this representation of the school by showing that, for example, the living conditions, social, cultural and national background, in a word, the specific 'past' of each pupil falsifies the rules of competition according to which each pupil supposedly is given an equal chance, except for differences in 'intellectual capacity'.[41]

The result of thus refusing to acknowledge the existence of differences is, as we have already seen, no less harmful than the xenophobic overemphasis on these differences.

But we can interpret the situation in another way. Indeed, racist behaviour can coexist with egalitarian principles. Other means are therefore needed to reveal such behaviour.

The best such means is observation based on the anthropological method we have already described. In this connection, G. Jackson and C. Cosca carried out an enormous study on some 500 classes in the southwestern United States in which there were both Mexican Americans and 'Yankee' students.[42] Reporting on the results of this study, M.D. Casserly and J.R. Garrett stated that 'Teachers praised, encouraged, accepted the ideas of, questioned, gave positive feedback and non-critically talked to more white than non-white students at a highly disproportionate level.'[43] The educative results are negative: little esteem or motivation for the academic system, slower learning, a feeling of not counting, increased tension, increased resentment between whites and non-whites. Hence, reinforcement of teacher stereotypes, and when open conflict occurs, automatic blaming of the victims.

However, things are not always quite this simple. An invaluable study by V. Washington[44] on the effects of segregation in American schools employing black and white teachers is one of the few of its kind to explore the relationship between opinions, attitudes and behaviours. The results are paradoxical. On one hand, the two groups of teachers, black and white, view their black students rather negatively, but black teachers to a lesser degree than white teachers. On the other hand, 'White teachers were more favorable in their instructional behaviors towards Afro-American children than black teachers were. Conversely, black teachers were more favorable in their instructional strategies toward white children than white teachers were.' The author concludes that there is 'a mirror effect in which teachers in integrated classrooms appear to be engaging in overcompensating behavior toward children of the other race'.[45] It must be added, however, that all of these teachers were volunteers for the study and, hence, 'well-intentioned'.

Another study conducted in France dealt with phenomena of attraction and repulsion based on a combination of processes and verbal and non-verbal codes:

the student's physical appearance, charm, voice, posture, courtesy, hygiene, ease, etc.[46] When school principals were presented with the objectives of the investigation 'there was a nearly unanimous outcry: never would a self-respecting teacher allow himself to judge children according to such criteria.'[47] As a result, only a minority of nursery and elementary school teachers accepted to judge 946 students on a scale of characteristics going from 'revolting, repulsive' to 'attractive and pleasant'. The results indicated that 'the children of working-class immigrants are always the least considered, with French working-class children next in the hierarchy and with privileged children on top.'[48] 'Nearly half of immigrant working-class children were consistently indifferent, antipathetic and sometimes repulsive.'[49] When one realizes to what extent norms nurturing these judgments are ingrained in cultural codes which themselves are linked to social and ethnic differences, one becomes aware of the powerful influence of cultural stereotypes on teacher-student relationships. As the author himself concludes,

even if it is definitely true that the majority of teachers attempt to help children for whom schools are ill-adapted to overcome their handicap, what can the real effect be when these teachers are preferentially attracted by the immense majority of privileged children, a simple majority of French working-class children, and by only a minority of immigrant working-class children?[50]

Finally, another type of investigation consists in asking subjects directly if they feel they are the victims of racist behaviour. We ourselves attempted to find this out by questioning 100 young Maghrebin immigrants from 16 to 25 years old in the Paris area.[51] According to them, their difficulties in relating stemmed in 10 per cent of cases from racial harassment in the true sense of the term, and in the remainder of cases (6 per cent) from rejection and mockery because of their difficulties in expressing themselves and other traits their French schoolmates considered to be signs of inferiority. It is significant that in the vast majority of cases the harassment was perceived not in horizontal relationships (with peers), but in vertical relationships: with superiors and especially teachers. Six per cent of replies indicated indifference or rejection on the part of teachers because of poor classroom performance, 28 per cent accused them of open racism, and 4 per cent of disparaging attitudes towards Arab students and strategies to encourage them. What is significant is the crystallization of the perception of racism around hierarchical relationships: these relationships foster tension and conflicts and constitute the terrain on which xenophobia objectively has the greatest chances of manifesting itself and where foreigners have the greatest tendency to give the situation a racist interpretation. However subjective this interpretation may be, it is yet another reason why teachers should guarantee that their relationships with students from ethnic minorities are perfectly clear, for as soon as a hint of racist rejection crops up, behaviour becomes confused and normal teaching becomes impossible.

This poses, as everyone agrees, the problem of teacher training and of how they can be made aware of these processes, of the existence of the cultural factor in general and of the many ways it affects the educational environment. A document of the Council of Europe[52] contains the final report by the Working Group on the Education of Migrant Workers' Children and a recommendation by the Committee of Ministers on Training Teachers to this effect. We will refer again to this at various stages of our discussion. For the time being, let us say that the recommendation contained three parts: to provide information about cultures and to inculcate the idea of cultural relativism; to highlight the sensitive areas in which this factor comes into play in educational situations and practices; to generate an ability to analyse oneself on this subject and to call oneself into question.

To conclude on the subject of teachers, we would like to mention a relevant observation made by M. Brossard:[53] the point at which stereotypes, ethnocentrism, racism and other 'culturally biased judgments' find their way into teaching practices is situated at the level of ignorance of the diversity and exact nature of learning mechanisms. This is why subjective judgments — especially those on the part of the teacher — of this kind, which have such disastrous consequences for children of ethnocultural or subcultural minorities, are especially frequent with respect to their learning problems: 'Judgments on individuals, based on social criteria, are substituted for the effort required in order to understand their learning difficulties.' Progress in the understanding of these mechanisms will make it possible for educational practice to become an 'intelligent practice' and not a 'lever of mechanistic social reproduction'.[54]

STUDENTS

As school attendance becomes more democratized in increasingly diversified societies, classrooms are being filled with young people of many different cultures and ethnic origins who bring their dissimilar representations and stereotypes learned on the outside where they were in daily contact in a common location. If one considers how important are the systems of images they form at this stage for their motivation, behaviour and aspirations in school, one realizes that the usual social models for explaining the effective influence of the sociocultural factor fall short. To clarify fully these systems of images would require a multitude of studies, yet such data are relatively rare.

It has been observed how children both in school and out tend to choose their friends and form groups according to natural affinities, hence finding themselves once again in their respective cultures and subcultures, and to become locked into their differences. A type of spontaneous segregation results,[55] even in desegregated institutions in the United States. Institutional measures, although necessary, are not alone sufficient to eliminate the negative effects of the cultural variable. However, the separation into groups is rarely absolute and the ways in which it comes about can be flexible.

It is important, therefore, that we go beyond stereotyped notions and try to carry out an empirical analysis of the consequences of inter-ethnic mix on school-goers. Such studies have been carried out in Australia[56] and the United States. Patchen,[57] for example, in a study on schools attended by very different ratios of blacks and whites found little correlation between the 'volume' of inter-ethnic contact and other variables, such as scholastic performance, or effort, or career and general culture-related aspirations. One significant finding was made, however: increased contacts resulted in an improvement in attitudes towards the other ethnic group, especially on the part of whites. Yet, as D. Rosenthal and S. Morrison pointed out,

the scant literature on the effects of interracial contact on attitudes is contradictory; increased interracial contact has been shown to improve attitudes, make them worse, or have no effect, in studies of all age groups, but positive findings are somewhat more frequently reported in younger white children and older blacks.[58]

One obvious conclusion can nonetheless be drawn: contact in itself does not necessarily improve attitudes. Y. Amir[59] compiled a list of conditions likely to help improve them: equal status between groups, positive stimulation or an atmosphere conducive to contact, induced rather than accidental interaction resulting in satisfaction or reward, pursuit of an objective common to both groups. N.H. St John, basing herself on an overview of the question,[60] felt that a plausible hypothesis, although untested by sufficient research, is that the performance of minority children is better in a desegregated environment in which the minority group has the support of authorities and is accepted by its peers.

Other studies deal with self-image as related to ethnic mix. According to Porter,[61] white children in predominantly black schools have a poor opinion of themselves. But for Powell, this is not the case between the seventh and twelfth grades. Rosenthal and Morrison found that the effects of ethnic mix on achievement and attitudes were ultimately small and inconsistent.[62]

The same authors, following in the footsteps of other investigators, conducted a study of this factor in Australia comparing three categories of schools with a large (80 per cent), average (50 per cent) and low (20 per cent) non-Anglo-Saxon immigrant attendance, respectively, in the sixth grade. This variable was shown to be a differentiating factor with respect to both performance and attitude.

Anglo-Saxon pupils are better at reading exercises when they are a majority, but this advantage does not apply to activities where language is not important (including mathematics). The language-related skills of nationals are therefore affected by the number of foreign language speaking immigrants present, but this may also be due to the teacher, who may adapt his language and teaching to the level of linguistic competence he finds among his foreign students.

On the other hand, however, scholastic motivation and intellectual curiosity in nationals decrease when they are greater in number, but increase when they are a minority. This may be due to the fact that, as other studies conducted in

Australia have shown, the educational aspirations of immigrant children are higher than those of their comrades. These aspirations appear in full force when the foreign peer group becomes a majority and elevates the general level of aspiration for the entire class.

The results of the Australian study confirm Porter's findings and show that the proportion of foreign pupils has no influence on their own cognitive performances, whether involving language skills or not. Foreign pupils are not even sensitive to the higher linguistic level established by nationals when the latter are the majority. It is possible that the minority status of immigrants makes them form a more compact group, impervious to outside influence. It is also possible that the level of teaching is beyond them, because it is adapted to the linguistic competence of the native majority. Ultimately the only changing variable among immigrants is their more positive attitude towards school activities when they are greater in number.

As the results obtained by Powell have also shown, the number of immigrant students does not affect self-image. However, attitudes to immigrants on the part of nationals varied as a function of 'degree of ethnic mix, with the most integrated group showing a more positive attitude'.[63] The views of N.H. St John are thus confirmed. Finally, surprisingly enough, it is in the group where the proportion of immigrants to nationals is equal that their cognitive performances are as good.

The reason for our detailed treatment of this study's conclusions is to give an idea of how complex this kind of analysis is. In addition, the conclusions drawn in this study are also more nuanced than those reached by some American authors[64] who assert that success on the part of ethnic minorities increases with the proportion of white children provided the white children come from privileged socio-economic backgrounds. These works have sparked a very lively scientific and methodological discussion. And this point is worth making. Did not N.H. St John, after reviewing all the literature on the subject, assert that the relationship between ethnic mix and scholastic success was extremely difficult to study? Indeed, classes used as samples differed not only with respect to the percentages of students of different origins but also with respect to an entire spectrum of other variables, not the least of which was social class.

Further research is thus needed and extreme caution must be exercised when interpreting the results, given the potential practical consequences. Is not the great fear on the part of native parents that scholastic levels will drop because of the presence of children of different ethnic backgrounds? The issues are emotional and are much like those related to the 'threshold of tolerance' towards immigrants in host societies. The scientific conclusions advanced on this point are worth thinking about because they are relevant to our topic. No one denies that national subgroups are likely to react to coexistence with foreigners, especially those of low socio-economic status, but these reactions vary according to subgroup. They may take the form of indifference, of acceptance, of comprehension, or even collaboration rather than simple rejection. And where there is intolerance, its manifestations are extremely diverse and occur at very different non-automatic thresholds, depending on the specific situation and the degree of variable interdependence.[65] The real task of this deluge of analyses, rather than making hasty and incorrect generalizations, is to sort out this tangle of variables as the only means of bringing about adjustments in teaching practices.

TEXTBOOKS

The various, rather less abundant, discussions, judging by our bibliographical investigations, on teaching materials will provide the basis for our treatment of a much discussed topic and one which directly concerns our subject, namely textbooks and primers.

Already at the national subcultural level some well-publicized observations have been made concerning, for example, the continued presence in readers used in France and other traditionally agricultural European countries of cultural depictions based on the traditional country landscape, in spite of the urban industrial revolution. The model of society they present city dwellers with is rural, the trades are 'archaic', work is idealized and industrial activity is virtually absent and always a source of hardship. This discrepancy between reality and the representation given to students was still prevalent in France long after the war.[66] Likewise, according to Spindler,[67] schools in the Federal Republic of Germany 'transmit romantic notions and identifications with the land and traditional village life and encourage children to choose modern, urban occupations'. The same is true in Japan. These observations remind us that every group, like each individual, has an 'ideal' ego or culture which diverges to varying degrees from cultural reality, making certain psychological outlets as daydreaming, compensation, alibis, etc, possible. Again we are confronted with the instrumental use of culture to various ends, in some cases going so far as to turn it into an ideology. This is even more apparent in the many reported observations concerning the 'sexist' outlook of textbooks, which is still prevalent.

Similar reports have been made concerning the ethnocentrism of school books, their silence on the subject of other ethnic groups or minorities and more often still, the deformed, stereotyped, negative images they give of them. Yet, as M. Laferrière[68] pointed out, books serve to redefine and reinforce communities by offering them images of others and themselves. Not only are the more or less unfavourable stereotypes and connotations about minority groups perceived by these groups as a source of irony, condescension, disdain and rejection, but they also prevent them from projecting themselves into, or identifying with, this material. This cannot avoid affecting their motivation to make use of it. Proposals have been made to modify this situation. For example, the Board of Education of the State of New York is trying to use elements of Haitian culture within bilingual programmes in its schools concerning Haitian students.

For example 'vévés' which are traditional figurines exhibited during voodoo ceremonies have, because of their symmetry, been used in geometry, art and religion courses.[69] It also happens that teachers use motivating materials for Indians or introduce studies on blacks. The danger in all of these cases is of another nature: that of introducing pseudo-adapted folkloric and itself stereotyped material based on preconceived ideas on ethnic groups. Precise anthropological knowledge clearly cannot be supplanted by the vulgarized conceptions popularized by the media.

We thus come by a supplementary path to the area of educational projects for students of cultural majorities. We will take up this subject again later.

The socio-economic variable and the cultural variable

A very lively debate is currently under way around the following topic: since ethnic minorities experiencing educational handicaps belong generally to a disfavoured social class, are not their supposedly ethnocultural difficulties really simply economic? Is there a specific relationship between the cultural variable and the socio-economic variable? Some say no, arguing on the basis of the similarities between the types of disadvantages affecting 'poor' children and ethnically different children, and the fact that upper-class students of foreign origin, the children of high-level immigrant white-collar workers, the liberal professions, etc do not experience these handicaps. On top of it all, the debate often takes on an ideological dimension. Is not culture an alibi for skirting the problem of the educational effects of economic inequality and social injustice? Is not reflecting on the institution of an educational system adapted to children from ethnic minorities a means of evading the more fundamental problem of what procedure to adopt for putting an end to the class-based school we spoke of in our discussion on the 'conflictualists'?[70]

It is undeniable that the cultural problem can be used as an alibi and is one of the adverse effects of cultural manipulation by social protagonists. However, such a practice is only possible on the basis of blind ignorance or theoretical errors. It is therefore necessary to situate the debate in the proper context using the following two observations as guidelines.

The absence of handicap among the 'ethnically different' from higher social classes is in no way proof of the nonexistence of the cultural parameter. It can be explained in many other ways. For example, successful acculturation, or effective means of overcoming the detrimental effects of cultural disparity.

It has been proven, and we have pointed this out in Chapter III, that an important element in the sociocultural variable consists precisely in the representations provided by anthropological culture. The handicaps experienced in school by children from disfavoured social classes are the result of a constellation or overall configuration where cultural differences dovetail with economic factors (as K.S. Chan and R. Rueda, in 1979, attempted a definition by putting them under the heading of 'poverty'). Presenting the two explanations — the sociocultural and the cultural — as mutually exclusive and requiring the choice between one or the other is completely unjustified.

So the only scientifically valid question becomes — at least at the theoretical level — somewhat secondary. 'Unskilled' immigrant workers and poor working-class people from the host society suffer the same effects of economic privation when confronted with the educational institution (with a more intense effect on immigrants because they are further down the social scale). But do the merely subcultural antagonisms of nationals have the same force, the same 'dysfunctional efficacy' as those involving the cultures of different ethnic groups? This is what is asserted by, for example, S. Boulot and D. Boyson-Fradet in France:

To claim that there is a specific situation in the disparity between the 'culture' of immigrant children and the 'dominant culture' of which the school is the vehicle is to forget the equally great gap beween the 'culture' of French children of the same social background and the scholastic norm.[71]

In saying this these authors show without ambiguity that their concern is of a practical nature:

To be sure, it would appear easier to introduce the 'culture of origin' of foreign children in schools — at least as the average Frenchman imagines it to be — than to ask schools to incorporate practices of popular origin in their materials and methods.[72]

The controversy thus cut down to size needs to be clarified through statistical data. Indeed, this is not easy, for the reference material is extremely mixed and unscientific. For example, official statistics include among nationals an unknown quantity of students who in terms of ethnoculture are foreign, but who have been legally naturalized. Nonetheless some of the material makes it possible to draw hard and fast conclusions. For example, official French figures show that 27.5 per cent of French working-class children going into the first year of secondary school make it through the second, long, high school cycle. In the case of foreign, working-class children, that figure is only 22.8 per cent. Given the sample size, this difference is statistically very significant, since it can be extrapolated with a margin of error well below 1 per cent. The difference would be even greater if criteria other than nationality were used to determine who was French.[73]

The genuinely valid evidence is provided by studies in which an attempt was made to isolate the socio-economic and cultural variables. Such studies have been carried out in the United States. One of the more recent ones[74] compares cognitive development in black children and white children, with each group equally composed of representatives of the middle class and the lower class, thus making it possible to distinguish factors related to ethnic origin and socio-economic status. The study involved 900 children from 6 to 9 years of age and had the rare advantage of being longitudinal. The results confirm those of

A.J. Jensen[75] and of S. Scarr. The latter compared 800 matched black children and white children from between 10 and 16 years old originating in the middle and lower classes. We can summarize the results as follows.

The scores achieved by children in most tests involving cognitive skills differed according to ethnic group on one hand, and with respect to social class on the other; the differences between groups were more significant in tests on intelligence than those on recall; the average performances of lower-class children were generally below those of middle-class children; the average performances of blacks were generally below those of whites.

There is therefore a specific, culturally determined source of handicaps in an ethnic minority situation, over and above those caused by socio-economic status. Everything is related to the types of tests used in American schools, leading S. Scarr to comment,

when black children are reared in the culture of the tests and the schools, they perform on intellectual tests as well as white children adopted into similar families; and the more culturally loaded the test, the larger the average racial difference in performance.[76]

We could also mention a study carried out in France[77] on the scholastic advancement of different groups of 14-year-old immigrant children of both sexes in several secondary schools compared to 'French children of the same age and the socio-economic status and socio-economic environment'.[78] The percentage of French children in the class corresponding to their age (ninth grade) was 34.9 per cent, 27.6 per cent and 49.4 per cent respectively in each of the three schools used. In the case of immigrants, these figures fell to 14.7 per cent, 6.4 per cent and 17.6 per cent. The discrepancy within the same social category is thus quite significant. The pattern can be seen in schools and classes in France as a whole, 'but where the drop in the number of foreign students in relation to French students becomes extremely evident is with respect to the number who have repeated twice'. If we take as a point of reference the number of children in the family, the proportion of oldest children compared to second children is around '29.03 per cent as compared to 5.44 per cent for families of 2–3 children; 33.03 as compared to 8.10 per cent for families of 4–5 children and, overall, 21.27 per cent against 12.9 per cent'.[79]

While the difference between the two groups with respect to their scholastic careers is significant, the differences between different nationalities of origin are equally important. Interestingly enough, Portuguese children are the furthest behind in school, as other studies have confirmed. This evidence seems to disprove the theory which claims that there are fewer handicaps the closer the foreign culture is to that of the host country. As E. Mullet stated,[80] there is no evidence to support this conclusion, for many variables other than 'cultural distance' are at play with respect to the various groups, such as the existence of a solid local community of the same nationality 'with the relative advantages and disadvantages which that implies'.[81] There is also the factor of whether the immigrant genuinely intends to return to his country or to establish himself permanently in the host country (North Africans are more established than Portuguese immigrants), interference between the educational system of the country of origin and that of the host country, etc. For example, Portuguese children are taken out of school in their country at the age of 12. It is thus necessary to identify these 'packaged variables' by the appropriate means before taking a stand.

Finally, the same investigator observed, based on a large sample, that there are consistently more immigrant students in 'special education' classes for slow learner pupils than their French comrades (12 per cent, 8 per cent and 2 per cent difference respectively for children of working-class parents, salaried employees and white-collar workers). After having analysed the various possible objections Mullet concluded that 'there exists a definite causality related to the child's immigrant working-class status, weighing equally from one category to another', at least with respect to enrolment in special education classes.[82]

Thus, despite the caution that the limited number of methodologically sound studies which have been carried out dictates, the tendency is to ascribe a more significant dysfunctional effect to ethnocultural differences than to those between different national subcultures.

The causes spoken of are often still based more on intuition or reasoning than the painstaking analysis which is needed. Accordingly, the linguistic difference comes to everyone's mind. We will see later that not everyone agrees on this point, depending on the alleged 'level' of assimilation of the linguistic code. It is also thought that conflicts of value between the dominant and the dominated cultures are markedly less acute for disfavoured nationals than for foreigners who, even if they are born in the host country, cannot possibly assimilate as well as natives the long cultural tradition which is unconsciously communicated by the family through a multitude of signs transmitted from generation to generation. No doubt all these factors have an impact on adaptation to the school, but further proof is needed.

Finally, the incidents which affect relations between individuals and groups, rather than between the cultures to which they belong per se, with the characteristic reactions of condescension, contempt, rejection or hate which result, are far more intense and spectacular for immigrants than for nationals from the poorest classes. How does this affect the young foreigner's attitudes to the educational demands of a society from which he and his group are alienated because of such a serious conflict? Complex observation protocols would be needed to find this out. In the meantime, specialists report numerous clinical cases of immigrant students which are totally different from those of nationals of the same social category. Let us take the example of Armindo, an 11-year-old Portuguese boy examined in France by J. Tourre for 'a state of anguish due to failure at school'. He demonstrated 'superior intelligence with a level of performance above 130 with a 30-point drop in the verbal score'.

The psychologist showed him a series of pictures and asked him to tell a story in Portuguese:

> The child, who had until then been in control of the situation, was suddenly shaken, grew red, looked at me with a lost expression, and asked me to repeat my question. So I repeated the question and added: 'You speak Portuguese and I understand your language.' He then did what I had asked, but in a barely audible voice and as concisely as possible. The violence of the emotional discharge caused by my request to express himself in Portuguese in my view is the key element in this case.[83]

It is thus clear that this foreign national is afflicted by his identity and the shame with which he surrounds it because of the relationship his community experiences with the host society. It is highly unlikely that the same would occur with an indigenous child, no matter what his position in the social hierarchy. Even if such an exceptional case should occur, never would it attain the same intensity.

What is interesting is that following that session, Armindo's behaviour in class changed and he began to assimilate French grammar: 'The basic concepts of the intermediate level first-year course are starting to become automatized.' This improvement went hand-in-hand with broader possibilities for speaking of his family, the vacations spent in his native country, his Portuguese context. 'I do not know what happened to me,' he told me, 'but now I'm completely different in class. I'm happy there now.' After two years 'he more than mastered all exercises involving the use of the French language.'[84]

Given these observations, and many others like them, and even if indisputable scientific evidence is scarce, it is difficult to liken, without some other form of investigation, the situation of the young immigrant to that of his national counterpart on the lower social scale. An oversimplified hypothesis like this is due to a failure to take into account a fundamental factor, namely, the child's different relationship with society. One thing is absolutely certain. Far from overlooking the socio-economic dimension, the cultural factor, because it is a constituent element of it, demands that that dimension is taken into consideration. Rather than unrealistically oppose one to the other, it would be more reasonable to ask that schools take into consideration their culture difference with respect to nationals, as well as the inappropriateness of their models for foreigners.

NOTES AND REFERENCES

1. Berthelier, R. *Identité, culture, langage, école... Journées d'études: enfants d'autres cultures dans la société française (11-14 janvier 1984)*. Paris, Centre d'entraînement aux méthodes d'éducation active, 1984, p. 10.
2. Alaluf, M. *Migrant culture and culture of origin*. Strasbourg, School Education Division, Council for Cultural Cooperation, Council of Europe, 1982. 52 p. (DECS/EGT (82) 4).

3. Centre de recherches interdisciplinaires de Vaucresson (CRIV), France. *Socialisation et déviance des jeunes immigrés: IV^{emes} Journées de criminologie comparée de la région méditerranéenne. Actes du Colloque de Syracuse, Italie, décembre 1982.* Vaucresson, France, 1984.
4. Malewska-Peyre, Hanna, éd. *Crise d'identité et déviance chez les jeunes immigrés.* Paris, La Documentation française, 1983.
5. L'immigration maghrébine en France: les faits et les mythes. *Les Temps modernes* (Paris), 40e année, nos. 452-4, mars-mai 1984, 2192 p.
6. Camilleri, C. Changements culturels, problèmes de socialisation et construction de l'identité. *In*: Centre de recherches interdisciplinaires, France. *Op. cit.*, pp. 35-66; Camilleri, C. Problèmes psychologiques de l'immigré maghrébin. *Les Temps modernes* (Paris), 40e année, nos. 452-4, mars-mai 1984, pp. 1877-901.
7. El-Andaloussi, K. *Contribution à l'étude du processus d'acculturation: le cas des parents migrants maghrébins.* Toulouse, France, Université de Toulouse, 1983, p. 107. [Thesis]
8. Vatz-Laâroussi, M. *Les pratiques et conception éducatives de parents maghrébins immigrés en France, leur impact sur les jeunes de la seconde génération: une étude comparative sur les régions de Tours en France et de Rabat au Maroc.* Paris, Université de Paris V, 1985. [Thesis].
9. Douville, O. *Processus d'acculturation chez les enfants et adolescents maghrébins de la seconde génération.* Paris, Université de Paris XIII, 1982. [Thesis]
10. Varro, G. *La femme transplantée: une étude du mariage franco-américain en France et le bilinguisme des enfants.* Lille, France, Presses universitaires de Lille, 1984.
11. Douville, O. *Op. cit.*
12. Myers, Linda, J. The nature of pluralism and the African American case. *Theory into practice* (Columbus, OH, Ohio State University), vol. 20, no. 1, Winter 1981, pp. 2-6.
13. *Ibid.*, p. 5.
14. *Ibid.*
15. Holtzman, W.H. Concepts and methods in the cross-cultural study of personality development. *Human development* (Basel, Switzerland), vol. 22, no. 5, 1979, pp. 281-95.
16. Castañeda, A.; James, R.L.; Webster, R. *The educational needs of minority groups.* Lincoln, NB, Professional Educators Publications, 1974, 112 p.
17. Cazden, C.B.; John, Vera, P. Learning in American Indian children. *In*: Wax, M.L.; Diamond, S.; Gearing, F.O., eds. *Anthropological perspectives on education.* New York, Basic Books, 1971, pp. 252-72.
18. Watson, L.C. Formal education in Calinatà: learning and the role of the Western school in a Guajiro community. *Anthropological quarterly* (Washington, DC), vol. 50, no. 2, 1977, pp. 91-7.
19. *Ibid.*, p. 95.
20. Vasquez, Ana. Quelques problèmes psychopédagogiques des enfants d'exilés. *International review of education* (The Hague), vol. 26, no. 1, 1980, pp. 66-75: Vasquez, Ana; Richard, Gabriela. Problèmes d'adaptation en France des enfants des réfugiés du Cône sud de l'Amérique latine. *Les Sciences de l'éducation* (Caen, France, Laboratoire de psychopédagogie, Université de Caen), no. 1, janvier-mars 1980, pp. 87-116; Vasquez, Ana. Temps social/temps culturel. *Enfance* (Paris), no. 5, novembre-décembre 1982, pp. 335-50; Vasquez, Ana; Proux, Michelle B. « La maîtresse dit que je suis lent »: représentation de l'école française dans le discours d'élèves immigrés. *International review of education* (The Hague), vol. 30, no. 2, 1984, pp. 155-70.
21. Berthelier, R. *Op. cit.*
22. Super, D.E. *The psychology of careers: an introduction to vocational development.* New York, Harper, 1957. 362 p.; Bloom, B.S. *Stability and change in human characteristics.* New York, Wiley, 1964.

23. Chan, K.S.; Rueda, R. Poverty and culture in education: separate but equal. *Exceptional children* (Reston, VA, Council for Exceptional Children), vol. 45, no. 6, March 1979, pp. 422-8.
24. Girod, R. Les adolescents sous-instruits dans les sociétés industrielle de l'Ouest. *Revue française de pédagogie* (Paris, Institut national de recherche et de documentation pédagogiques), no. 22, janvier-février-mars 1973, pp. 21-35; Forquin, J.-C. L'approche sociologique de la réussite et de l'échec scolaires: inégalités de réussite scolaire et appartenance sociale. *Revue française de pédagogie* (Paris, Institut national de recherche pédagogique), no. 59, avril-mai-juin 1982, pp. 52-75; no. 60, juillet-août-septembre 1982, pp. 51-70.
25. Myers, Linda J. *Op. cit.*; Melendez, D.; Melendez, Donna C.; Molina, Angela. Pluralism and the Hispanic student: challenge to educators. *Theory into practice* (Columbus, OH, Ohio State University), vol. 20, no. 1, Winter 1981, pp. 7-12; Laferrière, M. The education of West-Indian and Haitian students in the schools of Montreal: issues and prospects. *In*: Elliot, Jean L., ed. *Two nations, many cultures: ethnic groups in Canada.* 2nd ed. Scarborough, Ont. Canada, Prentice-Hall, 1983, pp. 158-72.
26. Central Advisory Council for Education, United Kingdom. *Children and their primary schools.* London, Department of Education and Science, 1967, 2 v.
27. Villa Nova, Roselyne de. L'information en milieu portugais. *Migrants formation* (Paris, Centre national de documentation pédagogique), no. 34, mai 1979, pp. E/7-E/12.
28. *Ibid.*, p. E/9.
29. *Ibid.*
30. Laferrière, M. The education of West-Indian and Haïtian students in the schools of Montreal: issues and prospects. *Op. cit.*
31. *Ibid.*, p. 166.
32. *Ibid.*, p. 167.
33. Chan, K.S.; Rueda R. *Op. cit.*, pp. 426-7.
34. Gilly, M. *Maître-élève: rôles institutionnels et représentations.* Paris, Presses universitaires de France, 1980. 304 p.
35. Meyer, R. Une méthode d'approche de l'image de l'enfant chez les enseignants de l'école maternelle. *Bulletin de psychologie* (Paris, Groupe d'études de psychologie, Université de Paris), vol. 35, no. 353, 1981, pp. 213-19.
36. *Ibid.*, p. 218.
37. Rosenthal, R.; Jacobson, Lenore. *Pygmalion in the classroom: teacher expectation and pupils' intellectual development.* New York, Holt, Rinehart and Winston, 1968. 240 p.
38. Rist, R. On understanding the processes of schooling: the contribution of labeling theory. *In*: Karabel, J.; Halsey, A.H., eds. *Power and ideology in education.* New York, Oxford University Press, 1977, pp. 292-305.
39. Zirotti, J.-P. Le jugement professoral: un système de classement «qui ne fait pas de différence». *Langage et société* (Paris), no. 4, 1980, pp. 3-42.
40. Bourdieu, P.; Saint-Martin, Monique de. Les catégories de l'entendement professoral. *Actes de la recherche en sciences sociales* (Paris), no. 3, 1975, pp. 68-93, p. 69.
41. Zirotti, J.-P. *Op. cit.*, p. 16.
42. Jackson, G.; Cosca, Cecilia. The inequality of educational opportunity in the Southwest: an observational study of ethnically mixed classrooms. *American educational research journal* (Washington, DC, American Educational Research Association), vol. 11, no. 3, Summer 1974, pp. 219-29.
43. Quoted by Casserly, M.D.; Garrett, J.R. Beyond the victim: new avenues for research on racism in education. *Educational theory* (Worcester, MA, University of Illinois), vol. 27, no. 3, Summer 1977, p. 199.
44. Washington, Valora. Teachers in integrated classrooms: profiles of attitudes, perceptions, and behavior. *The Elementary school journal* (Chicago, IL), vol. 80, no. 4, March 1980, pp. 193-201.

45. *Ibid.*, p. 200.
46. Zimmermann, D. Un langage non-verbal de classe: les processus d'attraction-répulsion des enseignants à l'égard des élèves en fonction de l'origine familiale de ces derniers. *Revue française de pédagogie* (Paris, Institut national de recherche pédagogique), no. 44, juillet-août-septembre 1978, pp. 46-70.
47. *Ibid.*, p. 48.
48. *Ibid.*, p. 49.
49. *Ibid.*, p. 58.
50. *Ibid.*, p. 69.
51. Camilleri, C. *Quelques facteurs psychologiques de la représentation du retour dans le pays d'origine chez les jeunes migrants maghrébins de la seconde génération.* Paris, Direction de la population et des migrations, Ministère du travail, 1979. [Mimeograph]
52. Council of Europe. Council for Cultural Cooperation, Working Group on the Education of Migrant Workers' Children – The Training of Teachers. *Final Report*, by Micheline Rey. Strasbourg, School Education Division, Council for Cultural Cooperation, Council of Europe, 1984. 21 p. (DECS/EGT (84) 84).
53. Brossard, M. Conduites verbales, activités cognitives et origine sociale. Bordeaux, France, Université de Bordeaux II, s.d.
54. *Ibid.*, p. 410.
55. Girod, R. *Op. cit.*
56. Rosenthal, Doreen; Morrison, Susan. On being a minority in the classroom: a study of the influence of ethnic mix on cognitive functioning and attitudes in working class children. The *Australian journal of education* (Hawthorn, Vic., Australian Council for Educational Research), vol. 22, no. 2, June 1978. pp. 144-60.
57. Patchen, M. *The relation of inter-racial contact and other factors to outcomes in the public high schools of Indianapolis.* Lafayette, IN, Institute for the Study of Social Change, Purdue University, 1975. [Unpublished manuscript]
58. Rosenthal, Doreen; Morrison, Susan. *Op. cit.*, p. 145.
59. Amir, Y. Contact hypothesis in ethnic relations. *In*: Brigham, J.C.; Weissbach, T.A., eds. *Racial attitudes in America.* New York, Harper and Row, 1972, pp. 245-9.
60. St John, Nancy H. Desegregation and minority group performance. *Review of educational research* (Washington, DC, American Educational Research Association), vol. 40, no. 1, February 1970, pp. 111-33.
61. Porter, Judith, D. *Black child, white child: the development of racial attitudes.* Cambridge, MA, Harvard University Press, 1971.
62. Rosenthal, Doreen; Morrison, Susan. *Op. cit.*, p. 145.
63. *Ibid.*, p. 158.
64. U.S. Office of Education. *Equality of educational opportunity*, by J.S. Coleman, et al. Washington, DC, 1966. 737 p.; Wilson, A.B. *The consequences of segregation: academic achievement in a Northern community.* Berkeley, CA, Glendessary Press, 1969; Jencks, C. The Coleman report and the conventional wisdom. *In:* Mosteller, F.; Moynihan, D.P., eds. *On equality of educational opportunity.* New York, Random House, 1972, pp. 69-115.
65. Le seuil de tolérance aux étrangers. *Sociologie du Sud-Est* (Aix-en-Provence, France, Université d'Aix-en-Provence), nos. 5-6, 1975.
66. Mollo, Suzanne. Participation de l'école à la formation culturelle de l'enfant. *In*: Chombart de Lauwe, P.H. *Images de la culture.* Paris, Les Editions Ouvrières, 1966, pp. 135-50.
67. G.D. Spindler, quoted by Foley, D.E. Anthropological studies of schooling in developing countries: some recent findings and trends. *Comparative education review* (Chicago, IL), vol. 21, nos. 2 and 3, June and October 1977, p. 318.
68. Laferrière, M. Lecture et situation minoritaire. *Lecture-jeunesse* (Paris), no. 21, janvier 1982, pp. 2-9.

69. Laferrière, M. The education of West-Indian and Haitian students in the schools of Montreal: issues and prospects. *Op. cit.*
70. Boulot, S.; Boyson-Fradet, Danielle. L'échec scolaire des enfants de travailleurs immigrés: un problème mal posé. *Les Temps modernes* (Paris), 40e année, nos. 452-4, mars-mai 1984, pp. 1902-14.
71. *Ibid.*, p. 1913.
72. *Ibid.*
73. Information memorandum of 8 August 1983 (M.E.N. – S.I.G.E.S.), quoted by S. Boulot and D. Boyson-Fradet. *Ibid.*, p. 1910.
74. Hall, V.C.; Kaye, D.B. Early patterns of cognitive development. *Monograph of the Society for Research in Child Development* (Chicago, IL), vol. 45, no. 2, Serial no. 184, 1980, pp. 1-83.
75. Jensen, A.J. How much can we boost IQ and scholastic achievement? *Harvard educational review* (Cambridge, MA, Harvard University), vol. 39, no. 1, 1969, pp. 1-123.
76. Scarr, Sandra. Commentary. *In*: Hall, V.C.; Kaye, D.B. *Op. cit.*, p. 82.
77. Gratiot-Alphandéry, Hélène; Chapuis, Elizabeth; Amselle, Sylvie. La progression scolaire des enfants étrangers en France. *L'Orientation scolaire et professionnelle* (Paris, Institut national d'études du travail et d'orientation professionnelle), vol. 9, no. 3, juillet-août-septembre 1980, pp. 253-66.
78. *Ibid.*, p. 254.
79. *Ibid.*, p. 262.
80. Mullet, E. Les enfants de travailleurs migrants et l'enseignement secondaire. *L'Orientation scolaire et professionnelle* (Paris, Institut national d'études du travail et d'orientation professionnelle), vol. 9, no. 3, juillet-août-septembre 1980, pp. 195-252.
81. *Ibid.*, p. 225.
82. *Ibid.*, p. 218.
83. Tourre, Jeanne. Désaveu d'identité. *Migrants formation* (Paris, Centre national de documentation pédagogique), no. 34, mai 1979, p. E/2.
84. *Ibid.*, p. E/4-5.

CHAPTER V

Culture and educational problems in the Third World

Typical situations

Most Third World countries encounter educational problems which are more intimately connected to dimensions of anthropological culture than in Western industrial societies, as we shall see. But the types of situation are diverse and at least two such kinds must be differentiated.

Latin American countries, generally considered to be 'developing', are a case that can easily be delineated. The European powers who had colonized them for centuries permanently implanted their civilizations in these countries. The former indigenous peoples — Indians — still occupy a marginal position, even more so than the millions of black slaves who had been imported to serve the dominant classes. These classes imposed their own culture at the same time as they attempted a radical 'deculturation' of non-whites. A certain number of native communities succeeded, however, in preserving their own languages, diverse traditions, rituals, religious beliefs, while at the same time the African influence consolidated itself. This influence introduced a very conspicuous component among popular segments of the population in the form of oral traditions, customs, rituals and characteristic types of music and beliefs.

The situation which resulted is as follows. First, Spanish culture enjoyed the status of an elite culture, officially disseminated by the education system, with contributions from Europe and the United States in the context of a type of relationship which, in the larger sense, was one of domination.

Thus, while the official culture had thus been undermined from above, it had also been affected from below 'with the influx of European immigrants who, for the most part, were from the lower class and almost none of whom was literate: they brought with them their "cultural experience" and elements of regional cultures (dances, songs, crafts, etc)'.[1]

Second, coloured ethnic communities, whether native or 'imported', undertook a process of 'cultural recovery and re-identification' based on their original models.[2] Given the magnitude of the wager and the strength of the antagonisms present, this phenomenon had a far different complexion from, for example, that with which Western European countries are familiar. The results were sweeping movements in which the social, economic and political dimensions became intertwined with the cultural and educational dimensions. What is more, these movements are often radicalized and strive towards, or attain, revolutionary goals. Consequently, although it may be possible in the industrial West to entertain the illusion of the separation between the social and the cultural dimensions, this is not possible in contemporary Third World countries. An educational reform project in these countries would commonly find itself linked to an explicit desire to redefine the collective identity via a given cultural model and the elaboration of a specific socio-political system.

Culture and the dominant school system in Latin America, therefore, are subjected to a dual series of pressures:

— those resulting from the ambivalent relationship with Western cultures, which are considered at one and the same time to be parent and dominator;
— those which develop through the contact between it and the various dominated communities, who, using models from everyday life which are still very much alive, attempt to elevate themselves to a plane of reflection by salvaging and formalizing elements from the original cultures. The goal is to promote them to a level of equality nationally, and to allow them to penetrate as deeply as possible into the education systems which penalize these communities severely for being 'different'.

The results of these efforts vary according to country, respective strengths and weaknesses, and the political system. However, in contrast to the principles and behaviours which held sway in the past, now at least currents exist which favour the promotion of these extremely disfavoured groups, including a good number of descendants of European immigrants of working-class origin. Hence, the launching of socio-educational projects such as that undertaken by P. Freire, well known for his views on 'functional literacy'.[3] One advantage of this theory is that it does not attempt to attack the problem from the outside and does not merely act upon 'cultural content'. Rather, focusing on methods, it tries to induce the subjects themselves to make the appropriate move towards the material to be assimilated. We know, for example, that Freire used drawings reflecting everyday life situations to create and stimulate dialogue, which for him was the fundamental strategy of non-directive literacy training.

Similarly, attempts have been made to foster change in groups in a situation of cultural domination using their own basic models. By way of example we can take C. Meyer's efforts to teach socioculturally disfavoured peoples (SCDP) of the southern Brazilian coast and rural northern Brazil.[4] He began by positing that 'development must be the work of the beneficiaries themselves; they must feel it is not a need imposed from the outside, but rather a necessity in its own right'. Yet, in the case of most programmes it is easy to see the 'magnitude of the contradiction between their objectives and the psycho-sociocultural identity of the populations concerned'.[5] The knowledge thus acquired is precarious or merely a 'pasted-on knowledge' which will soon become 'rusty' or simply unlearned, because it is foreign to both the psyche and the environment the subject claims as his. Obviously, this is not the case with what the individual recognizes as his tradition, hence the eminently educative character of that tradition, which, moreover, satisfies a sociological condition of prime importance which is widely disregarded in our industrialized societies, namely that 'education, insofar as it is a process directly involved in development, can only take place via the various official channels of the social environment. In this sense, schools are only one tool among others used in the educational process.'[6]

Thus, strategies for stimulating endogenous motivation need to be developed. Efforts to improve literacy, for example, 'must be based on the natural means of expression and communication of the people concerned'.[7] The problem, then, is that the written language in complex societies is conventional, that is, arbitrarily matched with the meaning it is supposed to express. We must make them aware of this by showing them, on the basis of their dances, codified corporal gestures, the graphic symbols contained in their religious, ritualistic and mythological symbolism and craftworks, that they too possess systems of writing and reading which are not different in essence from those they must learn for the sake of literacy.[8] 'Once they perceive and recognize in this language a new form of non-conventional 'writing', they will be capable of establishing a first link between their way of analysing and interpreting environmental indices and a way of *writing* per se, that is, written signs. This link, once established, will help create a positive attitude towards learning the written language.'[9] Indeed, a spontaneous transfer will be made between their situation of having to learn the elements of their own system to learning those of the 'written' culture as it exists in other societies.

These attempts to improve literacy can serve as prototypes for future attempts to satisfy a need which developing countries have insisted upon: although these countries recognize the necessity of accepting sociocultural change, they would like to become acquainted with the new culture, to integrate the new, the foreign culture by using their original culture, their own heritage as a starting point. This is precisely where the difficulty lies, as we will see when we consider societies – they are the majority – whose situation is different from that of South America. For these societies, which were once colonies of the European powers, recently achieved independence. Even if these groups see themselves as being different in various ways, they live together as if united on the basis of a common, original heritage and national vocation. It is within this framework that they strive to surmount the crisis spawned by their confrontation as independent nations with the new international environment.

We must, therefore, take a look at the aspects of this crisis which concern the relationship between the cultural and educational dimensions.

Decolonized societies in the Third World

Because these societies are dissimilar, and for the reasons mentioned in Chapter I, we will treat them in depth. Our discussion will concentrate essentially on the Arabo-Muslim countries of the Maghreb, the Middle East and Africa.

The violent shock of colonial domination on indigenous cultures could have permanently destroyed or disorganized them. However, the disintegrating effects remained limited, thanks to a vast movement of preservation using the customary defences. These include:

— Physical withdrawal from the dominating group: the colonized group takes refuge as much as possible in its own race.
— Manipulation of the colonizer's image, so as to make him less attractive and reduce the threat he represents for the original identity of the group. Thus it was commonly asserted that the superiority of the foreign culture did not reside in its moral, spiritual and intellectual values, but in technical expertise acquired by means of a morally dubious orientation of mental capabilities, producing mere brute material force, which, in any case, is capable of being learned:
— The symbolic preservation or accentuation of traits of the traditional culture, including many which a number of people found questionable. We might refer to this as 'reactional crystallization'.

Paradoxically, it was when independence was achieved and the foreigner left that movements occurred that would have been expected while he was still there: an opening up to his culture and close contact with many facets of it. With the departure of the dominator, a debate suddenly erupted as if it had been postponed because of various inhibitions. Another factor contributed to the pell-mell violence of the confrontation. As soon as independence was won, a 'pilot group' of these countries opted without hestitation for the construction of Western-style, industrialized economies, so completely had colonization spontaneously convinced them of the effectiveness of that model. This marked the launching of a 'modernization' effort which spread beyond the economic sector. Indeed, it was soon realized that, unlike what was previously thought, modernization could not be achieved simply through the acquisition of neutral knowledge and practical know-how without repercussions on the personality. Acquisition of this knowledge and the effective utilization of these techniques went hand in hand with culturally characteristic attitudes, representations and orientations vis-à-vis oneself and the environment, and for that very reason, called the importing countries' own systems into question.[10]

Accordingly, leaders and those they relied upon for support tended to encourage the adoption of these attitudes, which in many cases were quite different from or even diametrically opposed to traditional models. Yet, those who advocated simply abandoning the traditional model were few and far between. Even if this was what they actually thought, they could not have said so publicly. The popular masses and middle-class intellectuals would not have accepted it. The immense inequality which has always characterized North-South relations, with the dependence and threats which result, prevented these populations (and continues to do so) from considering cultural change as something historically normal and not to be dramatized. On the contrary, this would have been viewed as consenting to a betrayal which did not take place during the colonial period, acceptance of their own spiritual contamination and even annihilation. In these conditions, the claim to 'authenticity' was, and remains, fierce, showing to what extent the manner in which cultures and societies come into contact can be decisive. So, 'how can we have access to Western scientific progress and technology', a Moroccan intellectual exclaimed, 'without giving up ourselves, without subscribing to the underlying socio-cultural system?'.[11]

It is in this context that the conflictual situations which foster ambiguities and dysfunctions emerged, to the extent that, except for a minority which feels it can eliminate the antagonism between tradition and modernity by doing away with one or the other term, everyone endeavours to have a slice of both. To our view, many governments attempt to implement the strategy adopted by Algeria's leaders as described by B. Etienne:

The political leaders radically dissociate modernism of mores and modernization of society: the demands of modernism (the status of women, family planning, the cultural expression of young people) are minimized in relation to the demands of modernization (creation of an industrial infrastructure, rationalization of production, etc). The regime's dream society is modern (large public enterprises, advanced scientific activities, social mobility, increased job specialization), yet protected by the solid moral armour and austerity of habit attributed to Islam. They will accept, therefore, to place limits on modernism provided that it does not jeopardize modernization.[12]

In other words, we end up speaking in terms of 'limits', of grafting on to the process of change elements of the original identity. But on the basis of which criteria can these limits be justifiably defined and in a way obvious to everyone? The members of these societies, given the weakened state of traditional structures, are abnormally left to 'cope' for themselves and so attempt to reconcile the endogenous, foreign models in their own fashion. Obviously, not many of them obtain a coherent synthesis. Most of them end up with syncretic, 'makeshift' formations, determined by the whims of circumstances and experiences, with the contradictions and difficulties which can result.

We thus find ourselves confronted with a typical situation in which the two functions of culture, the ontological function (construction of the individual's identity around culturally determined significations) and the instrumental function (man's adaptation to his environment) become so dissociated that we must resort to two systems of models, because the original identity-building model can no longer ensure adaptation to an environment which no longer matches its code. From an educational point of view, rather than mutually reinforcing and enriching each other within the context of a single personalization model, systems of representations and spontaneous or intentional learning processes carried out synchronically (via the groups frequented) or diachronically (via the educational experiences undergone at different ages) risk culminating instead in a reciprocal negation and disintegration of the individual. Here we find ourselves confronted again, to some degree or other, with all the acculturational dysfunctions mentioned in our discussion on immigrants who are hemmed in within Western industrial societies, but on a larger scale, as well as the subsequent 'cultural manipulations' performed by subjects as described in the preceding chapter. It remains to see how this crisis, the constituent dimensions of which we have just given, affects areas directly related to education.

Education and the family

In the Third World, the family is generally a much more extensive and powerful social unit than in the industrial Western world. The crisis it is undergoing is therefore especially crucial, particularly because of the specific ties this institution has to the individual personality. Yet, at a time when young people are challenged to resolve the conflict of multiple cultural planes, the family rarely proves to be of much help to them and is sometimes a handicap. Bearing this in mind, what we are about to say with regard to the Arabo-Muslim family, Maghrebin, in particular, can be generally applied to other recently decolonized patriarchal societies.

Let us first mention a primary structural fact. In the case of the former communal family group, the particular psychological make-up of immediate relatives had little importance. The group made up for individual imperfections and relativized the incidents they caused. But the family's loss of importance (urbanization, structural changes in rural society) places the emphasis on the qualities and defects of parents and the peculiar structure of relationships within the smaller family group. New importance is placed on interactions between its members, which are more likely to be negative than positive, as the family environment is brutally upset by the present anomic situation. This is why it is important that we define the typical dysfunctions likely to affect relationships within it.[13]

As was the case with immigrants, we find here the same corrupting influence due to reinterpretations of the original cultural code plus the contaminating influence of Western values (the individual, money) having a disorienting impact on children: usurpation for individual profit of powers entrusted to him by the community, resulting in abuses when marriages are concluded or intervention in the private lives of young people and couples; exploitation of traditional rights and advantages, while overlooking the corresponding obligations with the negative consequences this may have for parents; mercantilization of relations, particularly matrimonial, with unfair practices on the part of fathers when collecting dowries. Like immigrants again, there is a tendency in these patriarchal societies to exercise 'differential permissiveness' owing to the traditional inclination to favour the son, to allow him a certain amount of 'modernistic' freedom not granted to daughters, or if so, with limitations or 'exceptions' which are often irrational. This leads to resentment and frustration in daughters or even stronger reactions.

Another set of tensions in parent-child relationships results from the application of the former code in situations for which it is no longer appropriate, because these situations do not afford the compensations they used to; because they are sometimes the opposite of what they formerly were (for example, the communal family which has become financially dependent on the married couple, yet claims the right to continue setting moral standards and values and to interfere in the upbringing of the children); because the older generation chooses to disregard new, modern legislation which affords young people greater autonomy.

Young people, however, in the current industrialized and urbanized environment, do not think of the communal family and its rules as absolutely necessary for individual survival. What they seek is not to destroy the traditional code, but to temper it so as to lighten the burden of parents and elders, to foster at the same time forms of individuality in several domains, to create less hierarchized relationships in which dialogue is more important than blind obedience, and in which informal affectivity is not crushed by formalized respect. They want, finally, an education which prepares children, boys and girls to confront the new environment rather than doom them to maladaptation.

Except in especially privileged segments of society, this desire is nowhere near being satisfied. First, there are the objective difficulties of the family situation, such as lack of space, leading to the expulsion into the street of masses of young people, of whom there is a huge number within the age pyramid. The world outside is no longer the socially structured and strongly integrating world of the village or camp under the constant control of a homogeneous group but, rather, the anonymous city street, both the product and reflection of the structural deficiencies, the contradictions, the anomie of the new, overburdened Third World city. The street will become the 'third milieu' next to the school and the home, posing special problems for the educator such as the weakening or complete loss of the fruits of previous schooling, the emergence of more widespread juvenile delinquency among both sexes, gravitating around the illicit satisfaction of heightened consumer needs in a context of predominant poverty.

These objective shortcomings are compounded by the parents' lack of education, which, as we have already seen, the disintegration of the traditional group makes evident by placing primary emphasis on their individuality. In addition to their dysfunctional behaviour within the family context we earlier mentioned, parents, especially in working-class circles, are completely without appropriate, educational techniques. How can we blame them, anyway, when we consider that they would have not only to guide their offspring through 'modern' situations beyond the reach of their traditional competences, but also through other, anomic, 'undefinable' situations with which even trained educators would be hard pressed to cope?

Young people readily feel pity for the educative behaviour of their parents: 'My mother only knows how to shout', 'to cry'. 'What can you say to a father who knows nothing but the Koran?' exclaimed a group of young Tunisians. Diametrically opposed to the traditional code, these deprecatory judgments made by young people about their elders are likely to become even more commonplace, now that, following national independence, more of them will receive a complete education, whereas their parents are for the most part illiterate or have been given only a very rudimentary education. Thus a rupture has taken place which, because of its suddenness and magnitude, is becoming a structural phenomenon, the consequences of which are far from at an end. It has spread to the most characteristic and most vital element of traditional societies in the Third World: the integrated relationship between generations.

All these factors contribute to a measurable increase in tension and frustration with the usual consequences that result, such as psychological problems and suicides or suicide attempts, which, in patriarchal societies are more common among girls. That is the picture as far as children are concerned. Parents, for their part, seeing their prerogatives challenged, will often react by taking a harder stand with respect to traditional values, which does not help the situation. Or else (this attitude can follow or alternate with the first) they abandon their educative vocation and the job of resolving the problems raised by their offspring to the State (made responsible for this state of 'anarchy' and these 'woeful times') or to schools.

However, researchers should not confine themselves to the analysis of dysfunctions alone, the dramatic moment and spectacular image of which arouse attention. To arrive at a more balanced picture, we must also take a look, as this author did for the Maghreb,[14] at the intelligent, psychological mechanisms which have been put into place, either spontaneously or more often unconsciously, to temper antagonisms within the family and the individual. For it would appear that, despite the crisis and the problems they give rise to, blood relations in these societies constitute the basic unit to which everyone remains attached. That is why, as we have seen, the vast majority of these young people do not seek to overturn the traditional cultural system, but rather to arrange it in various and often subtle ways.[15]

To illustrate this, let us cite several typical examples of these 'moderating mechanisms'.

First, there is 'open-ended traditionalism', which preserves traditional types of behaviour, but detaches them from their emotional involvement in principles considered to be sacred and inviolable. They are seen, rather, as belonging to the realm of the technical, the functional, the logically rational, and hence as being relative and potentially modifiable. In this way, parents and children can agree to safeguard certain traits of the original family, yet by justifying them differently and while belonging to different worlds.

Next, there is 'dissociation' whereby it is possible to safeguard the traditional principle by considering that anything which might jeopardize it is minor and incidental. For example, traditional education is vehemently criticized for its deficiencies and flaws, but parents continue to be respected because it would be unfair in view of their generation and their lack of schooling to blame them for these merely technical shortcomings. Or a list is made of all the grievances children have against their parents, but these ideal antagonisms are then set aside in the name of affective communion which affection for, devotion to, and solidarity with, the family justify.

Then there is 'relativism': the application of elements of the old or new code is relative, depending on the specific moment in time, the place and the individual's abilities. For example, only an educated girl will be allowed 'modern' autonomy, because she will be protected from the naïveté of those who are not. Boys will put up with the traditional system as long as they live at home, postponing the application of new models until they find their own families.

'Transposition' actually makes use of an original value to adopt a modern behaviour. For example, a girl will demand and receive an education so as to be better able to serve in the household and fulfil her traditional role as wife and mother.

Finally, there is the 'subjectification' of values. This involves keeping the 'spirit' rather than the 'letter' of traditional precepts in the form of values interiorized by the subject and freely applied in new situations. This is what is mainly involved in the relaxing of the original system in the home. For example, young people generally want to relieve parents of the precise, rigid powers they have over their marriage, their family life, etc. But to a certain extent parents recover what they have lost, for their children acknowledge their obligation to listen to them, to take their advice into account as concerns protecting the family reputation and interests. The values thus 'subjectified' and 'mobilized' are open to individual inventiveness, a precious advantage in a changing situation.

Education and the school

In newly independent Third World countries, it was the school which was immediately looked to to ensure development. Public investments in this institution are substantial, schools now exist throughout the national territories and expenditures for education represent as much as one-third of the overall State budget. For families, the new type of education and the diploma obtained by one of their members has for many years symbolized (and still does) the whole group's release from their century-old poverty and the realization of their long-awaited social and economic advancement.

It was originally thought that this result could be achieved by simply broadening access to knowledge-oriented learning processes, which were considered to be neutral and independent of any implication for the young person's innermost personality and hence of any cultural bias. This judgment had to be revised and the necessity of bringing the message, if it was to be retained and effective later on, in touch with the student's attitudes and motivations was recognized. But this realization still did not solve the problem. So that, after the optimism of the early years when education was virtually considered to be a panacea wore out, leaders and citizens began to raise questions which an African scholar summarized in three basic phrases:

Why, in spite of their spectacular development in the years between 1965 and 1970, do educational systems in Africa remain incapable of providing the skills required for economic, technological and scientific development? Are education and culture the appropriate means of bringing about the social and ideological changes which are indispensable for vanquishing the alienation of societies and men towards internal and external structures of dependence? If so, what is the relationship between education and development? ... The answers we are able to give to these questions will help us set up the conditions for a process of autonomous development, capable of attenuating the contradictions created by various structures of dependence.[16]

The same questions might be asked with regard to the so-called developing countries. We do not claim to be able to answer them, but only to make contributions to the central debate, based on an examination of the implication of culture in educational problems.

The difficulties which observers and researchers working along these lines identify can be organized into several categories.

SCHOOL AND THE ENVIRONMENT

One set of problems involves the school's contact with the environment. In all countries, the population receives the traditional message, of which ethnologists and sociologists have described the means of transmission.[17] Relative to this message, the 'modern' school, that is, the 'Western' type school, still represents a clean-cut break. Because it is less integrated into the society which surrounds it, is separated from its capital of knowledge and skills handed down through the generations, possesses an extremely formalized type of organization integrating the significant aspects of the Western, industrialized, cultural model, and provides the young person with less education and more pure information, which, moreover, is foreign to his milieu and handed down from above, this type of school is automatically regarded as being an 'exogenous' institution.[18] Yet it is the one that has been adopted everywhere, for, as one African leader explained, traditional education trained individuals who were 'closed to all scientific progress' and who even felt cut off from and excluded by the country's problems. Since independence was achieved, these problems were of a level of abstraction that made them inaccessible from the standpoint of the usual family and rural education.[19]

Whatever the case, children bring diverse cultural traditions into the classroom. Developing countries thus find themselves confronted with a situation of 'two culture stories'. But this situation is further complicated by the fact that this culture is never pure, but rather tainted in different ways by modernization models depending on the social background of the pupil. For the impact these models have will not be the same for a city person as for a rural person, or for a person from the middle class compared to one from the slums.[20]

The types of acculturation, therefore, undergone by these different groups are not all equally valid for succeeding in school (as in succeeding in life). The more the pupil's form of acculturation diverges from that of the group who established and left its imprint on the educational institution, the more it will represent a handicap for him and help him finish among the 'educational waste', the volume of which in these countries is, statistically speaking, startling. And the inescapable fact is that the privileged group that sets up and runs the school is generally that which is the most 'Westernized'. We will take up this point again when we discuss the problem of language in the classroom in the following chapter.

For the time being, a few overall observations will suffice. In order to understand better how the contemporary school affects the Third World student, some studies make an internal analysis of the culture they disseminate.

THE COMPOSITION OF CLASSROOM CULTURE

One way of focusing on this area is to analyse the 'ideological messages' contained in school readers. In this way we see how the information passed on in different languages — the language of the colonizer and the national language — institutionalizes ideologies rooted in cultural groups which are quite incompatible. Let us take, for example, the results of a study conducted by a Moroccan investigator[21] of 50 texts in Arabic and 50 texts in French, taken from readers used in elementary schools in Morocco, in the second year of the intermediate level.

The texts in Arabic were theocentrically oriented, presenting God as the cause of all things, exalting submission to His will, and minimizing suffering because it could be overcome through faith. Hence, the value of human activity was relativized. The French texts contained a humanistic ideology and placed emphasis on man's efficiency, while at the same time advising caution and the avoidance of danger, whereas the Arab texts preached assistance to one's fellow man and the giving of alms.

Unlike the French texts, the morality contained in the Arabic texts was very pronounced and extremely explicit (an abundance of maxims). The moralism of these texts constantly made references to religion, in contrast to the secularism of the morality contained in French texts.

The readings in Arabic contained lessons in virtue based on the acts of historical and institutional figures (the example coming from up above), while morality 'French style' was based mainly on interpersonal relationships between individuals in everyday life.

Arabic texts dwelt on the past, on the golden age of Islam, and on its culture and traditions. French texts concentrated on what was current, or 'modern'.

Adults, as portrayed in the Arabic readers, are highly esteemed, whereas the main focus is on children in French readers.

Arabic texts are loaded with indications from a patriarchal ideology. Consequently, they present an essentially masculine society in which there are six times as many men as women, 50 per cent of whom have very important positions (as opposed to 10 per cent of women). Father-son relationships by far outnumber father-mother or father-daughter relationships. The relationship nearly always goes from father to child and from chid to mother. Only the father 'acts' or intervenes. In contrast, 34 per cent of the figures presented in French texts are men and 28 per cent women (the remainder are unknown). Relationships are far more diversified and there is frequent brother-sister interaction.

This type of analysis was applied by J. Seux to all textbooks used in contemporary Moroccan schools. He found 'three essential contradictions' between textbooks in French and those in Arabic:

While texts in French address the young reader directly, texts in Arabic, which often ignore the child, do not; while French is used to describe a world of gaiety and joy, good example and seriousness pervade Arabic texts; while Arabic texts refer to a distant, bygone era, French texts give the pupil a vision of the contemporary world.[22]

These insights, which have the merit of being based on precise, empirical studies, give a good idea of the problem. The analysis of the effects of the day-to-day 'hammering away' of these two ideologically and culturally contradictory sources is far from exhausted.

Of course, the use of two languages from two different worlds is partly responsible for this situation. It would be wrong to assume that doing away with bilingualism would bring the problem to an end. Zoubida Haddab, basing himself on his 1979 analysis of textbooks used in Algeria, concludes that, above and beyond the linguistic dichotomy,

we are dealing with the successors of two groups who have been involved in a struggle for many years: one group is the product of colonial education and the other of traditional and, above all, reformistic indigenous schools. Each bases its respective social position (whether achieved through conversion or promotion) on the possession of a cultural heritage acquired through different systems which have always been rivals, despite the automatic advantage enjoyed by French schools. When the social realities were overturned following independence, the rivalry did not come to an end, but took on new shapes.[23]

We see, then, that this ideological and cultural ambiguity is at the very heart of the group which controls the educational system, the majority of whom come from the middle-middle and lower-middle classes which began to expand in the Third World following independence. Despite the language of unity contained in official texts and directives, this ambiguity is the reflection of genuine hesitations and conflicts among representatives of the ruling elite. But the situation gets more complicated yet, for, as we shall see, other phenomena can come into play in these rapidly changing societies.

Indeed, we cannot overlook the teacher. In these countries, as elsewhere, they have a role of primary importance in the dissemination of culture, but the effects are even greater than in the West, for differences and conflicts go well beyond those between subcultures of a given whole. A very significant example was provided by a study conducted between 1971 and 1972 by another Algerian, Mohamed Haddab. The study involved a sample chosen from among several thousand primary school monitors of both French and Arabic mother tongue, with an extremely low level of education (primary school leaving certificate) upon whom their government had to rely to replace European teachers who left when independence was proclaimed. They continued to serve for many years, with their number gradually diminishing. Observing these beginner instructors is especially indicated, because from their position at the bottom of the ladder their situation 'reveals some of the problems which arise in the relationship between schools and society'.[24]

Officially, the training these monitors received included moral, political and religious themes related to the significance of their task, as well as the technical knowledge needed for them to exercise their duties. But the guiding message they received had already been distorted upon transmission and, consequently, only part of the message which the monitor transmitted in turn came directly from that explicit source:

The most effective means of transmitting an entire cultural system with its hierarchies, specialities, prohibitions, performances, behaviour patterns, rules of language, etc, is, in fact, an entire arsenal of techniques which are often applied unconsciously or under the influence of diverse social processes. An ironic remark on the part of a fellow instructor or teacher, negative feedback from a school inspector or educational adviser, rumours circulating in different social circles, or the image of himself reflected in the social milieu in which he lives are all ways in which the dominant cultural system is imposed upon the monitor. This cultural aggregate, this mixture of scientism, of 'technophilia', of cultural values originating in Islam as well as in the secular tradition make up the cultural model that the dominant social groups propose and objectively impose and through which the appreciation – or rather depreciation – of the dominated social group takes place.[25]

While it is true that trainers are only partially responsible for transmitting the effectively dominant system, the relationship of those trained becomes, in turn, 'all the more complex because the group they make up is non-homogeneous and beset with tensions which undermine its cohesion'. As a result, we must be wary of oversimplification: 'We would commit the same error of reducing the problem to a dichotomy between modernism and tradition if we did not take into account the diverse backgrounds of the different groups which make up our team of monitors.'[26] Indeed, we must reckon with the diversity of their socio-economic origins (traditional peasantry in the case of Arabic-speaking monitors, modern sectors for French-speaking monitors, privileged, urban milieu for female monitors), their geographic origin, and their educational background. These teacher-apprentices must assimilate the elements which one tries to inculcate in them but operate certain changes in them, for the same objective behaviour does not have univocal significance. For example, 'to count on help from the family' refers to different things in different minds. For those with modernistic inclinations, the family environment is conceived as 'both separated from the school environment and capable of reinforcing the role of the teacher, provided the family has the means to provide the child with the psychological and material conditions to sustain his scholastic activities'. But, for those who have distanced themselves less from traditionalism, 'education tends to be regarded as an extension of family education', of which they expect 'reinforcement of the habits of discipline and good conduct they strive to teach themselves'.[27]

The study revealed some unexpected relationships, perhaps due to compensatory mechanisms. For example, monitors who pray regularly are more inclined than others 'to expose themselves to modern cultural instruments, to read books, to say that they are writing short stories, a novel, etc'.[28] We must above all not forget the influence exerted by the groups they hope to become part of. This explains the resistance of their spontaneous teaching practices to government efforts to train official teachers and the many obstacles in the way of the 'educational system's tendency to form a professional body of agents for disseminating the dominant culture in the most homogeneous way possible'.[29] We can, moreover, clearly comprehend the inadequacy of a few days of 'teacher training' or of 'practice lessons' in modifying these practices.

Finally, we must realize that

eliminating the monitor does not mean that all the difficulties revealed by our study of him will likewise disappear. Many of the traits and cultural norms incarnated by the monitor and which shed light on part of his behaviour and strategies, are manifestations of processes through which the sociocultural foundations of Algeria are being transformed at present.[30]

In a general way,

we have here the entire problem of cultural pluralism posed paradigmatically within the group of monitors, the same problem which is posed in various forms within the entire educational system, the social system, and in the relationship of one to the other.[31]

Indeed, it can safely be said that the process of change which the original culture in all of the decolonized societies of the Third World is currently undergoing is the result of a variety of manipulations which can be known only through empirical research. Thus, although we can generally speak of a 'traditionalist' or a 'modernist' dominant, the complex diversity of situations does not allow us to make a schematic representation of a cultural universe to two spheres.

At the grass roots level, the student in these countries is confronted with a situation which is not fundamentally different from that in the West. There too, as we have seen, to equate the culture of teachers and pupils to monolithic archetypes, or to reduce their 'cultural competence' (as defined by W.H. Goodenough) to mere familiarity with these archetypes would be an oversimplification. In modern complex societies, there is nothing simple in any field. But, in the societies we are dealing with, the processes under way concern far more dissimilar and discontinuous material because they go far beyond the subcultural level. Consequently, the reactions, manipulations and formations which result are apparently more complex, unexpected, fluid and tense for students and teachers alike. The difference is that students, because of their youth and lack of preparation and greater need because of their age for coherent identification models, are in a more difficult position.

Once again, the solutions called for go beyond educational science, especially in the present case, since it implies reconstructing the entire collective identity through total social dynamism. The situation would be much better if an awareness of these problems — rather widespread nowadays — led to something other than blanket definitions and verbal directives, leaving the protagonists alone in the dark to cope with concrete situations using unconscious mechanisms. At least it would be possible to incorporate cultural differences into textbooks and teacher training programmes. Generally speaking, a knowledge and understanding of the sociological and psychological mechanisms at play would make clear the nearly complete incapability of circulars and instructions handed down from above to change, to borrow an example from the Algerian A. Khellout, the extreme reserve on the part of numerous rural teachers with respect to teaching science subjects or educating women.[32]

CLASSROOM CULTURE AND COGNITIVE SKILLS IN THE CHILD

It would clearly be invaluable for the educator to have a rather precise knowledge of how children in these societies react to messages 'manipulated' in this way. According to our sources, we have no scientific studies on the subject, but only some rather vague observations based on the experience of teachers. One obvious guess would be that this splintered culture will cause distressing tensions in the child if he is directly implicated in the education he receives. It is worthwhile mentioning this fact. It shows that objective contradictions observed from the outside do not automatically correspond to conflicts in the life of the subject who is exposed to them. For this to occur, it is necessary for him to be involved.

It is precisely in this domain that scientific research would be extremely valuable, for the student seems to develop defence mechanisms which have a constant effect, namely to keep the message at a distance so that it does not attain the nucleus of his personality and identity. Do we not hear young people say — and we ourselves heard this in Tunisia — that they 'forget everything as soon as they leave the classroom'? In actual fact, they do not forget, but alternate: they change codes, systems of interpretation, and reactions when they leave the classroom, taking up those in tune with their social environment. In these conditions, learning risks becoming mere memorization and is transformed into 'pasted on knowledge' whose utility is purely instrumental and with no educative effect. It has been reported that this was especially the case among women. Sent to school to gain an 'education' as a matrimonial asset, they have already interiorized the model of the relationship to knowledge inculcated by their conservative families. The family enjoins them indirectly to retain the information which will be useful at the exam, and to ignore the modern significations contained in that information, because they could have negative effects on their profile as 'good wives', that is, well-educated, but at the same time possessing traditional know-how.

While there have been, to our knowledge, few scientific studies on the crucial question of the relationship between identity reactions and the acquisition of culturally-splintered knowledge, many have been carried out in the United States on its effect on the child's cognitive operations, or more precisely, on the formal structures involved in these operations. A review of the subject on the basis of cross-cultural research was presented by B. Rogoff.[33] For M. Cole, summarizing his results, cognitive skills

are widely believed to develop through schooling as follows:
1. Abstract thinking, because it is required for learning in schools.
2. Analytical skills (perceptual and conceptual) and analytical attitudes.
3. Skills of verbal description and explanation on external things and events and one's own internal psychological experience.
4. Basic intellectual skills, such as conservation.
5. Skills of logical reasoning.
6. Skills of searching for general rules, the universals and principles.
7. Skills of 'learning to learn'.
8. Acquisition and mental manipulation of concepts.
9. Knowledge of certain sets of problem formats.[34]

However, without denying the validity of these findings, their interest is limited as far as our subject here is concerned. For they concern the formal characteristics of the mind and tell us about the terminal phase of the school's influence. But observations, if they are to be pertinent for the point of view adopted here, must deal with the content of information and explanations presented by different cultures and creating a conflict in the mind of the subject, as well as with the manner in which the subject copes with this problem. In particular, with regard to the studies carried out in the United States, we would like to know what are the 'atypical' forms students might develop who have not succumbed to the influence of the model of the Western school.

The studies conducted by M. Richelle[35] came closer to this point of view, while the as yet unfinished study by A. Bouya deals with it directly and can serve as an example. This project involved 84 Congolese school children from Brazzaville from 7 to 13 years old who were asked what caused rain. The purpose was to find out which elements in the interpretation of this phenomenon were due to social and family tradition and which were a result of 'modern' knowledge from school. The author clearly indicated the originality of his undertaking compared with the usual studies one nearly always deals with: 'Our purpose was not to find out if the explanations given by Congolese children compare to those given two or three years later or earlier by Western children in classical investigations.'[36]

The findings are complex. With the 7-year-olds, the replies invoked the gods: 'There is a man in the sky who pours down water from a well.' We can suppose that this invention of the childish imagination is corroborated by traditional family and social explanations. For those between 8 and 10, 'Rain comes from the sky' in the vaguest sense. At 12, they designated clouds as the cause of rain. The majority of 13-year-olds (77.4 per cent) put forward the typical explanation received in school: evaporation of water from all parts forms clouds which cause rain. 'The evidence suggests,' the author comments, 'that, without schooling, the 13-year-old subjects would behave like their 12-year-old comrades, as shown by other studies conducted in a similar manner.'[37] No dominant theme is to be noted among the extremely dispersed responses of 11-year-olds: they preserve some characteristics from the earlier age groups and introduce new ones, characteristic of older subjects.

One interesting fact to be noted is that 7.1 per cent of the 13-year-olds believed in the ability of certain people to make it rain using 'fetishes' or other methods. According to the author, this may be due to secret, specialized initiation training by elders, selectively administered to adolescents. Often the 12- to 13-year-old group gave two types of explanation, one traditional and one academic. When these children, as well as all Congolese school children in general, were asked which of the two models was most 'credible', they opted for the school model: 'The explanation given in school' said one child, 'is the same in all the schools in the Congo and other countries'; 'The things they tell us in school are the same everywhere' (12 years old). Thus, these children recognize and accept the

notion of the universality of academic knowledge. Scholastic knowledge is the result of a broad consensus between scholars and the peoples of the world and consequently possesses a certain credibility. And yet, everything proceeds as if the Congolese – if not the African – school teacher incarnated for these students the authority formerly held by the Sage or the village Elder.[38]

In this situation, phenomena of conflict or rejection of one or the other explanation can be expected, with the difficulties that result. But the subject can also 'reconcile them in his own way'. He can

play on several planes at the same time. He adapts his personality to the expectations of his surroundings. At school, he will behave according to its norms. At home and in other extra-scholastic situations, he will adjust his actions accordingly... For school children in our country it is important to know with whom and where they are speaking about a given event.[39]

The pupils who gave a traditional explanation, meanwhile, either 'got the information from old people in their neighbourhood, from old people in the village during summer vacation, or from their comrades. To a certain extent, we have here the traditional chain of transmission of knowledge by elders.'[40]

According to A. Bouya, the confrontation of several types of causal interpretations can lead to

> a multiplication of the possibilities for explaining a given phenomenon. The older children are thus able to have several views on the same phenomenon and several directions in which to channel their analysis of events. If this is so, school-inspired explanations and those based on traditional beliefs can be considered to be eventualities. For example, children learned the mechanism of rain in school. But they also heard that someone could cause rain using fetishes, which does not necessarily mean that they believe this to be real. They simply situate themselves from another point of view, so as to multiply the possibilities and perspectives for explaining the phenomenon under consideration.[41]

And, obviously, this can lead to attempts at synthesis, such as in the case of this 8-year-old child: 'rainwater comes from the Congo river and reaches the sky at the horizon where the sky and the earth meet.'

This type of analysis, it must be allowed, by providing insights into the debate within the mind of the subject struggling with contradictory cultural models, is far more valuable than studies which merely indicate that a Western-type explanation is reached at a certain age or at the end of a child's school career. It would thus be worthwhile to use it more extensively.

These findings pose an incredible challenge for the educator. Indeed, he can no longer take his 'make-shift' notions to be psychologically and educationally equivalent to the logically coherent concepts every human being understands. Moreover, how effective can such 'manipulated' knowledge — if it survives — be in countries having opted for industrial technology and the underlying rational model. On the other hand, these notions enable the subject — and this is especially important for young people — to go about in his society in cultural crisis without jeopardizing his personal integrity. We must not, therefore, act hastily. This kind of analysis will have a positive effect if it makes this point clear, provided it also makes us realize that we cannot let the young person solve the problem alone by who knows what means, that we must invent a form of assistance to help him depending on the situation, to evolve beyond simple 'coping'. That is the crux of the problem for decolonized countries in the Third World, namely that the current level of knowledge cannot provide recipes for solutions, but it can help discern what should be avoided.

Under these conditions, any attempt at coherent synthesis between the ancient and the new will be welcome, even if it is not always possible to succeed. We have the example of an attempt made by G. Mbodj. By analysing traditional ludo-motor activities in Senegal, he observed that their replacement by Western-style sports resulted in a loss of educational riches. He thus attempted to combine the two in a plan he hopes to submit to his country's authorities.[42]

SCHOOL OUTPUTS AND THE CONSEQUENCES FOR SOCIETY

The specific cultural messages transmitted by schools compete with other educative processes to create new 'human products' capable of entering into continuity or discontinuity with the needs and requirements of local life. What does this mean exactly?

There are on the subject a number of general documents, of which an article by D.E. Foley (incomplete, since it only deals with studies in English) attempts to give us an idea.[43] In any case, his observation to us seems valid for the entire Third World. The consequences of this type of schooling are extremely diverse and even contradictory. According to many studies, it does not influence rural communities, but does affect members of the middle class, merchants, owners, white-collar workers, and civil servants. In these cases, the distance of school models from those of peasants and the relative proximity to those of the others are cited as the cause (usually without precise investigation). Thus, for Indians, these models represent a world divorced from reality. But in the other direction, according to other observations, rural schools have a considerable impact on ethnic identities by attempting to align them along the national identity. They also elevate the expectations of village dwellers and their children with respect to modern-day life. In this case, educational production would quickly surpass the country's economic and professional capacity, giving rise to masses of educated, unemployed 'cynics' and 'drunkards' lacking confidence in themselves, shunning manual work and rebelling against the family and political authority.

Alternatively, these schools increase class, ethnic and linguistic inequalities (with ethnic stereotypes, in particular, influencing the relationship between teachers and pupils). The up and coming middle class created since independence will be best able to evaluate and manipulate the system of admissions and promotions through tests. Paradoxes are pointed out: a religious education can prove to be extremely modern, while a lay, modern education can perpetuate traditional, social inequalities. According to anthropologists specializing in South East Asia, the Buddhist concept of salvation by merit has an effect similar to the Calvinistic tendency to encourage personal achievement through thrift and work, for it leads to the acquisition of riches for the many Buddhist activities. In other cases, the avowed goal of the school is to bring about change and yet it brings about stagnation in the old system. For example, in Iran under the monarchy, the official message in school extolled individual initiative, group cooperation and the value of manual work, but institutional behaviour blocked its effects. The educational system was a reflection of the Iranian bureaucracy of the time which was authoritarian, personalized, highly competitive, rigid and closed to all innovation.

What are we to think of this disconcerting variety of findings, each of which no doubt contains its parcel of truth? That the situations in which the school disseminates and consistently 'manipulates' its new message are varied, complex, composed of 'packaged variables' needing to be dissociated and carefully scrutinized, though this is rarely done. We can see this, for example, in observations on Japan. Everyone is focusing his attention on this country, because it is the brilliant example of a successful Third World society which could have been considered to be developing. Its success is primarily economic, and it remains to be seen whether the cultural sector is also concerned. However that might be, an attempt was made to establish the relationship between this country's success and its educational system.

According to J.M. Leclercq,[44] Japanese schools provide highly technical training combined with fierce competition for university degrees. To achieve this, it was necessary to do away with the feudal, clan-dominated system of social mobility which existed before Meiji's reform. Leclercq notes, however, that an equivalent to the clan system has reappeared in the form of a caste which knows how to prepare its children properly for obtaining the best diplomas in the most prestigious and expensive universities. In any case, given the system, students absorb a huge volume of knowledge. But, at the same time, schools must inculcate a system of values, and develop attitudes consistent with the efforts which will be demanded of each individual in professional life and which are essential to the dynamism of businesses. They fulfil this task perfectly, this author says, by relying on traditional values and concepts, to which there are abundant references in textbooks: the work ethic, a sense of discipline and of hierarchy; the idea that social solidarity must not be jeopardized by individual initiatives, and that meeting the needs of the community cannot be postponed. Moreover, the democratic ideal per se does not exclude aristocratic attitudes and the creation of allegiances, and this model is transposed spontaneously into the hierarchical organization of the modern enterprise. Finally, an acute sense of the unconditional value of the national interest survives because, given its success, the country is not depreciated, consciously or unconsciously. This configuration, which creates strong ties between the student and his endogenous heritage, makes possible the strong incitement to open up to other countries and to seek out and borrow information from them, without drawbacks.

One generally regards this model as living proof that effective acceptance of scientific positivism does not necessarily result in acceptance of the corpus of Western values, namely, individualism, rejection of community spirit, of authority, of hierarchies and disrespect for elders and certain traditions. In this way, Japan has succeeded in solving the structural problem with which developing countries are confronted: innovating from the inside, on the basis of an endogenous heritage capable of adjusting to normal changes from the outside.

All this gives food for thought. However, it must be said that the 'ingredients' which supposedly explain the success of the Japanese exist in the majority of Third World societies. They, too, have community values, and the rejection of individualism, a sense of respect for hierarchy and authority, and a strong attachment to the community are firmly rooted in their traditions and could serve as a positive mediator in the transition to a productive, dynamic system of modern capitalism or socialism. If this has not been done, or has been done poorly, the case of Japan and that of these other countries must involve other factors which need to be brought to light.

In the mean time, the most widespread situation of which most decolonized countries complain is that the school's outputs are inadequate, that the young people it trains are ill-prepared for the needs of the community they are theoretically meant to serve. According to J.K. Nyerere,[45] these individuals have an acute sense of belonging to an elite, despise the knowledge and culture of their ancestors, are often far removed from everyday reality, are irretrievable by their old rural community, and only aspire to material wealth and Western values. And the situation has been getting worse in the past ten years. These 'intellectuals' can no longer count on the spectacular social ascension they witnessed in the early days of independence. They will increasingly have to content themselves with inferior jobs or remain unemployed. They turn into, this author states, bitter individuals dominated by negative attitudes such as resentment, defeatism, resignation, *'arrivisme'* and escapism. All this points to the need for a multifaceted effort of reflection on the absolute necessity of a restructuring of the 'Western' educational model, and possibly of the original model as well. To illustrate this, we will confine ourselves to the analysis and recommendations made by P. Erny.

In a work published in 1977, P. Erny[46] reviewed the experiments in black Africa he regarded as the most significant, but whose achievements were feeble: the 1959 reform in Guinea, that of 1962 in Mali, the introduction of educational television, the education of rural areas in Burkina Fasso, the Harrambee movement in Kenya, and the practice of self-sufficiency in the United Republic of Tanzania. In 1981, he conducted an in-depth study in Rwanda.

He first emphasizes the radical educational inadequacy resulting from the failure to take socio-economic factors into account.

As long as the village dweller regards the school as a means of escaping poverty by abandoning one's condition, the rural exodus will continue and the educational edifice, no matter what the subject matter it provides, will be built on sand.

But 'it is equally true that a certain type of education can make an invaluable contribution to the goal of development'. The problem is clear: 'How can we design this type of training, and how can we gain acceptance for it?'[47]

Erny believes we must begin by calling the current system into question:

Is it not the school, as an artificial environment, which imposes segregation on young people and puts them on the fringe of social and economic life rather than in the middle, is it not the school because it is school and because it is scholastic which works against the very goal it was assigned to achieve?[48]

This does mean that we must reject the very concept of a specialized institution — which in the contemporary context cannot be done away with — but to differentiate it more distinctly from the current type of school. The principle is to break up the 'Western-style' school without regressing to total educational immersion in the life of the community, and in such a way that the 'adolescent continues to be fully part of his original environment, while at the same time being able to maintain a minimum distance between it and himself and to convert his daily experience into the bases of a general culture.'[49]

The author, quoting a report by Torsten Husén (1972) before the Organisation for Economic Cooperation and Development (OECD),[50] recommends utilization of all the educational resources available by means of a double transfusion, so to speak, of the educational benefits into everyday life and of the considerable volume of knowledge from the environment into the school. All forms of educational alternance are welcome. In this way a mentality can be created which 'aims not so much at creating islands for the purposes of education as to reinforce the educational dimension of social life as a whole'.[51] It is by making ourselves aware of the educational potentialities of the environment taken as a whole that we discover the resources of an educational approach based on custom. In the past, most educators in both black Africa and most other countries in the Third World took a negative view of this approach. Later, its indisputable influence on the child had to be recognized, because it constitutes the cultural substructure of his intelligence and personality. One is even astonished by the fascination he has for it compared to 'the superficial, disappointing effect the school has on him, despite the considerable means employed'[52]

The efficacy of traditional education can perhaps be explained by the fact that it is strongly integrated into everyday life, that it makes optimal use of the potentialities of the group of peers, that it transmits in a progressive and functional mode the cultural heritage via everyday circumstances, and that it knows how to utilize the person's affective resources and mobilize the system of symbols which communicates directly with the subconscious.

To 'return purely and simply to customary education' is, however, not an acceptable remedy. 'We can use it as a basis, but must also go beyond it.'[53] We thus find ourselves confronted with the same problem. Does P. Erny have more specific ideas about possible solutions, about which everyone formulates the basic conditions which they must meet?

In P. Erny's view, we must evolve from a static attitude on traditional education to a dynamic conception. On one hand, we content ourselves with highlighting 'content' alone, as is often the case when one is an ethnologist or desirous to restore ancient cultures. One can even resurrect ancient rituals, initiations, age associations and brotherhoods.

Such action seems from all points of view to be interesting and even necessary. But to regard traditional education in this way ... that is, inevitably in a static manner, is to archive it with things from the past and to liken it to folklore, the preservation of which will always be artificial in nature.

Cultures presented in this way tend to become 'show cultures', dead cultures. Yet, there exists another way of envisaging customary education which 'consists in understanding the mechanics, the functions and the dynamics'.[54] To rethink the native system from this point of view would be to reintegrate it in an act of educative creativity, rather than reproducing it as it existed in bygone days.

Other authors[55] have echoed this condemnation of the impasse resulting from the search for permanent identity in the attachment to static 'content'. They suggest that it be situated rather at the dynamic level of a set of organizational forms which would penetrate external contributions to which all societies are subject in the course of their history. But, again, it is easier said than done. For those who formulate the problem in this way do not hazard a guess as to what these forms might be which would enable us to assimilate new contents without creating a feeling of a structural break with identity. The reason is, no doubt, that this would involve an act of invention which, as such, cannot be 'spoken' in advance, and even less formulated from the outside of from 'above'. This is precisely how P. Erny sees it when he states that

it is on this score that the activity of schools conceived and imported from the outside has proven to be the most harmful: it relieved communities accustomed to social self-regulation of their educational responsibilities and dispensed them with having to invent anew.[56]

The criticism levelled at the educational and scholastic crisis in the 'new' societies of the Third World and the proposals made are far from being useless. But they will become a genuinely operational body of material once they are 'snatched up' and recast in a totally unique combination, not one proposed 'bureaucratically' by certain individuals, whether specialists or leaders, but constructed by society in a time of crisis and need. What needs to be done in order for science to become genuinely useful is beyond the scope of science: creating the local conditions for the community's effective involvement as a community in the educational process.

NOTES AND REFERENCES

1. Marquez, A.D.; Sobrino, E. L'Amérique latine et les Caraïbes: racines, apports, réidentification et projet culturel. *Education comparée* (Sèvres, France, Centre international d'études pédagogiques), no. 36, 1984, pp. 1-15.
2. *Ibid.*, p. 5.
3. Freire, P. Literacy and the possible dream. *Prospects* (Paris, Unesco), vol. VI, no. 1, 1976, pp. 68-71.
4. Meyer, C. Contribution du langage corporel et verbal à la création d'une méthode neuropsychomotrice d'enseigement de la langue écrite chez les P.S.C.D. *La Psychomotricité* (Paris), vol. 7, 1983, pp. 23-41; Meyer, C. Contribution des éléments graphico-symboliques de l'environnement physique et culturel à l'apprentissage du langage écrit chez les P.S.C.D. *La Psychomotricité* (Paris), vol. 7, 1983, pp. 57-79.
5. Meyer, C. Contribution des éléments graphico-symboliques...*Op. cit.*, p. 57.
6. *Ibid.*, p. 58.
7. Meyer. C. Contribution du langage corporel...*Op. cit.*, p. 31.

8. Zimmer, Anne; Zimmer, F. *Visual literacy in communication: designing for development*. Amersham, UK, Hulton Educational in co-operation with the International Institute for Adult Literacy Methods, 1978, 144 p.
9. Meyer, C. Contribution du langage corporel et verbal...*Op. cit.*, p. 32.
10. Berque, J. *Le rôle du facteur humain dans le développement des pays nouvellement indépendants*. Paris, Unesco, 1967. (Unesco/SHC/5)
11. Bennouna, M. Les décolonisés face à eux-mêmes. *Lamalif* (Casablanca, Morocco), no. 114, 1980, p. 30.
12. Etienne, B.; Leca, J. La politique culturelle de l'Algérie. *In*: Centre de recherches et d'études sur les sociétés méditerranéennes, France. *Annuaire de l'Afrique du Nord*, vol. 12, 1973. Paris, Eds du Centre national de la recherche scientifique, p. 75.
13. Camilleri, C. De quelques dysfonctions de la famille maghrébine contemporaine. *Annales de Vaucresson* (Vaucresson, France, Centre de recherches interdisciplinaires), 1979, no. spécial, pp. 173-87; Kacha, N. *La situation et les aspirations de la femme algérienne dans la région d'Alger*. Paris, Université de Paris V 1979. Mékidèche, N. *La représentation de soi des jeunes en situation de conflit culturel: le case de l'adolescente algérienne*. Paris, Université de Paris V, 1981.
14. Camilleri, C. *Jeunesse, famille et développement: essai sur le changement socio-culturel dans un pays du tiers-monde (Tunisie)*. Paris, Centre national de la recherche scientifique, 1973. 514 p.
15. Boutefnouchet, M. *La famille algérienne: évolution et caractéristiques récentes*. Algiers, Société nationale d'édition et de diffusion, 1979. 316 p.
16. Fadiga, K. *Problématique de l'autonomie par l'éducation*. Paris, Université de Paris V, 1984, p. 1.
17. Wagner, D.A. Indigenous education and literacy in the Third World. *In*: Wagner, D.A., ed. *Child development and international development: research-policy interface*. San Francisco, CA, Jossey-Bass, 1983.
18. Radtke, F.O.; Gestettner, P.; Streiffeler, F. Entkolonialisierung der Erziehung: das Beispiel der VR Kongo. *International review of education* (The Hague), vol. 27, no. 1, 1981, pp. 15-39.
19. Nyerere, J.K. *Independence and socialism*. Nairobi, Oxford University Press, 1968.
20. See, for example, Fitouri, C. *Biculturalisme, bilinguisme et éducation*. Neuchâtel, Switzerland, Delachaux et Niestlé, 1983. 300 p.
21. Ibaaquil, L. *Ecole et inculcation idélogique au Maroc*. Paris, Université de Paris V, 1977.
22. Seux, J. *L'image de l'enfant et de la société à travers les manuels scolaires au Maroc*. Paris, Université de Paris V, 1983, p. 466.
23. Haddab, Zoubida. Les variantes de la morale: la petite bourgeoisie et les manuels scolaires. *Actes de la recherche en sciences sociales* (Paris, Maison des sciences de l'homme et Ecole des hautes études en sciences sociales), no. 30, novembre 1979, p. 17.
24. Haddab, M. Les moniteurs de l'enseignement primaire en Algérie. *Actes de la recherche en sciences sociales* (Paris, Maison des sciences de l'homme et Ecole des hautes études en sciences sociales), no. 30, novembre 1979, p. 19.
25. *Ibid.*, p. 21.
26. *Ibid.*, p. 22.
27. *Ibid.*, p. 24.
28. *Ibid.*, p. 26.
29. *Ibid.*, p. 23.
30. *Ibid.*, p. 30.
31. *Ibid.*, p. 19.
32. Khellout, A. Les enseignants ruraux en face de l'école algérienne actuelle. *Psychologia educatio* (Constantine, Algeria, Université de Constantine), no. 8, 1980, pp. 21-7.

33. Rogoff, Barbara. Schooling and the development of cognitive skills. *In*: Triandis, H.C.; Heron, A., eds. *Handbook of cross-cultural psychology. Vol. 4.* Boston, MA, Allyn and Bacon, 1981, pp. 233-94.
34. Cole, M.; Wakai, K. *Cultural psychology and education: a draft outline.* Geneva, International Bureau of Education, 1984, p. 30. (UNESCO/BIE/ET/4.Sc. Ed./7) [Paper presented to the Seminar in Educational Sciences, 4th, Geneva, 1984.]
35. Richelle, M. Contribution à l'étude des mécanismes intellectuels chez les Africains du Katanga. *Problèmes sociaux congolais* (Elisabethville [Lubumbashi], Zaïre, Centre d'étude des problèmes sociaux indigènes), no. 45, juin 1959, pp. 3-69.
36. Bouya, A. Les représentations causales de l'enfant congolais. *Enfance* (Paris, Laboratoire de psycho-biologie de l'enfant), no. 3, juin-octobre 1981, p. 177.
37. *Ibid.*, p. 178.
38. *Ibid.*, pp. 181-2.
39. *Ibid.*, p. 182.
40. *Ibid.*, pp. 182-3.
41. *Ibid.*, pp. 183-4.
42. Mbodj, G. Place des activités ludomotrices de tradition dans l'education des conduites motrices à l'école élémentaire sénégalaise. *Psychologie et éducation* (Toulouse, Université de Toulouse-le-Mirail), vol. 6, no. 2, 1982, pp. 87-95.
43. Foley, D.E. Anthropological studies of schooling in developing countries: some recent findings and trends. *Comparative education review* (Chicago, IL), vol. 21, nos. 2 and 3, June and October 1977, pp. 311-28.
44. Leclercq. J.M. *Le Japon et son système éducatif.* Paris, La Documentation française, 1983. 120 p. (Notes et études documentaires. nos. 4747-8)
45. Nyerere, J.K. *Op. cit.*
46. Erny, P. *L'enseignement dans les pay pauvres: modèles et propositions.* Paris, L'Harmatan, 1977. 211 p.
47. Erny, P. *De l'éducation traditionnelle à l'enseignement moderne au Rwanda (1900-1975): un pays d'Afrique Noire en recherche pédagogique.* Lille, France, Service de reproduction des thèses, Université de Lille III, 1981, p. 649.
48. *Ibid.*
49. *Ibid.*, p. 650.
50. Husén, T. *Social background and educational career: research perspectives on equality of educational opportunity.* Paris, Centre for Educational Research and Innovation, Organization for Economic Cooperation and Development, 1972, 182 p.
51. Erny, P. *De l'éducation traditionnelle à l'enseignement moderne au Rwanda... Op. cit.,* p. 658.
52. *Ibid.*, p. 656.
53. *Ibid.*, p. 659.
54. *Ibid.*, p. 660.
55. Goguel, A.M. Identité à sauvegarder, identité à construire: l'enseignement à Madagascar de 1819 à 1979. *In*: Tap, P., éd. *Identité individuelle et personnalisation.* Toulouse, France, Privat, 1980, pp. 377-9.
56. Erny, P. *De l'éducation traditionnelle à l'enseignement moderne au Rwanda... Op. cit.,* p. 661.

CHAPTER VI

Special problems: language and testing

In this chapter we will focus on two problems which have proven to be closely linked to the cultural dimension, namely the uses of speech and language on one hand, and testing on the other. We will conclude by discussing attempts at what is called 'intercultural education'.

The influence of speech and other forms of language on culture

'Language (*la langue*) is the specific instrument of communication a community uses to analyse human experience. Language (*le langage*) is at once a product, a part, and a prerequisite of culture.'[1]

Indeed, language segments and interprets reality in accordance with a group's conceptual profile, needs and interests, according to the cultural models which govern them. Also, as the privileged medium of communication, it distributes these models in space from group member to group member. Finally, it is the main support of cultural reproduction through time.

We will define language as a code of communication based on conventional signs. Indeed, at the level of *significata* expressed via natural, unmodified signifiers, we are not yet dealing with culture. The reader may have noticed that P. Rambaud in the above quotation uses the French words '*langue*' and '*langage*' without distinction. While not wanting to become involved in a linguistic controversy, we will make the distinction which seems by and large to correspond to usage. We speak of the French 'language' (*langue*), but also say 'body language' or the 'language of a social class'. In the first case we are referring to a very precisely, collectively institutionalized and explicitly systematized code with its constraints and sanctions. In the second case these characteristics become more vague and more or less contaminated by the opposite characteristics: imprecision in its formalization, gaps in explanation, systematization and relative absence of constraints. Consequently, when speaking of language in this sense, we may be referring to codes which are completely independent of languages per se or to identifiable ways of using a language by different groups within a society.

NON-VERBAL COMMUNICATION

If we are to cover this subject exhaustively, it would be wisest to adopt the cautious definition given by C. Pujade-Renaud: 'I designate as non-verbal communication all procedures making it possible to establish contact by means other than through verbal language.'[2] This definition covers unconscious manifestations and behaviours of all types and on all levels, such as non-verbal, visual, auditive and corporal signals. Non-verbal channels involve the apparent, the implicit, the disguised: for example, how space is distributed, the manner in which roles and status are expressed.[3] As far as body language in particular is concerned, this category includes, according to the same author, 'all relational processes, whether institutional or not, in which the body is directly a producer of signs: faces, gestures, non-linguistic sound productions, looks, smells, changes in tension, heat diffusion, etc'.[4]

Anthropologists agree that all these signs are 'culturally subdetermined'[5] and condition individual reactions more strongly than words. Hence their exceptional importance in the educational relationship, especially in terms of rapport, where misinterpretations can lead to incomprehension of all kinds, and alter the impact of the verbal code, to the surprise of the interlocutors themselves, who are not aware that non-linguistic signals may be saying something different from — or even the opposite of — what they are expressing verbally. It is thus necessary that these languages come out of the dark where they function unconsciously, thus becoming deterministic mechanisms, and that intuition gives way to the illumination of science. Many recent works have been published on the subject of these codes, the most well known being E.T. Hall's of 1966.[6] They laid the foundations of disciplines whose task it is to identify and eliminate previously unrecognized obstacles to communication between subjects from different cultures, stimulating interest in a new breed of investigation into microcultures.[7]

Proxemics is the study of the differentiating significations attached to uses of space according to the group of which the subject is part. For example, the adjustment of distance as a function of the situation and of status is generally institutionalized. According to a given culture or educational norm, a certain distance is regarded as excessively close, while according to another, it is considered a friendly distance. Another discipline, *kinesics*, is the scientific study of communication based on movements and body positions. Children learn the diakinesic system at a very young age. It is thus important to be able to identify and understand the essential 'kinemes', which can be independent of that which is said or punctuate speech. W.S. Longstreet[8] incorporates these proxemic and kinesic units in the method of identifying and classifying pertinent cultural segments she suggests educators use to elaborate 'ethnic profiles' of their classes. This can be successfully accomplished with the help of tools such as films, videos or photography. She shows how this information, together with a knowledge of social value patterns and intellectual modes, can be a source of renewal in educational practice. She therefore includes these elements in the teacher training programmes she elaborates and tests.

Studies such as that by B. Kalish, which relate scholastic level to modes of corporal communication with the teacher and with peers, are not immediately relevant here. However, we are directly concerned by research into the link between infra-verbal language to a specific group and its effect on the teacher-student relationship in cases where they belong to the same group and in cases where they do not. Physical appearance, posture and way of dress belong to what Bourdieu and Passeron call 'the infinitely minute signals transmitted through style and manners, through accent and elocution, through posture and sign language, or even through clothing and make-up'.[9] These authors feel that such phenomena underlie, reinforce and contradict verbal language and constitute a 'class habitus'.

Unfortunately it appears that little has been done to identify and take these phenomena into consideration, particularly with respect to their relationship to the ethnic and social origin of the student. G. Snyders[10] mentions this plane of communication in reference to a point which directly concerns us, but only very briefly. He considers non-verbal communication, which includes gestures, mimics and actions in general to be the 'poor cousin' of verbal communication. He relates it to Bernstein's 'limited code' (which we define below) and, for this very reason, feels it plays a far more important role for working-class children than for those from privileged circles.

It was precisely with definition of this code as a 'class habitus' that D. Zimmermann took as his point of departure in the study we briefly mentioned in Chapter IV.[11] Positing the existence of a non-verbal class language, he, as the reader might recall, studied the way in which it dominated attraction-repulsion situations between teachers and students in kindergartens and elementary schools in France. The results were categorical. Scholastic success, of course, played a considerable role, and 'there appeared to exist', the author acknowledged, 'a definite, general connection between grades achieved and feelings of attraction and repulsion expressed by teachers'. But, he quickly adds, 'grades being equal, French working-class children and immigrant working-class children even more so, proved to be half as attractive as their well-to-do school fellows.'[12] The term 'repulsive' is never used in connection with this latter category of children; it first appears, like the words 'indifferent' and 'antipathetic', when we move to less privileged French children and then to ethnic minorities. Thus, judging that 'class membership strongly subtended empathetic reactions', the author concluded that there existed 'a non-verbal ghetto for a large majority of working-class children (made up of 40 per cent Frenchmen and 48 per cent foreigners). These children are literally set apart by the (dis-) regard of the teacher. They are the victims of effective segregation.'[13] In a more general way, reacting to G. Snyder's observations, Zimmermann concludes on the basis of his own observations that 'disfavoured children on a linguistic level are also disfavoured on a non-verbal level, even if in this situation of equivalent handicap, they use the non-verbal register more willingly.'[14] In contrast, in the case of economically privileged children, the positive effects are compounded.

The educational consequences of this type of discrimination were described by C. Pujade-Renaud, referring to body language:

> The student taken as *corpus*, as a body socialized according to norms which are ever so much more effective because not precisely formulated, will be better encouraged to assert his existence and himself, to dialogue with his teacher, and to communicate in every sense of the term. Yet, if the student feels his mode of physically moving, appearing and looking, if he feels the particular style which is both his own and that of his class, it will be difficult for him to enter into the world of communication and speech. The non-verbal channels of the Pygmalion effect need to be catalogued.[15]

Communication language and the school: national problems

COMMUNICATION AND CLASS

The connection between the forms of speech within a given language and the groups within a society who employ them has been accepted for many years. The fact that socio-economically modest groups were at a disadvantage and the privileged classes at an advantage because they imposed *their* linguistic norms in the country's schools was suspected and even denounced.

The first scientific analyses of this phenomenon were provided by the famous investigations of the Englishman Basil Bernstein and other researchers at the University of London Institute of Education.[16] This study owes its success to the fact that it is situated at the intersection of several fields of knowledge, that it establishes a link between theoretical and empirical findings,[17] and that it answers the questions raised in the 1960s. The most well-known component of this study is the two-code theory. As J.-C. Forquin, who analysed this theory in depth,[18] said,

> the linguistically and sociologically pertinent contrasts between two modes of linguistic use refer back to two modes of 'relating to language' and presuppose two different kinds of 'cognitive orientation', two ways of structuring experience with the world and to situate oneself in relation to the world: the physical world, the logical world, and the social world.[19]

This involves a 'limited code' and an 'elaborate code', which Bernstein defines on the basis of scrupulous empirical investigations, such as the analysis of speech samples of young children, mainly from commentaries on a series of pictures. The limited code proved to be used more frequently by working-class children, while the elaborate code was more common among middle- and upper-class children.

The limited code tends to refer to states rather than to processes and is an essentially descriptive language. It is strongly linked to the context and is harder to understand without its visual supports. The elaborate code, meanwhile, centres on relationships between things rather than on the objects themselves and tends to produce a self-sufficient account. For example, the way of presenting the rules of a game will be more general and more 'decontextualized' in the latter case than in the former. This distinction shows the contrast between a more particularistic cognitive orientation, dependent on substantive content and the existing situation, and one which is more universal and oriented towards generalization, formalization and the grasping of structures. The elaborate code appears to be linked to a more finely-tuned mastery and manipulation of the instruments and materials employed, giving rise to greater variety in the choice of words and greater flexibility in the use of grammatical categories. In speech situations, upper-class adolescents employ various subordinate clauses and more complex verb forms, the passive voice, and 'rare' adjectives, adverbs and conjunctions. Their language is thus richer from the semantic and syntactic points of view, and is more explicit and nuanced, whereas that of the other group is syntactically and lexically poorer, mixes facts and conclusions, is less demonstrative and more implicit. Words are often replaced by gestures. Because the limited code functions on a limited number of syntactic structures, it is hardly surprising that its form is extremely predictable, whereas in the case of the elaborate code, the form is much less predictable. It is perhaps because of this broader latitude and a greater concern for mastery of expression that the upper-class adolescent punctuates his speech with more numerous and longer pauses and hesitations. Generally speaking, we are dealing with a relationship to language which is more disciplined and better thought out, employing expressions such as 'It would appear that...' and other 'qualifiers'.

There is another interesting distinction. The limited code is a language in which the affective dimension reinforcing the feeling of membership in a social group predominates. It employs rhetorical devices of consent and consensus-seeking 'sociocentric' expressions such as 'Don't you agree?: or 'Do you see?' The other form of language, meanwhile, relies more frequently on 'egocentric' expressions and more frequent use of the personal pronoun 'I'. The elaborate code

facilitates the expressing and 'explicating' of the irreducibly individual part of experience and seems to go hand in hand with a type of 'sociality' in which personal originality is accepted and valued, whereas the limited code seems to correspond to group identification and affective conformity to the pragmatic demands of daily life.[20]

This is the language used 'among friends', at school, in the military, among intimates who share a large body of common experiences and expectations and do not need to 'dot the i's' or to 'expound' to be understood. It is the language of solidarity, of conformity, of community. This dual manner of using the linguistic tool, which, as we shall see later, does not necessarily correspond to inequalities in 'linguistic competence' and 'verbal intelligence', can have equally serious implications on the cognitive level as on the affective and social levels. The elaborate code 'seems to favour the expression of logical connections, the hierarchical ordering of concepts, and the apprehension or production of complex structures'.[21]

The consequences of these findings at the educational level are of paramount importance. They provide a solid argument against the conflictualist theory's accusations concerning school in the West. This is because it is obvious that the 'elaborate code' is the one which has been adopted, defended and imposed by educational institutions. This, then, is another means by which middle- and upper-class students are considerably advantaged, because they are dealing with a language which is generally used and encouraged in their social environment, extending and developing mental and socio-affective predispositions inculcated in them since early childhood. On the other hand, the working-class child will be confronted with the difficulties of a 'deculturizing' adaptation which could jeopardize his own identity and saddle him with an additional handicap in competition at school.

Before discussion, observations and criticism raised by Bernstein's theory, let us clarify several points. First of all, this author in no way intended his codes to be 'essences' consubstantially linked to two social classes. Everyone is able to make use of both, depending on the speech situation. For example, on the playground, all children, no matter what their social origin, use the limited code, as they do in all situations where the information is sufficiently clear to make a number of details superfluous. As M. Brossard said, it is a 'situational' language. In contrast, if it is necessary to tell or write a story in the absence of a frame of reference, and the real situation must be reconstructed at the linguistic level and the meanings must be given in detail, the elaborate code must be used. This is where the difference lies: children from privileged backgrounds do not experience difficulty in going from one to the other. For the others, this transition is by no means impossible, but on average is certainly more difficult. This is not due – and we arrive at our second point – to intellectual inferiority. Typical differences of expression between social classes are independent of intellectual levels measured by performance tests and even of verbal intelligence. In fact, it is the context in which the child normally operates that facilitates or not his orientation towards expository treatment of universal significations. We are dealing, as Bernstein was the first to admit, not with intellectual inequalities, but with different orientations of intelligence:

The resulting forms of language-use progressively orient the speakers to distinct and different types of relationships to objects and persons, irrespective of the level of measured intelligence. The role intelligence plays is to enable the speaker to exploit more successfully the possibilities symbolized by the socially determined forms of language-use.[22]

Having said this, comments on Bernstein's work take two main directions. The first is criticism of the modalities of the method used. On a linguistic level, the description criteria used are at times excessively vague and inconsistent.[23] This question was taken up again by R. Espéret[24] who turned his attention to the definition of the object (the language and linguistic practices), to what is understood as the variation of language, how we collect data and the measuring instruments used. The indicators that were used in this case to detect differences in language were those very ones to which the school and the upper class attribute the highest value: lexical range, complexity of syntax, accordance with the grammatical rules. This is relevant to illustrate whether educational standards have or have not been met, but it is not sufficient for a thorough and objective analysis of language and speech. Should science merely measure what the school measures?

Reactions with respect to his observations concerning the situational variable were more positive. Bernstein, as we have seen, accepted the principle of such a variable, but its effects seem to be more extensive than he thought. According to Brossard,[25] researchers agree that the 'variations to which the situation gives rise are more significant than the variations due to the social origin of the speakers'. C.B. Cazden goes even further to say that 'it may be wiser methodologically to accumulate the (social class) differences within contexts and to see what higher order generalizations can be made about them.'[26] A large number of variables are thus to be taken into consideration with regard to what determines the type of language used: the situation, the oral and written expression, the nature of the task and subject dealt with, and the status of the interlocutor.

D. Lawton,[27] for example, distinguishes several educational situations such as the individual conversation or group dynamics. He terms 'educationally structured', in contrast to 'open', a situation where the child is more or less required to use specific linguistic resources to perform the task demanded. For example, 'What do you do at school?' allows greater latitude than asking him to explain the rules of a game, which requires listing the conditions to be met for a team to win. Lawton found that linguistic differences were less significant in situations which were more formally constraining than those used by Bernstein. Conversely, Bernstein, in measuring the actual linguistic resources, used observation situations which were not natural enough and too inhibiting for children unfamiliar with experimentation and evaluation practices in which language use is to a certain extent artificial because it does not involve providing information, but showing that one knows how to speak. These criticisms were shared by Labov and Hardy,[28] as well as others.

Labov, in particular, by changing the context and materials involved in the task, obtained more complex results. The tests were given in a home rather than at school, the tasks involved subjects of emotional interest or even 'taboos', rather than the usual tedious topics. In these new situations, the language of black children became as complex, abstract and elaborate as that of speakers of standard English.

It thus seems that the theory that the child has 'one' language, from which it is possible to extract the static features, needs to be relativized if we are to avoid rigidifying differences. However, even though working-class children show that they are capable of using complex linguistic tools in structured situations when asked an abstract question, Lawton found that their responses were shorter, the time needed to answer was longer, and their hesitations, pauses and stops were more numerous. Apparently, the exercise is harder for them. Bernstein's hypothesis, therefore, which the conflictualists have made their own, remains valid, despite the attenuations imposed by subsequent research. Fortunately, this latter research prevents educators from giving in to pessimism and despair.

The second set of observations undertook a more in-depth study of the comparative value of either code. The study of the dialect of socially disfavoured groups in the 1960s led to serious doubts as to its educational value. Qualified as a mere emotional accompaniment to action,[29] it was regarded as lacking the necessary, formal properties for orderly thought processes and conceptualization. What was interpreted as a verbal 'deficiency' became, without further investigation, a 'cognitive' deficiency, affecting all working-class children. The natural conclusion was thus that in order to remedy the 'cultural deprivation'[30] of these subjects, one needed only to elaborate 'compensatory strategies', and many different such strategies were invented.[31]

The results, however, of these 'remedial programmes' proved to be disappointing.[32] So, beginning in the 1970s, there emerged what J.C. Forquin termed a wave of 'left-wing criticism' of this educational approach. We have already touched upon this topic in our discussion of popular subculture in opposition to that of the school. We will now look at objections raised with respect to the linguistic codes which are an integral part of that subculture.

These objections can be summarized as follows: quite beyond the fact that disparities between children of either social category are by and large created by the observational and experimental situation, and that the working classes are not consubstantially cut off from the code of the privileged classes, a second look must be taken before asserting that one is superior to the other. Even if genuine differences exist between these two types of language, it must be ascertained where the difference lies. Is it at the 'instrumental' level, at which a message is communicated, or at the 'emblematic' level, which is used to demonstrate one's ability 'to speak properly' or to gain social recognition?[33] Theoretically speaking, 'anormative' language is subject to the criterion of acceptability alone, that is, to the positive laws of linguistic discrimination. 'Normative' language, in contrast, obeys extralinguistic laws of a cultural order. It is a written language, governed by an imposed grammar. In the first case, the constraints are 'functional'; in the second they consist of 'supernorms' pertaining to language use among a certain social category.[34] It is precisely at the emblematic, normative and 'supernormative' levels that academic languages are situated. Some authors have gone so far as to reject the concept, shared by Bernstein, of 'levels of language' as minor variations of the common, median language, saying instead that there are two languages, the contradictory natures of which reflect the opposition of conflicting social classes.[35]

According to this point of view, the 'deficiency' theory would thus be quite incorrectly based on confusion of the grammatical norm and 'operativity', namely, between the linguistic and cognitive functions, which all recent research refutes.[36] Hence, the mode of expression of socially disfavoured children can only be considered to be extrinsically 'deficient' compared to the mode of expression used in schools, which merits further investigation. By using the linguistic and other arguments already discussed (cf Chapter III), the 'cultural deprivation' theory and its corollary, remedial education, would appear to be mere excuses for not challenging the cultural inculcation carried out by educational institutions.[37]

This reasoning, however, did not convince everyone. A certain number of authors, many of whom adopted a Marxist point of view, wondered whether this theory, which denies the genuine existence of handicaps, has not gone too far. Without rejecting the significant role of artificial 'supernorms' in symbolically distinguishing groups, can linguistic disparities between social classes be entirely reduced to differences of this order? To what extent are the differences described by Bernstein's team devoid of all instrumental value? Can it really be asserted that the language spoken in popular circles is always as functional as that of privileged circles?[38] Is it not possible to speak of the inferiority, if not the 'inferiorization', of children of certain backgrounds due to their living conditions?[39] These questions form the backdrop of the warning issued by G. Snyders:[40] cultural deprivation is not a figment of the imagination. The privileged classes have ensured themselves an effective 'extra' which should not be left to their exclusive enjoyment. We might add, that if it is the task of schools to share the riches of each culture present with everyone, then part of their role is also to redistribute the something 'extra' that the privileged classes have to everyone.

LANGUAGE AND REGIONAL CULTURAL GROUPS

In all countries, certain provinces use a specific dialect of the idiom which became the national language and, as such, is imposed or privileged at the educational institution level. The opposition of this language to the use of these dialects is a general occurrence. Governments have tried to eradicate them and schools have even penalized their use.

The new popularity of ethno-regional subcultures has given birth to a movement for their revival and introduction in schools. A number of arguments are used to defend rural 'patois' in Europe and, for example, Creole in the West Indies.

Rather than being poor 'patois' of no value, the languages of these cultural minorities are in fact languages in their own right, merely different from the national language and not a sign of 'backwardness'.

These tongues are the 'language of the heart'. This argument spurred a flourish of analyses on the use of the linguistic code for purposes heretofore masked by its instrumental function to the detriment of the affective function. Numerous psychoanalytic conjectures were spun around the equation 'mother tongue equals language of relationship between child and mother'. Studies focused on its role in personality development, namely on the formation of identity and experience. This involves 'cultural roots' of which language is the pre-eminent mediator. By this means, attention was henceforth concentrated on the symbolic force of the language's cultural link, responsible for the tight crystallization of identities around it. Hence the ideological and emotional implications of the movement to rehabilitate local idioms. This probably explains, initially at least, the fact that the movement 'often achieved more in the political and polemical areas, than at a strictly scientific level'.[41]

This brings us to the problem of bilingualism.

THE PROBLEM OF BILINGUALISM AMONG IMMIGRANTS

Bilingualism is broadly defined by A. Tabouret-Keller as 'all processes which are likely to manifest themselves in any situation in which two or more languages are spoken by a given individual or a group'.[42] Understanding this phenomenon, she goes on to say, requires relying

> not only on analysis of the strictly linguistic evidence, which in turn implies a structural study of the contact process and its consequences, but also on the psychological profile of the speaker and the original relationship between him and the different languages he speaks.[43]

Thus defined, bilingualism is seen as a total social phenomenon, and the full magnitude of the problem encountered by the immigrant and his children, especially, in the host society's schools becomes clear.

Reports as to the impact of this phenomenon on personality[44] show how more refined methods and the taking into account of various other variables can result in a more nuanced judgment. Some of them deal directly with the topic at hand, namely the importance of the status and significance of the languages used as a function of the context. This is precisely the crux of the problem in the case of both immigrant children and former colonies in the Third World. They find themselves in a situation of forced, discriminatory bilingualism, directly related to conflictual biculturalism. Even if it is true that bilingual acquisition depends on 'the manner in which both parents situate themselves in relation to the linguistic constraints they impose on their child' and 'the type of relationship they have with him',[45] we must also take into consideration the fact that parents themselves are prisoners of this context.

In such a situation, bilingual learning on the part of young immigrants is very likely to be both defective and difficult, and even have negative consequences for personality development. Some authors, who strive to prevent the educational system from disguising its flaws by using the cultural alibi, claimed that the problem no longer applies to the 'second generation'. This generation supposedly speak as well as their fellows from the host society.[46]

Various other authors have refuted this hypothesis,[47] based on evidence they gathered themselves and on the results of 'nearly every study conducted abroad by serious researchers'.[48] They found that the young immigrant, far from succeeding in his bilingual undertaking, most often achieves 'semi-lingualism', which is characterized by imperfect ability in both the native language and that of the host country. Those who dispute this assertion do not fully understand what is meant by the command of a language. Indeed, L. Dabène comments,

> in the case of the second generation pluriculturalism is not necessarily evident at the discourse level (full knowledge of the host language is apparently achieved, as various studies conducted in schools have shown), but at another level: mastery of the different functions of language, argumentative strategies, the general attitude to the language, etc.[49]

Deficiencies, observable even among those who apparently speak the best, are rooted, according to some scholars, in psychological factors, for the veritable mastery of a language implies total command of 'its symbolic, culturally determined architectonics'.[50] This is the most important consideration: a host society's language as well as that of origin symbolize for the young immigrant the conflict which separates the two communities in the situation of overall antagonism, cultural, in particular, which is imposed upon them. For him, learning two languages means learning two codes saturated with conflictual significations, involving both repulsion and attraction. We had an illustration of this in the case of Armindo, the young Portuguese boy living in France. Once his conflict had been resolved, it was precisely French which went from being his weakest subject to his strongest. This point of view was confirmed by M. Laferrière in the case of minority speakers of Creole and Indian languages in Quebec.[51]

Once these matters were understood, efforts to elaborate educational structures which are better adapted to ethnocultural minorities now place special emphasis on the linguistic dimension. Such is the case in Western Europe as a group of experts commissioned a few years ago by the Council of Europe was to report. Further institutional reform is still needed, however. In his final report, based on the notes of experts, L. Porcher inserted observations which he thought indispensable if satisfactory solutions to the problem were to be found.[52] These observations led to several recommendations on the training of teachers in authentic cross-cultural educational methods.

First of all, he warns against giving 'pre-eminence to "linguistico"-linguistics' which, in the mind of immigrants, will tend to impose itself as an institution. The underlying idea

> is a simple and apparently convincing one: that it is only language which differentiates migrant children from their native-born fellow pupils, so that if they are taught the language of the host country quickly and thoroughly they will be able to keep up with normal schooling.[53]

Language cannot be dissociated from the overall socio-psychological problem of which it is a part, and the schematic representation of this problem needs to be corrected to take into account a number of considerations.

Two complementary goals must be pursued: giving the foreign child the means to circulate freely in the host country and to integrate himself to whatever extent he desires, allowing him to preserve his own cultural roots within his native society. To ensure this, educators must concentrate on the 'liaison between teaching in the language of the host country and teaching in the native language.... On it depends the balance which the migrant child so deeply needs on both the psychological and sociocultural planes.'[54] In particular, 'the problems of teaching the languages concerned (that of the country of origin and that of the receiving country) must be elucidated jointly.'[55]

Respecting the same liaison implies shunning all 'universalist' methods (which apply without distinction to all countries, regardless of the language of origin of the learner) and training teachers in 'contrastive methodology', which 'makes the teacher alert to the relations between language and hence to the need to keep the first language in mind when evaluating a pupil's performance in the second'.[56]

The predominant tendency in school education

has always been to concentrate on the language itself as a closed whole, a body of material to be mastered; hence the ingurgitation of vocabulary lists, grammatical constructions, etc. The pupil must either submit or give up and has no voice in the matter.[57]

This archaic model must be abandoned for 'language is not only a system, it is primarily a social activity and it must be taught as such if the children are not to be imprisoned in a non-functional mould.'[58] This will have two kinds of consequence.

First, language teaching for everyone in general, but especially for the immigrant, must focus on developing communication, on forming what linguists call 'communicational competence'. For these skills will be required in all aspects of social life and in school. This concern should lead to the inclusion of socio-linguistics, that is, the study of relationships between linguistic activities and specific social situations, in teacher training programmes. For example,

the speakers' status and roles, the context in which the communication takes place, the cultural implications in the language itself, etc, all have a direct effect upon the use of language and must therefore enter into the learning of it.[59]

In the case of the children of migrant workers, reliance on this discipline is fundamental because they need not only to master the language, but also its code of utilization in the foreign society. In summary, it is the 'situational language' which they must master.

Second, regarding language as a social activity should lead the teacher to centre his teaching on the learner. This will force him to take into account, initially at least, the learner's individual characteristics, needs and motivations.

In teaching the young immigrant, it will be important to know the parameters which define him, his specific manner of situating himself in relation to the codes with which he is in contact, as well as possible fears, ambivalences and blocks preventing him from mastering these codes in a conflictual context.

Finally, from the point of view of language teaching, the teacher must be aware of several characteristics of the host language. For migrant pupils, this is a foreign language, but, unlike the usual situation, it is the main language spoken outside the school. 'The trainee teacher must therefore be brought to distinguish fundamentally between: — his language as mother tongue and his language as a foreign one ... — his language as a foreign one outside his country.'[60] Another characteristic of this language is that it is both the object and vehicle of teaching. It is a language with which migrant pupils 'are confronted in a wide variety of socio-linguistic situations'[61] which need to be taken into consideration.

These, then, are the main factors, according to L. Porcher, which condition the learning of the host language by the migrant child. As we can see, it was worthwhile highlighting their complexity.

THE PROBLEMS OF PLURILINGUALISM IN THE THIRD WORLD

As we know, these problems are due to the continued use by these ex-colonies of the language of the colonizer at the institutional — educational, in particular — level after independence was achieved. Indeed, to ensure the success of their technical and economic development towards modern industrialization, the privileged use of these languages seemed especially indicated. On one hand, it was the most effective means of staying in contact with international scientific developments upon which this effort depended. On the other, as was explicitly stated at the outset, this made it possible to modify 'traditional' ways of thinking, to eradicate and rectify certain former attitudes and representations standing in the way of change, thanks to the alternative representations suggested by Western cultures, of which the foreign language was the vehicle. In some countries, this language was even proclaimed the 'cultural language'.

In some cases, the tongue of the former colonizer represented the only universal language, in contrast to the multitude of different native dialects.

Thus, paradoxically, thanks to the intense educational effort undertaken in these countries since their liberation, the language and, with it, the exogenous cultural model of the colonizer have penetrated (and continue to do so) strata of the population to a far greater extent than in the colonial period.

A debate was quickly launched. This led to a redefinition of bilingualism, because of the way and the circumstances in which it is practised in these countries, as a global phenomenon involving numerous factors. This was clearly brought out in a study carried out by C. Fitouri.[62] Basing himself on actual research on Tunisia and, in particular, on the long-term follow-up of a large cohort of pupils until the end of their elementary education — a rare feature not to be underestimated — Fitouri succeeded in providing a general analysis of this phenomenon, which by extrapolation can be applied to the majority of Third World countries. This study both highlighted the reasons for the importance of plurilingualism and 'debsubstanciated' it. Indeed, this phenomenon appears to be just a single but special indicator within a complex whole. The degree to which it is real depends on the situation of which it is part and can only be defined on the basis of an analysis of that situation. What stood out in the case studied by the author, as well as in the case of nearly all ex-colonies in the Third World, was the contradictory duality which characterizes the economies, the objective structures and institutions, and the anthropological and promotional cultures of these countries. Nearly all aspects of their social dynamics which can be given the prefix 'bi' as a coefficient (as well as lingualism) are interrelated and reinforce each other.

At the educational level, many questions were raised in these countries concerning the least favourable conditions for the simultaneous learning of the foreign and national languages. They only concern us here to the extent that they compound problems related to poorly integrated biculturalism which is the usual context to which they apply, as many authors have pointed out. Here are the most salient characteristics.

Simultaneous deterioration of both languages. It is well known that two languages can be learned in parallel without jeopardizing one or the other, *in the proper circumstances.* However, everyone agrees that such circumstances are only rarely achieved. This means that most often the result is an incomplete mastery of both languages and rather shocking 'makeshift' solutions.

Unequal status of the two languages, employed institutionally for the teaching of different disciplines and contents, the foreign idiom being used for scientific subjects. In the Maghreb, for example, 'with time, the pupil develops a Pavlovian reflex whereby the very sound of French automatically foreshadows something rational, modern and efficient', whereas Arabic has the opposite effect.[63]

The splitting of the speaker's personality, depending upon which language he uses. This, in fact, brings us to the main methodological problem: the need to separate the effects related specifically to the simultaneous learning of two languages from phenomena for which, because of circumstances, it merely serves as a vehicle. In particular, can the blame for the dissociation and alienation of of the individual be placed, as is commonly done, on bilingual teaching? It is to these questions that a study by M. Riguet[64] attempted — quite commendably — to reply, based on a series of detailed investigations into the comparative behaviour of young, monolingual, Arabic-speaking or French-speaking Tunisians, on one hand, and bilingual subjects on the other.

The findings were nuanced. It was found that the use of one or the other language by bilingual subjects had only little influence on the opinions expressed and the values asserted, whether traditional or modern. For example, Westernized attitudes noted when the subjects expressed themselves in French persisted when the subjects spoke in Arabic. In other words, the problem of the structure and unity or splintering of the personality is related to the broader problem of the bicultural situation as a whole (which involves many other factors than language) and its particular characteristics. Similarly, performance levels and cognitive operations depended according to this study on schooling and not on the language employed.

Other variables were more significant than the languae of expression in determining a choice of one set of values over another: for example, the speaker's group affiliation and personal characteristics such as sex and living environment, the field or subject of interest taken up, or whether there was a real or imaginary interlocutor. In all of these cases, the language used is itself dominated by other more fundamental parameters, the causal role of which is indisputable. In contrast, however, the language used influences the way in which reality is approached: according to the author, bilingual pupils expressing themselves in French take on a more 'intellectualist', more objective, more affective and less extremist attitude than when speaking Arabic.

The link between language use and the interests of various social groups in the country: the ruling classes, able to handle the foreign language and culture with greater ease are accused of deliberately maintaining the bilingual system to preserve their dominant position. C. Fitouri thus speaks of a Tunisian elite 'torn between the demands of the masses and the political, economic and cultural prerogatives they do not want to abandon'.[65] In addition, bilingualism is accused of placing a barrier between rich and poor, between city dwellers and rural people.[66] Basically, we find ourselves in a situation of utilization of the cultural asset for special purposes, which authors have attacked in the case of Western societies. Here, not only do privileged groups rely on different language and subculture to distance themselves from the masses, but even resort to foreign languages and cultures.

Similarly, the ease in learning demonstrated by children from these privileged groups is reinforced by the linguistico-cultural factor, which helps them succeed, while the extremely high failure rate of those originating in the lower classes is worsening for the same reasons. Paradoxically, those who remain within the original cultural and linguistic world are generally penalized. Here again, C. Fitouri made an interesting discovery. Although children brought up in an entirely Arabic environment experience the greatest difficulty in adjusting to bilingualism at school, those who belong to the traditional, literate, Arabic elite do better than pupils coming from groups who are economically and socially uprooted because of current changes. We thus see the difference between a 'degraded' subculture, which is of little help to the second group of children, and the 'authentic traditional culture', which affords the first group a coherent point of reference and resources for adapting. He concludes that an individual is more privileged the more 'authentic' the culture which he endorses. More substantial research in this extremely interesting area is needed to bring out the different variables involved.

For the author, in any case, culture is the springboard for the linguistic factor. The solution of the models crisis and the endorsement of a vigorous system of education would make it possible to open up without risk to plurilingualism and the riches it can bring. 'In the framework of an educational system based on bilingualism and biculturalism, the Tunisian pupil — and, by extension, the Maghrebin pupil — cannot triumph over the inherent difficulties of such a system, unless his is deeply rooted in an original culture.'[67] In this way, he achieves a dialectical reconciliation of two theses which originally appeared contradictory. Rather than reject pluriculturalism, he sees it as the universal way of the future and, in an apparently paradoxical fashion, as a remedy against acculturation. But we are not talking about just any kind of biculturalism or acculturation: 'Struggling against the effects of colonial acculturation... consists, as the close of the present century approaches, in pursuing bicultural education as a necessity which populations must freely accept rather than have imposed upon them.'[68] Moreover, pluriculturalism, far from being opposed to the original system, presupposes that it occupies the central stage: 'Just as mastery of the mother tongue is a necessary condition to the learning of a foreign language, a firm footing in the original culture is a prerequisite for any initiation into another culture.'[69]

Meanwhile, a number of decolonized Third World countries have, in a more or less radical, progressive fashion, undertaken the complete 'nationalization' of the language of learning. Apart from the symbolic satisfaction this has achieved, it also remedies certain dysfunctions caused by a considerably flaw-ridden bilingualism. Other problems arise, however, which it would of interest to mention briefly.

The national language thus instituted is very often a learned language far removed from the local idioms used by pupils in their families. The problems of bilingualism are not totally eliminated, but take on another form.

This language must be brought to assure the same functions as the language rejected, to avoid negative consequences in various spheres of the national existence.

Since teachers trained in the language of the colonizer will experience numerous difficulties in undergoing retraining, during an interim period, personnel will be recruited whose competence is limited to ease of expression in the national idiom, their scientific and educational skills leaving much to be desired, leading to a drop in the level of instruction.

If a system of teaching is not set up which ensures a broad, effective command of an international foreign language, students, researchers, businessmen and technicians will find themselves with access to a rather scanty library of documentation in the national language, thus risking to fall behind with respect to the world's capital of useful information.

Testing and culture

The use of tests, as we know, has become general practice in every field and is an institutionalized part of every scholastic career. Used to identify and 'measure' various aspects of the subject's personality, including his skills, testing can, in many cases, have extremely serious consequences. For example, on the basis of tests used as a diagnostic instrument or for formulating prognoses, orientations are decided upon and critical choices are even made with respect to the curriculum the child will follow and to his future.

This raises a serious question: do tests attain and measure what they claim to strive for and measure, in particular, skill, 'intelligence', 'recall', alertness, etc? It is not at all certain that they indeed do, for achieving this objective is neither easy nor rapid. First, there are difficulties involved in identifying and defining the objective sought: what is intelligence, for example? Moreover, the situation in which the exam is administered can present several factors which prevent the condition to be measured from appearing either purely or completely, or both at the same time.

Among these variables, there are those which are culturally related. How did we come to think of them? The question was first raised in the countries which 'invented' these tests, that is, countries in the West, based on odd statistical results which cropped up regularly when administered to people, including ethnic minorities.

TESTS, SOCIO-PROFESSIONAL CATEGORY AND ETHNIC MINORITIES IN THE WEST

It was the large-scale administration of aptitude tests, especially intelligence (IQ) tests, which first drew attention, because of the institutional consequences they can have for young people in school and in later life. As F. Aubret-Bény and J. Pelnard-Considère said, after summarizing the most significant studies on intellectual development tests,

> We found that the mean success rates per socio-professional category among children tested agree not only in space (we could have based ourselves on studies conducted outside the United States, France or the United Kingdom – in Sweden, for example), but also in time, from the first measures taken immediately after the Second World War to the most recent tests.[70]

Everywhere, the scores fall the 'lower' we go down the socio-economic scale. The authors also insist on the 'consistency of this difference' for both adults and children from 'early infancy to the end of adolescence'.[71]

Of the studies which reveal and interpret these results, we will indicate just a few by way of example.

In France, national studies on the level of intelligence of school-age children conducted by the National Institute of Demographic Studies (INED) and published in 1950 and 1973,[72] and works by M. de Montmollin[73] on prisoners, by M. Reuchlin and F. Bacher[74] on secondary-school children, and a report presented at the XIIIth Congress of the French Scientific Psychology Association in 1970.[75]

In the United Kingdom, works by L.M. Terman and M.A. Merill[76] on the standardization of the Stanford Scale, by C. Burt[77] and J. Conway.[78]

In the United States, the wide-scale study on army recruits[79] and N. Stewart's study[80] on a subset of them, research by H. Seashore et al.[81] on the standardization of the Wechsler Intelligence Scale, and that by G.R. Medinnus and R.C. Johnson,[82] a major study by a group of researchers of the Chicago School headed by K. Eells,[83] and lastly, an already rather dated review of the subject by A. Anastasi.[84]

The Chicago research team, using nine usual collective intelligence tests graded in terms of IQs, carried out their 1948 study in the average sized town of Rockford, Illinois. It involved more than 5,000 children aged 9 and 10, and 13 and 14. Information about their ethnic background and social status was obtained and scaled. The most interesting comparison concerned two contrasting groups: American-born, upper-class and lower-class individuals. The researchers used techniques enabling them to compare and correlate intelligence tests and the socio-economic scale. Their main hypothesis was that tests widely used measure not only innate aptitudes, but a combination of such aptitudes and a number of cultural advantages.

Their findings confirmed those of others and provided additional information. They have been reproduced many times and are discussed in detail by M. Demangeon et al.,[85] and are clearly summarized in a document vehemently condemning IQs, published in France by M. Tort.[86] There is a very significant link between the socio-economic variable and the tests measuring cognitive development, with success rates diminishing as one goes down the social scale. The force of this correlation varies depending on the test considered. The most marked differences involve verbal scores, in which the social gap was most pronounced, followed by numerical, geometric and visual (abstract or figurative drawings) tests. There are also non-verbal items which are strongly linked to social category.

The more an item involved knowledge acquired through schools or books, the more socially differentiating it was because it referred to objects and experiences which are more familiar to upper- and middle-class children than to working-class children.

The kinds of errors made vary measurably according to social class. Errors made by upper-class children very frequently centred around a nearly correct reply; those made by disfavoured children, in contrast, tended to be evenly distributed over all wrong answers generally.

The percentage of unanswered questions was higher in the case of working-class children.

Finally, the study showed once again that variations based on social background increased with age. As we have already seen, the averages between groups are much closer for children than for adults. A study by C. Burt,[87] which has the rare advantage of comparing children and adults, reveals that for children 'there is a difference of a little over 20 points (that is, approximately half the difference in the case of parents) betwen the upper and lower groups.'[88] This points to the cumulative influence of social background.

We might add that everything we have just said is valid in terms of averages, for individual variations within groups are significant: According to D.A. Kennedy, 'it is well known that the variability within any given ethnic, racial or socio-economic status group is greater than the mean difference between groups.'[89] In fact, the extremes within different categories widely overlap.

If this is the case, how do we interpret the results? Why is there a link between IQ and social status? As M. Demangeon said,

> If intelligence is an innate aptitude, does this relation translate the genetic superiority of individuals from the upper class? If intelligence is at least partially acquired, can we say that an upper-class social background is more stimulating than another social level for intellectual development? Finally, does this relation merely indicate a bias with respect to the content of the test, rather than a genuine difference between groups?[90]

Eells and his colleagues opted for the latter solution. The inequality of success rates, they felt, was due to the fact that the test included values which are relatively distinct from one class to another. The implications of this assertion, as formulated by this team and other authors,[91] are the following.

Each social level has its own predominant type of mentality, that is, different values and concepts, ways of approaching problems and intellectual habits. Thus, the emphasis placed on competition and individual achievement in these tests (the 'go for it' cult), the abstract, artificial nature of the problem and the type of intellectual activity it demands correspond to the subculture of the privileged classes, not to that of the lower class.

The same can be said about the objects, experiences and realities to which these problems refer: they are familiar to children of the first group, but represent an 'alien' world to the second group.

The interview with the examiner, which is just as formal as the exam situation set-up, inhibits and intimidates lower-class children who become edgy when dealing with any form of abstract reality.

The language used in tests is the same as that used at school. We have seen how this language is different from that of members of the disfavoured classes and we can imagine the misunderstandings which can result, for example, with respect to the test directions. Based on what we said at the beginning of this chapter, we can easily see how these children are especially penalized by verbal items and problems.

It is not surprising, therefore, that working-class children, with the bulk of these difficulties concentrated on them, are penalized by the time limits and the speed generally imposed by these tests (and included in the final score). It is no less surprising that they are less motivated towards this kind of exam: the importance of motivation in these tests has been clearly demonstrated.

Analogous observations have been made and similar conclusions drawn with respect to the administration of standardized tests to ethnic minorities in the United States and other industrialized countries. Here the socio-economic factor is compounded with the effects of ethnic culture. If the two variables are dissociated, the results become more diversified, the more of them there are.[92] This is only natural, if one considers that the subjects tested are not the representatives of a pure culture, attached to the very nature of all members of their group but, rather, are diversely situated with respect to the host culture, and this point needs to be examined closely, as most authors have failed to do. However, as has often been pointed out, classes for slow learners in the United States are attended by a disproportionately high number of children from ethnic minorities, and this has accentuated the dispute over the potentially biased nature of IQ tests. Thus, the Association of Black Psychologists has asked that psychological testing for educational purposes be completely abandoned in the United States.[93] Such tests have been banned in schools in some cities such as New York.

It was naturally felt that cultural bias be eliminated and tests be developed which made legitimate comparison between subjects from different cultures or subcultures so as not to unjustly harm or favour their scholastic careers. This has been done in the United States since 1910 with the so-called culture-free tests.[94] It was revealed, however, that this goal has never been completely achieved, since no test can be considered to be totally independent of culture. For intelligence cannot function without content, of which environmental elements are a vehicle and culture is automatically a part. We can still, however, attempt to develop culturally unbiased tests, representing what M. Reuchlin referred to as a faithful 'cross-section' of mental systems used in real life by normal children of all socio-economic levels. Such tests would be balanced, because they would favour no one subculture – they would be 'culture fair'.

R.B. Cattell[95] proposed one such test. He began by defining intelligence as a general factor (the G factor), in the sense used by Spearman, which comes into play 'in the utilization of all specific aptitudes and involves especially the ability to reason', that is, 'to deduce relationships and correlates'.[96] This factor, considered to be hereditary, is coupled with others which influence the testing situation: development of this ability through class influence (dG); the relationship between the cultural content of the test and the subject's experience (C), which corresponds to Eells' 'cultural bias'; familiarity with tests and testing situations (t). Both the factors t and C need to be reduced.

To do this, Cattell considered using elements common to all cultures: different objects, actions and processes presented especially via schematic, geometric shapes and figures to avoid using words. The cultural content was further reduced by the relative absence of verbal instructions, the exercise being explained essentially by graduated examples and the elimination of time limits when dealing with non-Western subjects.

Cattell evaluated his test by comparing it to other tests. The results were inconclusive. Other authors[97] subsequently based themselves on the same principles to judge the validity of a certain number of intelligence tests used to compare subjects from different social classes. The results were more convincing, leading M. Demangeon to say, 'It seems that so-called G factor tests constitute intelligence tests whose content is much more culturally independent than verbal tests.'[95]

Another well-known attempt was made by Eells and his team in Chicago, using elements common only to the specific cultures involved. As a result, problems were selected in such a way that the specific knowledge and background necessary to solve them were equally developed among the social classes represented. In this way the intelligence test could be defined as an instrument for measuring the aptitude for solving difficult problems within the cultural group to which the subject belonged. Moreover, testing conditions, as was also the case with Cattell, neutralized the effect of variables likely to differentiate these classes: reading skills (oral instructions), speed (time limits were mainly per item) and comprehension of instructions (simple vocabulary and numerous practice exercises). Finally, unlike Cattell, Eells and his team tried to stimulate optimal motivations for all children: choosing problems which were interesting to everyone, concrete, and based on everyday life; presenting the test as a game; and creating a relaxed atmosphere.

Despite all these precautions, the results of the application of this instrument were relatively disappointing. A certain number of studies have shown that the differences are generally attenuated when Davis-Eells games and other culture-free tests are used instead of classic school-type exams, but not entirely eliminated. At the same time, compared to normal school-type exams (reading, reading comprehension, basic knowledge), they are significantly less valid than classic, more verbally-oriented intelligence tests, which is understandable since the changes introduced aimed precisely at eliminating discriminatory aspects of the classroom subculture.[99]

This poses the problem of how to interpret these results, a sensitive issue because of its emotional and ideological implications. The logical possibilities are, however, well defined.

1. On one hand, we can assume that these culture-free and culture-fair tests have indeed eliminated cultural bias. This would mean that, given the persistent inequality of the results of these tests, there is an *effective* hierarchy of intellectual aptitudes, independent of cultural factors and maintained in function of the socio-economic scale. The increasing inferiority as we go down the social class scale would then be due to either or both of the factors involved in the exercise of intelligence once the cultural factor has been removed:

The G factor as genetic potential dependent on hereditary transmission.

To prove the existence of this factor, one cites

the fact that identical twins raised apart from infancy are more alike in IQ than fraternal twins raised together, and that the intellectual-academic development of children adopted at infancy is considerably closer to that of their natural parents than to that of their adoptive parents.[100]

On this basis, several assumptions are made. One line of reasoning consists in saying that subjects from the lower class are intellectually deficient and are doomed to remain so. Another is that 'deficient' members of the upper class will eventually move towards the bottom of the scale. This explains the presence among the economically disfavoured of a higher proportion of 'intellectually poor' individuals. A.R. Jensen rekindled the political and scientific debate with an article published in 1969.[101] He suggested that the at least partial influence of the hereditary factor could explain the poor results achieved by a systematic policy of 'remedial' teaching.

The dG factor, that is, the actualization of hereditary potential, the development of the faculty of intelligence and its universal biological traits (in the Piagetian sense, for example). This development will be more difficult to achieve, the more the social environment is unstimulating or even inhibiting: this is what is commonly believed to occur as we go down the social ladder (on average, at least).

2. On the other hand, it is deemed impossible ever to separate intelligence from the cultural parameter completely. This theme can be presented in a radical form, as with M. Tort: 'A test is by nature socially selective', for 'it is a bourgeois test.'[102] Indeed, whatever improvements are made in these tests to eliminate these factors, they will continue to offer an accumulation of easily recognizable tricks: exercises divorced from problems encountered in reality; the requiring of a special type of intelligence and specific operations which are not those of rural people or workers in their daily lives and work (upon whom 'certificates of intelligence' are not conferred); the artificial character of situations. In short, the test will continue to be, no matter what we do, the most 'artificial' of constructs so frequently condemned. It

really involves the caricaturized transformation of the learning exercise, which in itself is nothing more than a specific, historical form of learning, the very structure of which incorporates class characteristics with no relation to the socially-situated work of intelligence.[103]

It remains, therefore, a concentrate of 'bourgeois culture', slightly sweetened by the refinements introduced by the designers of culture-free instruments. Besides, could these authors, when putting these instruments together, shed their own middle- or upper-class models and genuinely confront those of working-class children?

At a more modest level, we might ask ourselves to what extent, other than by definition, can the factors we spoke of — hereditary aptitude, development of this aptitude during the person's lifetime, and situational factors such as cultures and subcultures — be separated? The G and dG factors, when one tries to enter into detail with respect to the characteristics attributed to them, are not always *absolutely* dissociable from specific learning situations confronted by the individual, hence from environmental parameters.[104] The conclusion, then, is that the cultural dimension cannot be completely severed from functions of the active man, and that aptitude-situation interaction cannot be completely done away with. As a result, culture-free tests were not able fully to achieve their goal of eliminating inequalities due to culture.

As we can see, the debate over testing ties in with another one we have encountered several times: are the handicaps of disfavoured groups entirely imaginary or real, or a little of both?

This debate, in any case, has certainly not been in vain. It made it possible to further our understanding of the connection between culture and cognitive functions. In addition, from the practical point of view, these tests, which could be more aptly called 'culturally simplified', are far from being of no value. As M. Tort stated, 'since 1951, most test developers take the findings of the Rockford study into account.'[105] This helps reduce, although not eliminate, inequalities due to social and ethnic origin. Finally, by revealing cultural biases and identifying other distorting factors, these efforts have led to greater vigilance with respect to these powerful instruments and reinforced the awareness that they must not be the sole instrument upon which diagnoses and prognoses are based.

TESTS AND CULTURE IN THE THIRD WORLD

As we can well imagine, the instruments invented in the West cannot be transposed to radically different cultures without complications, as is generally the case in the Third World. To show this, we will use a report made by S. Benouniche on the Algerian situation, and this will serve as a typical example of the situation in all countries grappling with this problem.[106]

The first facet of his critical examination concerns the relational aspect of the testing situation. The Algerian child (we know to what extent this observation can be applied elsewhere) is influenced by the original model:

Adults know, he does not, adults can do, he must do; adults command, he obeys; adults think, he repeats; adults speak, he listens; adults act, he undergoes. Yet, in a test situation, the child is asked to know, to be able to, to think, to speak, and to act. What is more, he finds an adult who speaks, waits and perhaps expects to learn something from him. There is total incongruity between the two scenarios.[107]

Completely confused, the child will 'take refuge in his usual model, but adopting caricature-like attitudes: paralysed and inhibited, he is unable to answer the psychologist's questions.'[108] The subject matter used, moreover,

more closely resembles educational games and involves manipulatory activity. But what does it mean to an Algerian child to play or to manipulate? In Algeria, games are not recognized as a fundamental means of personality expression.... Because of this, adults rarely participate in childrens' game activities.

The situation is thus the opposite of that of the test in which 'the psychologist places value on the game and takes part in it, which reinforces the inhabitual aspect of the relationship'. As far as the material used is concerned, either the young Algerian 'considers it to be a strange object, is wary of it and transfers this wariness to the entire relationship' or 'to be a coveted object... and, hence, overestimates it'. Thus, 'the relationship has to be rethought if we do not wish to obtain invalid results.'[109]

Examination of the 'notional' content of tests resulted in similar judgments. Given the concept of time in Maghrebin culture, we must ask ourselves what meaning 'concepts such as efficiency, yield over a limited time, etc which refer to an appropriation of time by the individual in competition or simply in a work situation, might have for the subject. When a child is told "Work as fast and as well as you can", what is he to understand, given his way of life and the relationship and material of the test?'[110] In addition, the Algerian child is confined to a very limited space and then, without transition, as soon as he is able to walk, he has access to the street and the world outside. Does this mean that theories on acquisition of the corporal scheme and spatial structuring upon which these tests are based apply to him? What is more, 'the problem of space appropriation is compounded by that of the organization and orientation of perception.' For the youngster will first learn Arabic (which is written from right to left) and then French 'requiring him to reverse his way of writing, while continuing to use what he learned first'. So, 'will he choose one or the other of these reference models, and if so, which?'[111]

The Arabic language and its use likewise pose complex problems. Arab dialects, Berber, educated Arabic, French: the Algerian child is subjected to multilingualism. Under these conditions, how are we to communicate with him in tests? The mother tongue reduces the two interlocutors to the restrained possibilities of Bernstein's 'limited code'. The other languages break with 'the spontaneous communication of personal experiences' and pose problems related to comprehension, not to mention the different systems of thought of which they are each the vehicle. Adapting instructions and translating them into different levels of language can facilitate understanding but also 'introduce a bias at the very substratum level of the test'; difficulty climaxes when dealing with the 'tests themselves, that is, the verbal exercises'. Other dangers related to grading can also arise.

In trying to measure the level of intellectual development, the psychologist may only measure 'linguistic level... which is part of the problem of learning'.[112] This danger is further aggravated by the use of a foreign language like French.

Confronted with material expressed in non-spontaneous, stereotyped language, he risks interpreting it 'not as difficulty in expressing himself in the cultural language, but as an intrinsic characteristic' of the subject being tested. This is to be especially borne in mind when administering personality tests. Indeed, 'whereas the mother tongue refers to the most intimate, emotional experiences, use of the cultural language can create a distance. As such, language serves as a defence mechanism....'

Thus, 'characteristics of our environment force us to rethink the very principles upon which these tests are based.'[113] But this is not the end of the problem because the environment itself is in a crisis of change. So, when the child is presented as 'having problems', this seems to imply a maladjustment. 'But where is the maladjustment?...Maladjusted to what? Is he too far ahead of the times or too far behind?' Similarly, in a composite school which has not yet achieved a stable point of reference 'what is the meaning of the ideas of failure and of slowness in school?' We must, therefore define each time the standard against which we are comparing to determine what is abnormal and in relation to what. 'Hence questions raised with respect to the tools in our possession to help us identify the problems and to solve them'.[114]

Because these tools are borrowed from foreign societies in a situation of relative stability, it is clear that they need to be replaced by 'original tests, adapted in terms of their theoretical bases, to their material environment and cultural support'. To create such tests, it

is indispensable that research be done to understand better the environment and its impact on the child's psychological development, his progress at school, and his social and cultural integration. Research is also needed as to what the child experiences in a testing situation when confronted with a specific type of material and an adult whose role is misunderstood.[115]

All specialists in recently decolonized Third World countries agree that the results of such analyses could be applied to many if not all of them.

In conclusion, let us merely say that such studies have begun and have resulted in adjustments — provisionally at least — in a certain number of aptitude and personality tests. An example is to be found in the changes made in the Murray Thematic Apperception Test (TAT) to correspond to cultural groups.[116]

NOTES AND REFERENCES

1. Rambaud. P. *Société rurale et urbanisation.* Paris, Seuil, 1969, p. 108.
2. Pujade-Renaud, Claude. Du corps enseignant. *Revue française de pédagogie* (Paris, Institut national de recherche pédagogique), no. 40, juillet-août-septembre 1977, p. 45.
3. Pujade-Renaud, Claude; Zimmermann, D. *Voies non verbales de la relation pédagogique.* Paris, Editions sociales françaises, 1976. 120 p.
4. Pujade-Renaud, Claude. Du corps enseignant. *Op. cit.*, p. 45.
5. Berthelier, R. *Identité, culture, langage, école... Journées d'études: enfants d'autres cultures dans la société française (11-14 janvier 1984).* Paris, Centre d'entraînement aux méthodes d'éducation active, 1984.
6. Hall, E.T. *The hidden dimension.* New York, Doubleday, 1966; Hall, E.T. *Beyond culture.* New York, Doubleday, 1977; Hall, E.T. Cultural models in transcultural communication. *In:* Wolfgang, A., ed. *Nonverbal behavior: applications and cultural implications.* New York, Academic Press, 1979, pp. xi-xvii.

7. Taft, R. Coping with unfamiliar cultures. *In*: Warren, N., ed. *Studies in cross-cultural psychology*, vol. 1. London, Academic Press, 1977, pp. 121-53; Weeks, W.H.; Pederson, P.B.; Brislin, R.W., eds. *A manual of structured experiences for cross-cultural learning*. Chicago, IL, Intercultural Press, 1977. 134 p.
8. Longstreet, Wilma, S. *Aspects of ethnicity: understanding differences in pluralistic classrooms*. New York, Teacher's College Press, 1978. 196 p.
9. Bourdieu, P.; Passeron, J.-C. *Reproduction in education, society and culture*. London, Sage, 1977. p. 162.
10. Snyders, G. *Ecole, classe et lutte de classes*. Paris, Presses universitaires de France, 1976. 384 p.
11. Zimmermann, D. Un langage non-verbal de classe: les processus d'attraction-répulsion des enseignants à l'égard des élèves en fonction de l'origine familiale de ces derniers. *Revue française de pédagogie* (Paris, Institut national de recherche pédagogique), no. 44, juillet-août-septembre 1978, pp. 46-70.
12. *Ibid*., p. 62.
13. *Ibid*., p. 58.
14. *Ibid*., p. 46.
15. Pujade-Renaud, Claude. Du corps enseignant. *Op. cit*., p. 47.
16. Bernstein, B. Social class and linguistic development: a theory of social learning. *In*: Halsey, A.M.; Floud, Jean; Anderson, C.A., eds. *Education, economy and society*. Glencoe, IL, The Free Press, 1961, pp. 288-314; Bernstein, B. *Class, codes and Control, vol. 1*. London, Routledge and Kegan Paul, 1971. 266 p.; Bernstein, B. *Class and pedagogies, visible and invisible*. Paris, Organization for Economic Cooperation and Development, 1975. 36 p. (Studies in the learning sciences, no. 2.)
17. Cherkaoui, M. Structures de classes, performances linguistiques et types de socialisation: «Bernstein et son école». *Revue française de sociologie* (Paris, Centre national de la recherche scientifique), vol. 15, no. 4, novembre-décembre 1974, pp. 585-99.
18. Forquin, J.-C. L'approche sociologique de la réussite et de l'échec scolaires: inégalités de réussite scolaire et appartenance sociale. *Revue française de pédagogie* (Paris, Institut national de recherche pédagogique), no. 59, avril-mai-juin 1982, pp. 52-75; no. 60, juillet-août-septembre 1982, pp. 51-70.
19. *Ibid*., no. 60, p. 51.
20. *Ibid*., p. 52.
21. *Ibid*.
22. Bernstein, B. *Class, codes and control, vol. 1*. *Op. cit*., p. 61.
23. Lawton, D. *Social class, language and education*. London, Routledge and Kegan Paul, 1968. 181 p.
24. Espéret, R. Langage et origine sociale des élèves. Berne, Lang, 1979. 281 p.
25. Brossard, M. *Conduites verbales, activités cognitives et origine sociale*. Bordeaux, France, Université de Bordeaux II, s.d., Thesis, p. 101.
26. Cazden, C.B. The situation: a neglected source of social class differences in language use. *In*: Pride, J.B.; Holmes, Janet., eds. *Sociolinguistics: selected readings*. Harmondsworth, Penguin, 1972, p. 296, quoting Robinson, W.P. *Restricted codes in sociolinguistics and the sociology of education*. Dar-es-salaam, University College, 1968, p. 6. [Paper presented at the Ninth International Seminar]
27. Lawton, D. *Op. cit*.
28. Labov, W. *The logic of nonstandard English*. Washington, DC, Georgetown University, 1969. (Georgetown monographs in languages and linguistics, no. 22); Hardy, M.; Platone, F.; Dannequin, C. Langage et classes sociales: quelques problèmes méthodologiques. *Psychologie française* (Paris, Société française de psychologie), 1977 vol. 22, nos. 1-2, pp. 37-46.
29. Deutsch, M.; Katz, I.; Jensen, A.R., eds. *Social class, race and psychological development*. New York, Holt, Rinehart and Winston, 1968.

30. Passow, A.H.; Goldberg, Miriam; Tannenbaum, A.J., eds. *Education of the disadvantaged*. New York, Holt, Rinehart and Winston, 1967. 503 p.
31. De Coster, W. Le handicap socio-culturel et sa compensation: différentes approches-problèmes. *In*: Belgique. Ministère de l'éducation nationale et de la culture française. Direction générale de l'organisation des études. *Recherches convergentes sur le diagnostic et la compensation des handicaps socio-culturels affectant des enfants de 0 à 7-8 ans*. Bruxelles, 1973, pp. 17-35.
32. Westinghouse Learning Corporation. *The impact of Head Start: an evaluation of the effects of Head Start on children's cognitive and affective development*. New York, Westinghouse Learning Corporation; Athens, OH, Ohio University, 1969. 11 p. [Microfiche ERIC ED036321]; Tyler, W. *The sociology of educational opportunity*. London, Methuen, 1977. 143 p.
33. Cf. Dannequin, C.; Hardy, M.; Platone, F. Le concept de handicap linguistique: examen critique. *Travaux du CRESAS* (Paris, Centre de recherche de l'éducation spécialisée et de l'adaptation scolaire), no. 12, 1975, pp. 1-45.
34. François, F. Classe sociale et langue de l'enfant. *La Pensée* (Paris), no. 190, 1976, pp. 75-92; François, F. Analyse linguistique, normes scolaires et différenciations socio-culturelles. *Langages* (Paris), vol. 14, no. 59, 1980. pp. 25-52.
35. Bernard, R. *Ecole, culture et langue française: éléments pour une approche sociologique*. Paris, Tema Formation, 1972. 311 p.
36. Brossard, M. Langage, opérativité, milieu culturel. *Enfance* (Paris, Laboratoire de psycho-biologie de l'enfant), no. 5, septembre-décembre 1972, pp. 455-68; Brossard, M. Développement cognitif, langage et classes sociales: quelques hypothèses. *La Pensée* (Paris), no. 190, 1976, pp. 5-16.
37. Burguière, Evelyne; Isambert-Jamati, Viviane. Handicap et différence en question. *L'Ecole et la nation* (Paris, Parti communiste français), no. 287, décembre 1978, pp. 28-32.
38. Goodnow, Jacqueline J. Problems in research on culture and thought. *In*: Elkind, D.; Flavell, J.H., eds. *Studies in cognitive development*. New York, Oxford University Press, 1969, pp. 439-62; Brossard, M. Milieu social, situation de verbalisation et capacités linguistiques. *Revue française de pédagogie* (Paris, Institut national de recherche pédagogique), no. 44, juillet-août-septembre 1978, pp. 38-45.
39. Le Ny, J.F. Capacités cognitives et différenciation de classe. *La Pensée* (Paris), no. 190, 1976, pp. 17-30.
40. Snyders, G. *Op. cit*.
41. Tabouret-Keller, Andrée. Plurilinguisme: revue des travaux français de 1945 à 1973. *Linguistique* (Paris), vol. 11, no. 2, 1975, p. 126.
42. *Ibid*., p. 124.
43. *Ibid*.
44. For example: Landry, R.J. Le bilinguisme: le facteur répétition. *Canadian modern language review* (Welland, Ont., Ontario Modern Language Teachers' Association), vol. 34, no. 3, February 1978, pp. 548-76.
45. Tabouret-Keller, Andrée. *Op. cit*., p. 129.
46. Boulot, S.; Boyson-Fradet, Danielle. L'échec scolaire des enfants de travailleurs immigrés: un problème mal posé. *Les Temps modernes* (Paris), 40e année, nos. 452-4, mars-mai 1984, pp. 1902-14.
47. Gratiot-Alphandery, Hélène; Lambiotte-Fekkar, B. [La scolarisation des enfants de travailleurs migrants dans le département de la Seine-Saint Denis]. *In*: Centre international de l'enfance. *Les enfants de travailleurs migrants en Europe: santé, scolarité, adaptation sociale*. Paris, les Editions ESF, 1974, pp. 68-71; Berthelier, R. *Op. cit*.; Dabène, L. Contribution de l'analyse linguistique à l'étude des phénomènes de pluralisme culturel. 1981. [Document presented to the European Science Foundation

Additional Activity in Migration, Analytical and Methodological Seminar, Sophia-Antipolis, France, 28 September-3 October 1981]
48. Berthelier, R. *Op. cit.*, p. 2.
49. Dabène, L. *Op. cit.*, p. 3.
50. Berthelier, R. *Op. cit.*, p. 13.
51. Laferrière, M. The education of West-Indian and Haitian students in the schools of Montreal: issues and prospects. *In*: Elliot, Jean, L., ed. *Two nations, many cultures: ethnic groups in Canada*. 2nd ed. Scarborough, Ont., Canada, Prentice-Hall, 1983, pp. 158-72.
52. Porcher, L. *The education of the children of migrant workers in Europe: interculturalism and teacher training*. Strasbourg, School Education Division, Council for Cultural Cooperation, Council of Europe, 1981. 176 p.
53. *Ibid.*, pp. 34-5.
54. *Ibid.*, p. 40.
55. *Ibid.*, p. 30.
56. *Ibid.*, p. 84.
57. *Ibid.*, p. 85.
58. *Ibid.*, p. 35.
59. *Ibid.*, p. 86.
60. *Ibid.*, p. 30.
61. *Ibid.*, p. 82.
62. Fitouri, C. *Biculturalisme, bilinguisme et éducation: analyse du cas tunisien*. Paris, Université René Descartes, 1980. 2 v; Fitouri, C. *Biculturalisme, bilinguisme et éducation*. Neuchâtel, Suisse, Delachaux et Niestlé, 1983. 300 p.
63. Lahjomri, A. Langue et société dans le Maroc contemporain. *Pro-C* (Rabat), nos. 13-14, 1979. p. 3.
64. Riguet, M. *Attitudes et représentations liées à l'emploi du bilinguisme: analyse du cas tunisien*. Paris, Publications de la Sorbonne, 1984. 382 p.
65. Fitouri, C. *Biculturalisme, bilinguisme et éducation: analyse du cas tunisien*. *Op. cit.*, p. 325.
66. Jenaïstar, A. Ecole, famille et société au Maroc. *Lamalif* (Casablanca, Morocco), no. 116, mai 1980, pp. 49-57.
67. Fitouri, C. *Biculturalisme, bilinguisme et éducation*. *Op. cit.*, p. 279.
68. *Ibid.*, p. 285.
69. *Ibid.*, p. 279.
70. Aubret-Bény, F.; Pelnard-Considère, Jacqueline. La liaison entre appartenance socio-économique et développement. *In*: Reuchlin, M., éd. *Cultures et conduites*. Paris, Presses universitaires de France, 1976, pp. 28-9.
71. *Ibid.*, p. 25.
72. Institut national d'études démographiques. *Enquête nationale sur le niveau intellectuel des enfants d'âge scolaire*, 1. Paris, 1954, 212 p; Vallot, F.; Courgeau, D.; Clerc, P. *Enquête nationale sur le niveau intellectuel des enfants d'âge scolaire*, 2. Paris, Institut national d'études démographiques, 1973. 198 p.
73. Montmollin, M. de. Le niveau intellectuel des recrues du contingent. *Population* (Paris, Institut national d'études démographiques), vol. 14, no. 2, avril-juin 1959, pp. 233-52.
74. Reuchlin, M.; Bacher, Françoise. *L'orientation à la fin du premier cycle secondaire*. Paris, Presses universitaires de France, 1969, 369 p.
75. Reuchlin, M. Les facteurs socio-économiques du développement cognitif. *In*: Association de psychologie scientifique de langue française. Symposium, XIIIe, Lille, 1970. *Milieu et développement*, par F. Duyckaerts, et al. Paris, Presses universitaires de France, 1972, pp. 69-136.
76. Terman, L.M.; Merill, Maud A. *Measuring intelligence*. Boston, MA, Houghton, Mifflin, 1937; London, Harrap, 1939. 461 p.

77. Burt, C. Class differences in intelligence, III. *British journal of statistical psychology* (London, British Psychological Society), vol. 12, Part 1, May 1959, pp. 15-34; Burt, C. Intelligence and social mobility. *British journal of statistical psychology* (London, British Psychological Society), vol. 14, Part 1, May 1961, pp. 3-24.
78. Conway, J. Class differences in intelligence, II. *British journal of statistical psychology* (London, British Psychological Society), vol. 12, Part 1, May 1959, pp. 5-14.
79. Bingham, M.V. Inequalities in adult capacity, from military data. *Science* (Washington, DC, American Association for the Advancement of Science), vol. 104, no. 2694, 16 August 1946, pp. 147-52.
80. Stewart, Naomi, A.G.C.T. scores of army personnel grouped by occupation. *Occupations* (Easton, PA, National Vocational Guidance Association), vol. 26, no. 1, October 1947, pp. 5-41.
81. Seashore, H.; Wesman, A.; Doppelt, J. The standardization of the Wechsler Intelligence Scale for Children. *Journal of consulting and clinical psychology* (Washington, DC, American Psychological Association), vol. 14, April 1950, pp. 99-110.
82. Medinnus, G.; Johnson. R.C. *Child and adolescent psychology: behavior and development*. New York, Wiley, 1969.
83. Eells, K.W. et al. *Intelligence and cultural differences: a study of cultural learning and problem-solving*. Chicago, IL, University of Chicago Press, 1969.
84. Anastasi, Anne. *Differential psychology: individual and group differences in behavior*. 3rd. ed. New York, Macmillan, 1958.
85. Demangeon, M.; Larcebeau, S.; Nguyen Xuan, A. Mesure de l'intelligence et facteurs de milieu: constats analytiques. *In*: Reuchlin, M., éd. *Cultures et conduites*. Paris, Presses universitaires de France, 1976, pp. 63-145.
86. Tort, M. *Le quotient intellectuel*. Paris, Maspéro, 1974. 205 p.
87. Burt, C. Class differences in general intelligence. II. *Op. cit.*; Burt, C. Intelligence and social mobility. *Op. cit.*
88. Aubret-Bény, F.; Pelnard-Considère, Jacqueline. *Op. cit.*, p.24.
89. Kennedy, D.A. Rationality, emotionality, and testing. *Journal of school psychology* (New York), vol. 16, no. 1, Spring 1978, p. 21.
90. Demangeon, M.; Larcebeau, S.; Nguyen Xuan, A. *Op. cit.*, p. 71.
91. Clarizio, H.F. Nonbiased assessment of minority group children. *Measurement and evaluation in guidance* (Falls Church, VA), vol. 11, no. 2, July 1978, pp. 106-13.
92. Willard, Louisa A. A comparison of culture fair test scores with group and individual intelligence test scores of disadvantaged Negro children. *Journal of learning disabilities* (Chicago, IL), vol. 1, October 1968, pp. 584-9; Gaudia, G. Race, social class and age of achievement of conservation on Piaget's tasks. *Development psychology* (Washington, DC, American Psychological Association), vol. 6, no. 1, January 1972, pp. 158-65; Jensen, A.R. How biased are culture-loaded tests? *Genetic psychology monographs* (Provincetown, MA), vol. 90, no. 2, November 1974, pp. 185-244; Jensen, A.R. *Test bias and construct validity*. 1975. 31 p. [Document presented at the annual meeting of the American Psychological Association, 83e, Chicago, IL, September 1975] [Microfiche ERIC ED 114 415]; Jensen, A.R. IQ tests are not culturally biased for blacks and whites. *Phi Delta Kappa* (Bloomington, IN), vol. 57, no. 10, June 1976, p. 676; Anastasi, Anne. *Psychological testing*, 4th ed. New York, Macmillan, 1976. 750 p.; Clarizio, H.F. *Op. cit.*
93. Jackson, G.D. Comment: On the report of the Ad hoc Committee on Educational Uses of Tests with Disadvantaged Students: another psychological view from the Association of Black Psychologists. *American psychologist* (Washington, DC, American Psychological Association), vol. 30, no. 1, January 1975, pp. 88-93.
94. Anastasi, Anne. *Psychological testing. Op. cit.*
95. Cattell, R.B. A culture-free intelligence test, I. *Journal of educational psychology*

(Baltimore, MD), vol. 31, no. 3, March 1940, pp. 161-79; Cattell, R.B.; Flingold, S.N.; Sarason, S.B. A culture-free intelligence test, II: evaluation of cultural influence on test performance. *Journal of educational psychology* (Baltimore, MD), vol. 32, no. 2, February 1941, pp. 81-100.
96. Demangeon, M.; Larcebeau, S.; Nguyen Xuan, A. *Op. cit.*, p. 91.
97. MacArthur, R.S.; Elley, W.B. The reduction of socioeconomic bias in intelligence testing. *British journal of educational psychology* (London), vol. 33, Part, 2, June 1963, pp. 107-19.
98. Demangeon, M.; Larcebeau, S.; Nguyen Xuan, A. *Op. cit.*, p. 95.
99. Larcebeau, S. Le problème de la validité des tests d'intelligence. *In*: Reuchlin, M., éd. *Cultures et conduites*. Paris, Presses universitaires de France, 1976, pp. 101-20.
100. Kennedy, D.A. *Op. cit.*, p. 21.
101. Jensen, A.R. How much can we boost IQ and scholastic achievement? *Harvard educational review* (Cambridge, MA, Harvard University), vol. 39, no. 1, Winter 1969, pp. 1-23.
102. Tort, M. *Op. cit.*, p. 33.
103. *Ibid.*, p. 14.
104. See, for example, Pelnard-Considère, Jacqueline; Levasseur, Jacqueline. Pédagogie nouvelle en mathématiques et développement intellectuel. *Revue française de pédagogie* (Paris, Institut national de recherche pédagogique), no. 23, avril-mai-juin 1973, pp. 5-30.
105. Tort, *Op. cit.*, p. 31.
106. Benouniche, Samia. Pratique actuelle de la méthode des tests en Algérie. *Psychologie française* (Paris, Société française de psychologie), vol. 25, nos. 3-4, 1980, pp. 265-74.
107. *Ibid.*, p. 267.
108. *Ibid.*
109. *Ibid.*
110. *Ibid.*, p. 268.
111. *Ibid.*, pp. 268-9.
112. *Ibid.*, pp. 269-70.
113. *Ibid.*
114. *Ibid.*, p. 271.
115. *Ibid.*, p. 273.
116. Jacquemin, A. Les variantes du «thematic apperception test» pour l'étude des groupes culturels. *Revue belge de psychologie et de pédagogie* (Bruxelles), vol. 44, no. 180, décembre 1982, pp. 135-44.

CONCLUSION

Towards intercultural teaching

The foregoing demonstrates to what extent a misunderstanding of the cultural parameter can have negative effects in a number of educational areas. To decide to take it into account intelligently is to opt for the constant, wholesome inclusion of this dimension in educational practice. But this still does not necessarily imply the use of so-called cross-cultural teaching methods. This option was first recognized as a possibility in the United States, and then in Europe, as the place occupied by young people from different ethnic groups in schools became more significant. Was it possible to set up an educational system adapted to the diversity of their cultures?

The ambition is legitimate, but the difficulties involved in achieving it are many. How can cultural relativism be translated into the classroom, which could not survive the disparity of messages unless, at one level or the other, it culminates in synthesis or a Tower of Babel, to use M. Laferrière's expression.[1] Many attempts have been made, systems have been set up based on individual or institutional initiatives in various countries, accompanied by a vast amount of literature.[2]

We shall *not* treat in detail the wealth of data these operations produced.[3] However, we will try to extract from them what to us appears to be the necessary elements of genuinely cross-cultural teaching. We will pass over the problem of language teaching which was treated in our last chapter.

As M.A. Gibson noted, 'the purpose of the first approach to multicultural education is to equalize opportunity for culturally different students.'[4] The first direction taken, however, was that of .'remedial education' which had been inspired, as we well know, by a doubly egocentric concern.

First, because of its objective, namely to avoid wasting the unexploited abilitites of disfavoured groups. According to A. Little and G. Smith, who treated the subject extensively, this movement was spawned by the concern aroused in American political circles by the launching of the first 'sputnik' by the USSR. It was consequently necessary 'to locate potentially talented youngsters at an early age and provide special training for them, particularly in scientific subjects'.[5]

Second, because of its ideological basis, namely to consider the educational deficiencies of ethnic minorities and disfavoured social groups to be the result of the weaknesses of their cultures. The goal of remedial programmes is to bring them up to the level of the avant-garde culture of Western countries.

Remedial education in the United States led to a number of programmes which distinguished themselves by their brevity, for the initial optimism quickly subsided with the disappointing results achieved.

This movement has at its nucleus an ideology which not only rejects the hierarchical ranking of cultures, and speaks in terms of differences rather than inequalities, but also regards these differences as a source of richness and fulfilment. This is the primary justification, as M. Rey-Von Allmen[4] observed, for the term 'intercultural education'. For, the term 'by giving the prefix "inter-" its full meaning, necessarily implies interaction, exchange, decompartmentalization, reciprocity, objective solidarity'. It also implies,

by lending to the term 'culture' its full meaning, recognition of values, life-styles, and symbolic representations which human beings use as a frame of reference...in their relationships with others and in their perception of the world, their recognition of their own importance, their diversity, and the interactions between the various strata of a given culture, as well as between different cultures.[6]

Yet the problem is precisely the way in which the reappreciation of cultural differences is conceived and put into practice, because it could: jeopardize social consensus and even the national unity;[7] indelibly trace the map of cultural differences; straitjacket each individual within the society;[8] and make of each group a monolithic entity and a prisoner of its distinctive cultural traits.[9] Because of this we would run the risk of not noticing the similarities between groups. We would especially fail to see the diversity within these groups themselves, for it is well known that in complex societies, individuals perform their own manipulations and organize their own 'cultural pool', variously situated with respect to the majority culture. We would run the risk of antagonizing school children and even more so their parents by lumping everyone together according to our personal, abstract conception of their cultural model, without taking into account the actual position of 'culturally peripheral' groups.

Completely doing away with the concept of inequality in favour of mere diversity would imply certain risks: that of denying the possibility of assembling a body of objective knowledge, officialized by science and hence preferable to other types of knowledge which a given culture might contain, but which are erroneous or less objective. As D. Lawton said, attacking what he regarded as excessive relativism, 'If all knowledge is of equal worth, then why have schools at all?'[10] That of denying the existence of a universal, human, 'genetic programme' of aptitude development and the fact that anthropological cultures are, depending on the content and learning processes they encourage or avoid, capable of stimulating or slowing skill acquisition differentially. By treating all cultures as equal, we would be encouraging the skill inequalities they institute.

A practical objection can be added to this list of theoretical objections: how can education be adapted to cultural differences without splitting up groups which are culturally distinct, that is, without arriving at the same effects of segregation and non-communication of racist educational models? In other words, rehabilitating differences per se will naturally elevate them to the status of an absolute and again, like racism, convert them into a dead-end.

In the final analysis, as M. Rey-Von Allmen stated, 'the cross-cultural dimension is constantly threatened in daily life by Manichaeism and by both those who reject it and those who are its champions.'[11]

Indeed, the foregoing objections clearly illustrate the main difficulty, that of how to deal satisfactorily with differences. They show how necessary it is to elaborate an approach which is dialectical rather than mechanical, that is, which enables them to surpass themselves, to promote more authentic communication because it is informed rather than naive: what we mean by this is that it is informed about these differences, particularly their nature and their importance. This can help us to extricate the principles for a response to these objections.

With respect to *conflicts of values between various cultures*, a distinction needs to be made. We might first take into consideration the problem of the basic philosophical values upon which moral principles governing the lives of every individual are based. Two lines of argument are possible in this connection: anthropology has established statistically that the majority of values are common to different cultures, that is, their values agree more often than they conflict. There is, therefore, a broad potential basis of consensus among culturally different students. If residual conflicting values subsist, the problem has to be dealt with at school as in any democratic society: open confrontation is to be accepted, which in turn makes the obligation to submit to the will of the majority legitimate. The problem is thus social, which shows that cultural education does not depend on schools alone and is hardly imaginable outside certain forms of society.

In the second — far more frequent — case, we could be dealing with different educational models and learning systems, depending on the culture of the child. How can these conflicts be resolved? Several principles can be suggested.

First, it is generally agreed that culturally different groups should not be physically separated. This is not, as we have already seen, only for the mutual enrichment of students. It involves something even more essential: no one can succeed in making his differentness a positive factor in his identity development if it is not accepted and recognized by others. The identity a person prescribes for himself is nothing if it does not coincide with that prescribed by others. Isolating oneself with one's own kind within a given society will make acceptance by others more difficult. This well known psychological truth is but one facet of a more general principle: the value of de facto differences depends on the use that people make of them. Subjects, through their interaction, weight them to various degrees, make them murderously real, or attenuate them to the point of extinction. As M. Abdallah-Pretceille, commenting on the usual dichotomy of native children-immigrant children, said 'the interactionist outlook defines differences not as a natural fact, like an objective statistical fact, but as the dynamic relationship between two entities which make each other mutually meaningful.'[12] It is thus clear that any approach which chooses to overlook the effective interaction between communities deprives it of both its prefix and its reality: 'It is this process of mutal mirroring,' the same author wrote, 'which provides the basis for cross-cultural dialogue, whatever its field of application'. In this way, 'the objective of cross-culturalism distinguishes itself from pluriculturalism which contents itself with a cultural mosaic.'[13] This is also reformulated by L. Porcher who at a practical level in his report to the Council of Europe said:

If the intercultural policy is to be coherent and really effective, it must be adopted generally and for everyone. If it is applied to only part of the school population, it will immediately become contradictory and impracticable and create new kinds of segregation for those whom it is sought precisely to release from their present isolation. The test of hard facts reveals the true role of interculturalism in education, which is to address itself to everyone.[14]

Hence the new, currently popular approach: the intercultural option is not a programme aimed at isolated groups, but can only be effectively implemented by educating everyone including non-minorities in the cultural dimension, in a spirit of reciprocal opportunity. It becomes 'education about cultural differences rather than education for the so-called culturally different'.[15] It transcends the mere treatment of educational problems because it teaches human relations of a specific type: one which is needed for the fulfilment of the individual through his acceptance of his individuality under specific conditions by others.

It is thus evident that we cannot judge the success or failure of intercultural education only according to the quality of the results achieved by minorities at school. But it is likely that, if the relationship with peers and teachers corresponds to this model and eliminates prejudices, a good number of educational handicaps will disappear.

The best means of avoiding the labelling of the stigmatization of subjects is to integrate the adaptation to cultural and subcultural (ie existing within one society) distinctions into an educational programme which takes into account other differences among students and is cognizant of the other planes of diversity in their personalities. To do this, institutional avenues must be reorganized, meaning that the problem of the education of minorities 'is not only a problem of specific target groups. It exemplifies all the questions which the educational authorities will have to ask themselves.'[16]

It is not up to us to say what these avenues are to be. But the objective seems to call for educational systems centred on learners, capable of avoiding institutional segregation by promoting the conditions for expressing diversity within the classroom itself. The various so-called 'active' methods are precisely the ones suggested for these purposes: adopting this direction rather than that of traditional teaching systems will most improve the chances of success.

By moulding curricula and structures of advancement 'to measure' within the class will help solve a problem which often arises: how can different categories of students (among nationals as well as foreigners) be educated together, while simultaneously avoiding overburdening some with a common curriculum and eliminating the negative effects of coexistence of disparate groups? The spontaneous evolution of these groups will bring out similarities and differences as *perceived* by students themselves rather than postulated on the outside. Students will thus be able to situate themselves in relationship to others as a function of their 'cultural pool'. For,

it is not the school's role to determine what is the identity of students, nor to choose an identity for them (neither that of origin or of the host country). But it must give them the means to diversify their points of reference and to live legitimately according to the diverse cultural modes of their environment.[17]

Next, for both students and teachers, intercultural education must include information on cultures which is not only descriptive, but also *genetic and explanatory*. Cultures are to be presented as entities elaborated by societies to cope with the challenges of the environment. Consequently — and this is important — they *naturally change* as the nature of the challenges posed by the environment changes (as history shows). It would be excellent as well to show this using the national culture as an example. Many similarities could be discovered with respect to analogous problems and in the collective reactions of communities: this would help eliminate certain stereotypes and superiority or inferiority complexes on both sides.

This type of training would contribute to the reduction of moral judgments which are generally hierarchically inclined and constitute the privileged breeding ground for ethnocentrism and xenophobia, in favour of a technical, expository analysis. Accordingly, all cultures will be globally legitimized on one hand, even if they are not adopted, since the technical approach makes it possible to interiorize cultural relativism fully. On the other hand, we would avoid attributing to cultures the sacred status which currently paralyses them. This would significantly foster the unhampered development of the subject's sense of identity, including those from ethnic minorities, without the frustrations and guilt feelings psychologists are familiar with.

Subsidiarily, intercultural education, which we consider to be the most essential element of the multidisciplinary training that teachers — and through them students — are to receive, would eliminate the folkloric manifestations and exotic formulations to which some intercultural programmes are reduced.

With respect to curriculum development, the intercultural option must distinguish between 'content' and the means to assimilate it. We do not imply that all content is of equal value: to be credible, relativism needs to be criticized.[18] Of course, the sociology of knowledge retains its cathartic function, demystifying the idea of an intemporal body of knowledge elevated to the status of a dogma. But although nothing is absolute 'truth', it is reasonable to at least take into account a body of scientific knowledge which centuries of practical, multifaceted success on a broad scale have designated as less subjective than other types offered in schools all over the world. Thus, taking cultural truth into account does not refer to knowledge itself, wherever it exists, but to elaborating the means and educational avenues for attaining it. As Lawton[19] asserted, sociological analysis encourages us to *adapt* the programme to the characteristics of students, not to *adopt* a given programme for reasons unrelated to knowledge. It is not up to sociology to define it, but to epistemology. Sociologists and psychologists are only there to make it accessible: they are the specialists of communication, that is, of the art of rendering things common. Of course, that requires special vigilance with respect to the methodological approaches making it possible to distinguish that which is scientific from that which is not.

Finally, the most important point, perhaps, concerns the ambiguity which to our view surrounds the idea of 'cultural competence' as defined by W.H. Goodenough.[20] Experience has shown, and a study by C. Tapia[21] confirms the fact, that one can very well be an intellectual expert with respect to a given culture and nurture a degree of antipathy for the groups and individuals who are part of it: the psychology of xenophobia and racism makes it possible to understand it. We cannot, therefore, content ourselves with bringing students to a level of cultural competence in the same way as we would teach them botany or geology. It must be borne in mind that they are exposed to arguments in their families relative to different ethnic communities and that they have interiorized surrounding stereotypes and prejudices intertwined with social and personal interests and reactions.

Because of this, intercultural education will no doubt stir up emotional conflicts and arouse various rivalries, for it does not belong to the realm of pure knowledge, independent of other facets of the personality. If the emotional aspect is not articulated, it is likely that this is simply due to a communication block. If we stop here, we will have achieved only 'paper thin' intercultural education, doomed to be ineffective and probably futureless. It therefore seems useful to us to bring the debate out into the open and to guide it along. This is why *complete* intercultural education contains risks, not the least of which is that the student 'intead of adopting a receptive attitude...will come to feel at home nowhere'.[22]

These considerations should not lead us to be discouraged. They tell us that much research is needed, as well as the on-the-spot observations of teachers and educational practitioners to master conceptually the enormous mass of experiments under way, to extract the variables involved, and to ensure that, gradually, a better grasp of the phenomenon is achieved. In the process, periodic reassessments (like the one we have just made) of the proper theoretical foundations and the risks of the operation would have a positive impact if they achieved one aim: to make us more aware of what we are doing, to make us understand better why the results obtained are poor, and to help us find the means of improving them.

NOTES AND REFERENCES

1. Laferrière, M. Les idéologies ethniques de la société canadienne: du conformisme colonial au multiculturalisme. *In*: Lecomte, Monique; Thomas, Claudine, éds. *Le facteur ethnique aux Etats-Unis et au Canada*. Lille, France, Presses universitaires de Lille, 1984, p. 209.
2. Gibson, Margaret Alison. Approaches to multi-cultural education in the United States: some concepts and assumptions. *Anthropology and education quarterly* (Washington, DC, Council on Anthropology and Education), vol. 7, no. 4, November 1976, pp. 7-18; Baker, Gwendolyn C. Policy issues in multicultural education in the United States. *The Journal of Negro education* (Washington, DC, Howard University), vol. 48, no. 3, Summer 1979, pp. 253-66; Banks, J.A. Shaping the future of multicultural education. *The Journal of Negro education* (Washington, DC, Howard University), vol. 48, no. 3, Summer 1979, pp. 237-52; Lecomte, Monique; Thomas, Claudine. *Le facteur ethnique aux Etats-Unis et au Canada*. Lille, France, Presses universitaires de Lille, 1984, 260 p.
3. L'éducation interculturelle. *Migrants formation* (Paris, Centre national de documentation pédagogique), no. 45, juin 1981, 151 p.; Scolarisation des enfants de migrants dans quelques pays européens. *Migrants formation* (Paris, Centre national de documentation pédagogique), no. 46, octobre 1981, p. 346; Colloquy on 'Migrant Culture in a Changing Society: Multicultural Europe by the Year 2000', Strasbourg, 1983. *General Report*, by Micheline Rey. Strasbourg, School Education Division, Council for Cultural Cooperation, Council of Europe, 1983, 63, v p. (DECS/EGT (83) 10); Council of Europe. Council for Cultural Cooperation. Working Group on the Education of Migrant Workers' Children – the Training of Teachers. *Final* Report, by Micheline Rey. Strasbourg, School Education Division, Council for Cultural Cooperation, Council of Europe, 1984. 21 p. (DECS/EGT (84) 84); Rey, Micheline, ed. *Une pédagogie interculturelle*. Berne, Commission nationale suisse pour l'Unesco, 1984; Rey-Von Allmen, Micheline. Pièges et défis de l'interculturalisme. *Education permanente* (Paris, Université de Paris-Dauphine), no. 75, septembre 1984, pp. 11-21; Riguet, M. *Eléments de synthèse pour une réflexion sur l'école française interculturelle*. Paris, Laboratoire de psychologie sociale appliquée, Section interculturelle, Institut de psychologie, Université de Paris V, 1985.
4. Gibson, Margaret Alison. *Op. cit.*, p. 7.
5. Little, A.; Smith, G. *Strategies of compensation: a review of educational projects for the disadvantaged in the United States*. Paris, Centre for Educational Research and Innovation, Organization for Economic Cooperation and Development, 1971, p. 13.
6. Rey-Von Allmen, Micheline. Pièges et défis de l'interculturalisme. *Op. cit.*, p. 12.
7. Banks, J.A. *Op. cit.*, p. 242; Baker, Gwendolyn C. *Op. cit.*, p. 256.
8. Pettigrew, L. Eudora. Competency-based teacher education: teacher training for multicultural education. *In*: Hunter, W.A., ed. *Multicultural education through competency-based teacher education*. Washington, DC, American Association of Colleges for Teacher Education, 1974, pp. 72-94 [Microfiche ERIC ED 098 226].
9. Garcia, E. Chicano cultural diversity: implications for CBTE. *In*: Hunger, W.A., ed.

Multicultural education through competency-based teacher education. Washington, DC, American Association of Colleges for Teacher Education, 1974, pp. 146-57 [Microfiche ERIC ED 098 226].
10. Lawton, D. *Class, culture and the curriculum.* London, Routledge and Kegan Paul, 1975, p. 69.
11. Rey-Von Allmen, Micheline. Pièges et défis de l'interculturalisme. *Op. cit.*, p. 15.
12. Abdallah-Pretceille, M. Pédagogie interculturelle: de la pratique à la théorie. Réflexions à partir de la situation française. *In*: Rey, Micheline. *Une pédagogie interculturelle.* Berne, Commission nationale suisse pour l'Unesco, 1984, p. 42.
13. *Ibid.*
14. Porcher, L. *The education of the children of migrant workers in Europe: interculturalism and teaching training.* Strasbourg, School Education Division, Council for Cultural Cooperation, Council of Europe, 1981, p. 47.
15. Gibson, Margaret Alison. *Op. cit.*, p. 9.
16. Porcher, L. *Op. cit.*, p. 48.
17. Rey, Micheline, ed. *Une pédagogie interculturelle. Op. cit.*, p. 17.
18. Kleinfield, Judith. Positive stereotyping: the cultural relativist in the classroom. *Human organization* (Boulder, CO, Institute of Behavioral Science, University of Colorado), vol. 34, no. 3, Fall 1975, pp. 269-74.
19. Lawton, D. *Op. cit.*
20. Goodenough, W.H. Multiculturalism as the normal human experience. *Anthropology and education quarterly* (Washington, DC, Council on Anthropology and Education), vol. 7, no. 4, November 1976, pp. 4-7.
21. Tapia, C. Contacts interculturels dans un quartier de Paris. *Cahiers internationaux de sociologie* (Paris), vol. 20, no. 54, janvier-juin 1973. pp. 127-58.
22. Porcher, L. *Op. cit.*, p. 46.

APPENDIX

Additional reading

Althusser, L. Idéologie et appareils idéologiques d'Etat: notes pour une recherche. *La Pensée* (Paris), no. 151, mai-juin 1970, pp. 3-38.
Barré de Miniac, C. Déficience ou différence? Principales thèses en présence concernant les difficultés linguistiques des élèves issus de milieux défavorisés. *Bref* (Paris), no. 18, 1979, pp. 33-51.
Baudelot, C.; Establet, R. *L'école primaire divise.* Paris, Maspero, 1975. 128 p.
Bloom, B.S.; Davis, Allison; Hess, R. *Compensatory education for cultural deprivation.* New York, Holt, Rinehart and Winston, 1967. 179 p.
Boudon, R. Analyse critique: la sociologie des inégalités dans l'impasse? En marge du livre de Christopher Jencks: *Inequality. Analyse et prévision* (Paris, Société d'études et de documentation économiques, industrielles et sociales), vol. 17, no. 1, janvier 1974, pp. 83-95.
Bourdieu, P.; Passeron, J.-C. *The inheritors: French students and their relation to culture,* Chicago, IL, University of Chicago Press, 1979. 158 p.
Burnett, Jacquetta H., et al. *Anthropology and education: an annotated bibliographic guide.* Snyder, NY, Human Relations Area File Press, 1974.
Cauthen, N.; Robinson, E.; Krauss, H. Stereotypes: a review of the literature, 1926-1968. *Journal of social psychology* (Provincetown, MA), vol. 84, no. 1, June 1971, pp. 103-25.
Cole, M.; Scribner, Sylvia. Developmental theories applied to cross-cultural cognitive research. *In:* Adler, Leonore L., ed. *Cross-cultural research at issue.* New York, Academic Press, 1982, pp. 3-21.
Collier, J. *Alaskan Eskimo education: a film analysis of cultural confrontation in the schools.* New York, Holt, Rinehart and Winston, 1973.
Coslin, P.; Winnykamen, F. Contribution à l'étude de la genèse des stéréotypes: attribution d'actes négatifs ou positifs en fonction de l'aspect vestimentaire et de l'appartenance ethnique. *Psychologie française* (Paris, Société française de psychologie), vol. 26, no. 1, 1981, pp. 39-45.
Forbes, J.D. *The education of the culturally different: a multi-cultural approach.* Rev. ed. Washington, DC, U.S. Govt. Print. Off. for the Far West Laboratory for Educational Research and Development, 1969. 65 p. [Microfiche ERIC ED075 142]
Freire, P. *Pedagogy of the oppressed.* New York, Herder and Herder, 1970. 186 p.; Conscientization and liberation: a conversation with Paulo Freire. *IDAC document* (Geneva Institute of Cultural Action), no. 1, 1973.

Gearing, F. Where we are and where we might to: steps towards a general theory of cultural transmission. *Newsletter. Council on Anthropology and Education* (Washington, DC), vol. 4, nos. 1-19, 1973.
Gintis, H. Education, technology and the characteristics of worker productivity. *The American economic review* (Menasha, WI, American Economic Association), vol. 61, no. 2, May 1971, pp. 266-79.
Grandguillaume, G. Politiques d'enseignement au Maghreb: quelles perspectives? *Maghreb-Machrek* (Paris, Fondation nationale des politiques et Direction de la documentation), no. 80, avril-mai-juin 1978, pp. 54-5.
Halsey, A.H. Towards meritocracy? The case of Britain. *In*: Karabel, J.; Halsey, A.H. *Power and ideology in education.* New York, Oxford University Press, 1977, pp. 173-86.
Harrington, C. *Psychological anthropology and education: a delineation of a field of inquiry.* New York, AMS Press, 1978. 232 p.
Huteau, M.; Lautrey, J. Artefact et réalité dans la mesure de l'intelligence (à propos du livre de Michel Tort: «Le QI»). *L'Orientation scolaire et professionnelle* (Paris, Institut national d'étude du travail et d'orientation professionalle), vol. 4, no. 2, 1975, pp. 169-87.
Levine, R.A.; Campbell, D.T. *Ethnocentrism: theories of conflict, ethnic attitudes and group behavior.* New York, Wiley, 1972, 310 p.
Lévy-Strauss, C. *Anthropologie structurale.* Paris, Plon, 1958.
Linton, R. *The study of man.* New York, Appleton-Century-Crofts, 1936.
Linton, R. *The cultural background of personality.* New York, Appleton-Century-Crofts, 1945.
Malassis, L. *The rural world: education and development.* London, Croom Helm, Paris, The Unesco Press, 1976. 128 p.
Moatassime, A. Le «bilinguisme sauvage»: blocage linguistique, sous-développement et coopération hypothéquée. L'example maghrébin: cas du Maroc. *Tiers monde* (Paris, Institut d'étude du développement économique et social, Université de Paris), t. XV, nos. 59-60, juillet-décembre 1974, pp. 619-70.
Sayad, A. Santé et éequilibre social chez les immigrés. *Psychologie médicale* (Paris), vol. 13, no. 11, octobre 1981, pp. 1747-75.
Scribner, Sylvia; Cole, M. *The psychology of literacy.* Cambridge, MA, Harvard University Press, 1981. 335 p.
Spindler, G.D., ed. *Education and cultural processes: toward an anthropology of education.* New York, Holt, Rinehart and Winston, 1974. 561 p.
Tajfel, H. La catégorisation sociale. *In*: Moscovici, S. *Introduction à la psychologie sociale.* Vol. 1. Paris, Larousse, 1972, pp. 272-302.
Triandis, H.C.; Lambert, W.W. *Handbook of cross-cultural psychology, Vol. 1.* Boston, Allyn and Bacon, 1980. 392 p.
Tyler, E.B. *Primitive culture.* London, J. Murray, 1871. 2 v.
Wax M.L.; Diamond, S.; Gearing, F.O. *Anthropological perspectives on education.* New York, Basic Books, 1971.